STO

ACF
P9-EEN-449
DISCARDED

SEP 27 '74

TANTE MARIE'S FRENCH KITCHEN

TANTE MARIE'S

French Kitchen

TRANSLATED AND ADAPTED

BY CHARLOTTE TURGEON

Decorated by Julian Brazelton

NEW YORK

OXFORD UNIVERSITY PRESS

1949

Copyright 1949 by Oxford University Press, Inc.
Printed in the United States of America

Contents

La Véritable Cuisine de Famille par Tante Marie, more commonly known as *Tante Marie,* has been used by generations of French families. The fact that few changes have been made in the many editions that have been published bears witness to the fundamental secrets of French cooking—timelessness and simplicity. The French cuisine, despite its reputation for quality and artistry, is basically simple. It is true that an able French chef can produce culinary wonders of *haute cuisine* that seem extremely complicated, but these complexities are usually matters of decoration and presentation, not of cooking.

French home cooking includes a wide variety of foods. This volume contains recipes for everything from hors-d'œuvre to homemade liqueurs, but there is nothing in it too difficult for an American housewife. Admirers of French cuisine often despair of trying to reproduce it in their own kitchens, fearing that the herbs and ingredients cannot be found in this country. Actually, with the exception of some fish and game peculiar to Europe, there is no ingredient that cannot be found in a good grocery store or grown in a home garden.

The French housewife of many generations ago was aware of the importance of time and money in cooking, as the modern American is today. She knew nothing of frozen or packaged foods or even modern vitamin theories, but the French have instinctively known for centuries how to get the most in flavor and nutrition out of every food. The economical and high-in-vitamin parts of animals, such as liver, brains, and sweetbreads, have long been common in the everyday diet; vegetables have always been cooked in as little water as possible and the vegetable water used in a variety of ways.

This cookbook is written for homes where one is obliged to consider time and money. All the recipes are given in the clearest and simplest terms possible, so that even those entirely unaccustomed to cooking may readily understand.

Liberties of addition and omission have been taken in preparing this cookbook for use in the United States. Measurements and methods have been adapted to the American kitchen. For those who know certain dishes by their French name only, or who enjoy presenting their culinary efforts under a French title, we have given both English and French recipe names. Most of the recipes are designed for 4 people. Some of the dinner-party recipes are obviously planned for 8 to 10 guests.

The French proverbs scattered throughout were added in the designing of the book and do not appear in the original *Tante Marie.*

In the following words Tante Marie presents her cookbook:

AVIS

Ce livre de cuisine s'adresse aux intérieurs modestes où l'on est obligé de compter avec le temps et l'argent.

Toutes nos recettes sont formulées en termes simples et compréhensibles pour les personnes les plus étrangères à la cuisine. De plus, ces recettes sont peu coûteuses et donnent les quantités pour trois ou quatre personnes.

Quelle est aussi la maîtresse de maison qui n'adresse pas, quinze fois par mois, cette question à son mari: 'Dis-moi donc ce que je pourrais faire aujourd'hui pour dîner?' Et le mari de répondre invariablement: 'Fais ce que tu voudras.'

*   *   *

NOTA BENE. *Afin d'être absolument clair dans nos recettes, nous n'avons pas craint de répéter plusieurs fois un même mot dans une phrase. Nos lecteurs nous sauront gré d'avoir évité les recherches de style dans un ouvrage qui n'en comporte pas.*

TANTE MARIE'S FRENCH KITCHEN

Good sauces are an indispensable part of good cooking. The more one knows about their preparation, the greater the variety in one's cooking. This does not mean that the sauces need be complicated or expensive. We shall show our readers how to master this art and thereby discover the secret of French cooking.

TANTE MARIE

TO BIND SAUCES: The purpose of binding sauces is to make them thicker or richer. One must take care that the eggs and flour used do not spoil rather than improve the sauces. This means careful preparation. Soups are thickened in the same manner.

BINDING WITH EGGS: Take one or more eggs according to the amount of sauce. One egg is enough for a pint of sauce. Separate the yolks from the whites. Beat the yolks slightly, adding 1 tablespoon of water per yolk. Stir in a little of the hot sauce that is to be thickened, mix well, and pour the egg mixture into the rest of the sauce, which has been removed

3

from the fire. Blend the mixture thoroughly. Stir over a very low flame or in the top of a double boiler until the sauce has reached the desired thickness. The sauce must not boil or the eggs will curdle.

BINDING WITH EGGS AND CREAM: Follow directions for BINDING WITH EGGS, but substitute cream for the water.

BINDING WITH BUTTER AND FLOUR: Mix 1 tablespoon of flour with 1 tablespoon of softened butter. Form tiny balls of the mixture and gradually drop them into the hot sauce. Let the sauce simmer for several minutes but do not let it boil.

BINDING WITH BUTTER AND STARCH (CORN OR POTATO): Substitute the starch for the flour and follow directions in the preceding paragraph. Do not let the sauce simmer more than 2 minutes.

BINDING WITH FLOUR: Take 1 teaspoon of flour per 2 cups sauce. Blend with ½ cup of the hot sauce until perfectly smooth. Stir into the rest of the sauce. Continue stirring a moment over a low fire, and serve immediately.

BINDING WITH STARCH (CORN OR POTATO): Mix 1 teaspoon of starch with 2 tablespoons of water. Add a little of the hot sauce. When it is thoroughly blended, add to the rest of the sauce. Stir over a low fire until the sauce is very hot. Serve immediately.

BINDING WITH BLOOD: This form of thickening is used in sauces served with wild game. Add the blood of the animal to the liver, which has been crushed to a paste. Add gradually to the sauce, stirring constantly. Reheat the sauce but do not let it boil. Serve immediately.

1. Béchamel Sauce   *Sauce béchamel*

2 tablespoons butter $\frac{1}{4}$ teaspoon salt
2 tablespoons flour $\frac{1}{8}$ teaspoon pepper
1 cup warm milk

Melt the butter. Add the flour and stir over fire until very light brown. Add the warm milk and stir until sauce is thick. Season with salt and pepper.

2. Cream Sauce   *Sauce à la crème*

2 tablespoons butter $\frac{1}{4}$ teaspoon salt
2 tablespoons flour $\frac{1}{8}$ teaspoon white pepper
1 cup scalded cream   1 teaspoon chopped scallion or
1 teaspoon chopped parsley   onion

Melt the butter. Stir in flour and, when thoroughly blended, add cream, scallions, salt, pepper, and parsley. Stir over low heat until the sauce is very thick.

3. White Sauce   *Sauce blanche*

2 tablespoons butter   1 egg yolk beaten with
2 tablespoons flour $\frac{1}{2}$ teaspoon vinegar
1 cup hot water $\frac{1}{4}$ teaspoon salt
                              $\frac{1}{8}$ teaspoon white pepper

Melt the butter and stir in the flour. Add the water and, when the sauce is smooth, add the egg yolk little by little, stirring constantly and taking care that the sauce does not boil. Season with salt and pepper.

4. Caper Sauce   *Sauce blanche aux câpres*

Make a White Sauce (3) but do not use the vinegar. Add $\frac{1}{2}$ cup of capers just before serving.

5. Brown Sauce I   *Roux brun*

2 tablespoons butter
2 tablespoons flour
1 cup hot stock or water

¼ teaspoon salt
dash of freshly ground black
   pepper

Melt the butter and stir in flour. Continue stirring until mixture is light brown. Add the liquid and seasonings. Cook until the sauce is thick. If this sauce is too thick for the particular recipe calling for it, add more liquid.

6. Brown Sauce II   *Roux blanc*

This sauce is made in the same way as Brown Sauce I except that the heated liquid is added as soon as the flour and butter are blended. It is, therefore, lighter in color.

7. Blanquette Sauce   *Sauce blanquette*

Follow directions for Cream Sauce (2), but substitute water for the cream.

8. Poulette Sauce   *Sauce poulette*

Follow directions for Cream Sauce (2), but substitute water for the cream and thicken with an egg (page 3). Add 1 teaspoon chopped parsley.

9. Maître d'hôtel Sauce   *Sauce maître d'hôtel*

3 tablespoons butter
1 teaspoon chopped parsley
1 teaspoon chopped scallion
½ teaspoon salt

1 tablespoon wine vinegar
⅛ teaspoon black pepper
1 teaspoon lemon juice (or ¼
   teaspoon vinegar)

Heat all the ingredients together but do not let them boil.
Serve very hot.

10. Hollandaise Sauce   *Sauce hollandaise aux œufs*

½ cup butter   1 tablespoon wine vinegar
2 egg yolks   ½ teaspoon salt

Melt the butter in the top of a double boiler. Add the other
ingredients, stirring constantly until the sauce thickens. This
is a fairly tart hollandaise. Less vinegar may be used for a
milder flavor.

11. Butter Sauce   *Sauce hollandaise au beurre*

½ cup butter   1 teaspoon salt

Melt the butter over a low flame. Add the salt and beat vigorously with a wire whisk. The butter should be almost boiling. Serve in a heated sauce-boat. This sauce is served with
boiled fish.

12. Piquant Sauce   *Sauce piquante*

3 tablespoons wine vinegar   1 teaspoon chopped parsley
¼ teaspoon black pepper   1 tablespoon butter
1 teaspoon chopped shallot (or   2 tablespoons chopped pickle
   grated onion)   2 cups Brown Sauce I (5)

Mix the vinegar, pepper, shallot, parsley, and butter. Heat
until the butter is melted. Add to the Brown Sauce, and just
before serving add the pickle. This sauce is used with various
pork and beef dishes.

13. Madeira Sauce   *Sauce Madère*

2 cups Brown Sauce I (5)   salt and pepper
bouquet garni (42)   3 tablespoons Madeira wine

Prepare the Brown Sauce, using stock instead of water. Canned consommé or bouillon cubes dissolved in water may be used. Allow the *bouquet garni* to simmer in the sauce for 30 minutes. Just before serving remove the *bouquet garni* and add the wine. This sauce is excellent with roast beef, steak, and beef kidneys.

14. Black Butter Sauce   *Beurre noir*

½ cup butter   3 sprigs of parsley
2 tablespoons wine vinegar

Melt the butter and heat until dark brown. Take care that it does not burn. Throw in the parsley and let it fry for a moment or two. Pour this over the food that is to be served. Return the pan to the flame and put in the vinegar. As soon as the vinegar is hot—which is a matter of seconds—pour over the same food. This sauce is used for fish, brains, and egg dishes.

15. Poor Man's Sauce   *Sauce au pauvre homme*

5 shallots (or tiny onions),   1 teaspoon chopped parsley
   chopped fine   salt and pepper
2 cups stock or water

Mix the ingredients and let them simmer until the shallots are tender. This sauce is good with left-overs.

16. Robert Sauce   *Sauce Robert*

2 tablespoons butter	2 tablespoons flour
2 onions, chopped fine	1 cup stock (or consommé)
1 tablespoon strong prepared mustard	1 teaspoon wine vinegar
	salt and pepper

Fry the onions in the butter until they are pale yellow. Add the flour and stir in well. Stir in the liquid and let the sauce simmer for 5 minutes or longer. Just before serving add mustard and vinegar and season with salt and pepper. This sauce is excellent with left-over meat and poultry and with lamb or mutton chops.

17. Mayonnaise   *Sauce mayonnaise*

1 egg yolk	1 teaspoon wine vinegar (or lemon juice)
½ teaspoon salt	
¼ teaspoon white pepper	1 cup olive oil

Combine egg yolk, salt, pepper, and vinegar or lemon juice in a deep bowl. Add the olive oil drop by drop, beating constantly until the sauce is thick and all the oil has been used. If the sauce tastes too oily, add more vinegar or lemon juice. Tante Marie recommends the use of a silver fork or spoon. It is more easily and quickly made, however, with a rotary (hand or electric) beater. The secret is in adding the oil very slowly.

18. Green Mayonnaise   *Sauce mayonnaise verte*

Prepare Mayonnaise (17). Add 1 teaspoon chopped parsley, 1 teaspoon chopped chives, and 1 or 2 drops of green vegetable coloring.

19. Pepper Sauce   *Sauce poivrade*

Brown Sauce I (5)
2 teaspoons wine vinegar
1 teaspoon chopped shallot (or
    small onion)
1 teaspoon chopped parsley
1 teaspoon chopped chives
bouquet garni (42)
¼ teaspoon salt
½ teaspoon freshly ground
    black pepper

Combine all the ingredients and simmer 30 minutes. Strain
and serve. This sauce is excellent with cold meats, especially
pork.

20. Tartar Sauce   *Sauce tartare*

1 egg yolk
3 shallots (or very small
    onions), chopped fine
1 teaspoon chopped parsley
1 teaspoon chopped tarragon
1 teaspoon wine vinegar
½ teaspoon prepared mustard
1 cup olive oil
½ teaspoon salt
¼ teaspoon white pepper

Beat the egg yolk slightly. Add the shallots, herbs, vinegar
and mustard, salt and pepper. Add the oil, drop by drop,
beating constantly until the sauce is thick. See directions for
making Mayonnaise (17). Another way to achieve almost
the same result is to combine the various herbs and mustard
with 1 cup previously prepared or bought mayonnaise. Homemade mayonnaise is always better.

21. Tomato Sauce   *Sauce tomate*

8 large tomatoes
1 onion, sliced thin
a sprig of thyme (or ¼ tea-
    spoon powdered thyme)
½ bay leaf
1 clove garlic
1 tablespoon butter
1 teaspoon cornstarch
salt and pepper

Crush the tomatoes in a heavy saucepan. Add onion, thyme, bay leaf, and garlic and simmer until the tomatoes are soft. Take care that they do not burn. Force the tomatoes through a strainer or food mill. Work the cornstarch into the butter and add to the tomato purée. Season with salt and pepper and simmer 15 or 20 minutes more.

22. Italian Tomato Sauce *Sauce tomate à l'italienne*

2 tablespoons butter (or 2
    tablespoons olive oil)
1 onion chopped fine
1 clove garlic, chopped fine
salt and pepper

1 can tomato paste
4 fresh tomatoes (or 1 can of
    tomatoes)
½ cup red wine
1 teaspoon sugar

Fry the onion and garlic in the butter or olive oil until the onion is transparent. Add the rest of the ingredients and let the sauce simmer 2 to 3 hours over a very low flame. The sauce should be quite thick. Variations of this sauce are made by adding lean meat, clams, shrimps, or lobster meat. The meat, veal or beef, can be chopped or ground and fried with the onions. The clams, shrimps, or pieces of lobster meat are added 15 minutes before the sauce is served.

23. Rémoulade Sauce *Sauce rémoulade*

8 tarragon leaves
5 tablespoons watercress leaves
2 teaspoons chopped chives
1 small clove of garlic

2 teaspoons chopped parsley
½ teaspoon strong prepared
    mustard
1 cup Mayonnaise (17)

Pound the tarragon, watercress, chives, garlic, and parsley to a smooth paste. Combine the paste with the mustard and mayonnaise.

24. Ravigote Sauce   *Sauce ravigote*

8 tarragon leaves	salt and pepper
5 tablespoons watercress leaves	½ teaspoon prepared mustard
2 teaspoons chopped chives	2 tablespoons wine vinegar
1 small clove of garlic	¾ cup olive oil
2 teaspoons chopped parsley	

Pound the tarragon, watercress, chives, garlic, and parsley to a smooth paste. Mix thoroughly with mustard, oil, and vinegar and season with salt and pepper. This is an excellent sauce for cold meats.

25. Curry Sauce   *Sauce au kari*

2 tablespoons butter	1 teaspoon curry powder
2 tablespoons flour	1 cup of stock

Melt the butter. Add flour and curry powder. Mix well but do not allow it to brown. Add the stock. Simmer 2 to 3 minutes. Strain and serve. This sauce is good for wild game.

26. Italian Herb Sauce   *Sauce italienne*

1 teaspoon chopped parsley	1 teaspoon olive oil
1 teaspoon chopped shallots (or tiny onions)	1 teaspoon cornstarch
1 clove of garlic, chopped fine	1 teaspoon butter
½ cup chopped mushrooms	½ teaspoon salt
½ cup white wine (dry)	¼ teaspoon black pepper

Simmer the parsley, shallots, garlic, and mushrooms in the wine for 20 minutes. Add oil, salt, and pepper. Mix the butter and cornstarch and gradually stir into the sauce. Simmer for a moment longer.

27. Truffle Sauce   *Sauce Périgueux*

2 truffles
6 large mushrooms
½ clove of garlic
1 teaspoon chopped parsley
1 teaspoon chopped chives
1 teaspoon olive oil

1 tablespoon flour
¼ cup hot water
¼ cup white wine (dry)
½ teaspoon salt
few grains of freshly ground
  black pepper

Chop the truffles, mushrooms, garlic, parsley, and chives together until they make a smooth paste. Add oil and heat over a slow flame. Add the flour and, when it is well blended, add the water, wine, salt, and pepper. Simmer 20 minutes. Skim off the fat and serve.

28. Anchovy Butter   *Beurre d'anchois*

6 anchovy fillets (or 1 tablespoon anchovy paste)

2 tablespoons butter

Pound the fillets to a paste or use the prepared paste. Mix with the butter, which has been softened but not melted, using a fork or a mortar and pestle.

29. Financière Sauce   *Sauce financière*

4 lamb kidneys
2 chicken livers
2 cockscombs (if possible)
1 sweetbread
1 cup stock
1 tablespoon butter
1 tablespoon lemon juice
Brown Sauce II (6)

bouquet garni (42)
½ cup mushrooms
2 truffles
6 *quenelles* (38)
½ teaspoon salt
few grains freshly ground black
  pepper

Split kidneys and remove the hard core of fat. Cut kidneys, livers, cockscombs, and sweetbread into small pieces. Soak in cold water for 3 hours. Drain well and cook slowly in stock, lemon juice and butter for 30 minutes. Drain and use the liquor to make Brown Sauce II. Add the meats, *bouquet garni,* mushrooms, and truffles, sliced thin, and *quenelles* (these may be omitted). Season with salt and pepper and cook slowly for 1 hour. This sauce is used with vol-au-vents, chicken fricassee, and macaroni rings.

30. Béarnaise Sauce   *Sauce Béarnaise*

3 tablespoons wine vinegar
2 tablespoons water
1 scallion, chopped fine
1 teaspoon parsley, chopped
  fine
⅛ teaspoon black pepper

3 egg yolks
4 tablespoons butter
½ teaspoon salt
1 teaspoon chopped parsley
1 teaspoon chopped tarragon
  leaves

Combine the vinegar, water, scallion, parsley, and pepper. Simmer 5 minutes. Meanwhile melt the butter in the top of a double boiler. Add the egg yolks and stir until the mixture thickens. Gradually add the hot vinegar, which has been strained, stirring constantly so that the eggs will not curdle.

Season with salt. Just before serving, add chopped parsley and tarragon leaves. This is delicious with steak.

31. French Dressing   *Sauce vinaigrette*

1 teaspoon chopped onion	$\frac{1}{4}$ teaspoon freshly ground
1 teaspoon chopped chives	black pepper
1 teaspoon chopped parsley	2 tablespoons wine vinegar
1 teaspoon salt	$\frac{3}{4}$ cup olive oil

Mix all the seasonings with the vinegar and allow them to stand several minutes before combining with the oil. Mix thoroughly before serving.

32. Marinating Dressing   *Marinade*

$\frac{1}{4}$ cup olive oil	a sprig of thyme
1 tablespoon wine vinegar	$\frac{1}{2}$ bay leaf
1 clove of garlic, chopped fine	2 tablespoons chopped parsley

Place the ingredients in a shallow dish in which the food is to be marinated. The thyme and bay leaf should be crushed. Place the meat to be marinated in the platter and spoon the sauce over the meat several times a day. The meat should be turned from time to time. Some meats are marinated as long as 6 days before cooking.

33. Garlic Sauce   *Sauce méridionale*

2 cloves of garlic	$\frac{1}{2}$ cup milk
1 slice dry bread	1 cup Mayonnaise (17)

Pound the garlic to a smooth paste. Remove the crusts from the bread and soak in milk. Squeeze out the milk and mix the bread with the garlic. Add this mixture to the mayonnaise. This sauce is excellent with cold beef, lamb, or poultry.

34. Onion Sauce   *Sauce Soubise*

8 large onions
3 tablespoons butter
3 tablespoons flour

1 cup hot water
1 teaspoon salt
½ teaspoon pepper

Slice the onions as thin as possible. Fry the onions in butter over a low flame until they are yellow. Sprinkle the flour over the onions and stir in gently. Add water, salt, and pepper and simmer for 20 minutes. Serve with pork or lamb chops.

35. Spanish Pimento Sauce   *Sauce rouge au piment*

4 cloves of garlic
2 red peppers
1 cup olive oil

½ teaspoon salt
¼ teaspoon freshly ground black pepper

Parboil the peppers until they are soft, or use canned peppers. Pound the garlic and peppers together until they form a smooth paste. Heat the oil and stir into the garlic and pepper mixture. Season with salt and pepper. This sauce is used with large fish.

36. Meat Essence   *Jus*

Jus is indispensable in real French cooking. It is made and sold commercially in France. It adds greatly to the richness of sauces. Canned consommé or bouillon cubes may be used as a substitute, but they do not give the same quality to a sauce that *jus* does. It can be made and kept in the icebox for a very long time.

½ pound stew beef
½ pound stew veal

1 calf's foot (or 1 beef knuckle, sawed in 4 pieces)

2 onions
2 carrots
bouquet garni (42)
2 cloves

1 teaspoon salt
$\frac{1}{4}$ teaspoon pepper
water

Place the beef, veal, onions, carrots, cloves, *bouquet garni,* salt, and pepper in a heavy saucepan that has a cover. Add one cup of water and cook until the meat juices begin to stick to the pan and the vegetables begin to brown. Add 2 cups of water and put in the calf's foot or knuckle. Any meat or poultry trimmings may also be added. Cook over a very low flame for 3 hours. Strain the liquid into a shallow pan and skim off the fat as it cools. A hard jelly will form. A small square of this will do wonders for a sauce.

37. Aspic

Many beautiful and delicious dishes may be prepared *en aspic.* 2 cups of Meat Essence (36) make a perfect aspic. Rich meat, poultry, or fish stock combined with granulated gelatine (1 tablespoon gelatine to 1 cup liquid) is very satisfactory.

TO CLARIFY STOCK: It is the clarity of the jelly that gives aspic its particular splendor. When the stock that is to be used has been properly seasoned and the gelatine has been added, the following method is used to clarify it: Beat 2 egg whites until foamy. Add $\frac{1}{2}$ teaspoon salt, 1 teaspoon wine vinegar, and 1 teaspoon cooking brandy. Stir this mixture into the stock and heat to the boiling point. Remove from the fire quickly and pour the stock through a double thickness of cheesecloth or a clean dish towel. If the jelly is pale, add a little coloring.

TO LINE MOLDS: Enough jelly should be prepared so that the mold may be filled. Fill a chilled mold with the liquid, which should be lukewarm. Place in the refrigerator for a few moments. When a thin layer of jelly has adhered to the bottom and sides of the mold, pour off the rest of the liquid. Place on this first layer of jelly the decorations called for or the first layer of food. The liquid should now be cool enough so that the first layer of jelly will not melt when the second is added. Pour in the second layer and let it jell. The rest of the food is then placed in the mold. Pour the rest of the jelly over the food. Care should be taken that there is a layer of jelly between the food and the mold. Let the mold stand in a cold place until the jelly is firm. When the time comes to serve the mold, place it on a serving platter. Cover with a hot towel and the mold will slip off easily.

38. Forcemeat   *Quenelles*

½ pound lean veal or uncooked chicken

½ cup bread crumbs soaked in ¼ cup milk

½ cup softened butter

2 eggs

salt and pepper

Force the meat through a meat chopper, using the finest blade. Drain the bread crumbs and mix with the butter and meat. Pound the mixture to a smooth paste. Separate the yolks and whites of the eggs. Stir the yolks into the paste. Season with salt and pepper. Fold in egg whites, beaten stiff. The traditional shape of *quenelles* is that of a small link sausage. Form by making little balls of the mixture and rolling them on a floured bread board. Drop into boiling salted water and cook 15 minutes.

39. Fish Forcemeat   *Quenelles maigres*

Substitute fish for meat in the preceding recipe.

40. Frying Batter   *Pâte à frire*

1 cup flour	½ cup water
½ teaspoon salt	1 egg
1 teaspoon salad oil	1 teaspoon brandy (optional)

Beat the egg well and combine with the other ingredients. The batter should be smooth and quite thick. If a lighter batter is preferred, beat the yolk and the white separately. Fold in the stiffly beaten egg white after the other ingredients have been well blended.

41. Deep Fat Frying

It is advisable to have a special pan reserved for deep fat frying. A deep iron or aluminum one is excellent. It is convenient to have a fat thermometer and frying basket. Lard, vegetable fats, and oil are all suitable for frying. The same fat may be used several times, although it should be poured out of the frying pan and stored in a cool place between times. To clean the fat, drop several slices of raw potato into the hot fat. The potato will absorb the odors, and extraneous matter will stick to it. It is poor economy not to use enough fat. The temperature should be kept as near constant as possible; otherwise the food will absorb the fat. The proper temperature will be indicated in each recipe. Fried food should be drained on absorbent paper and served immediately.

42. *Bouquet garni*

Bouquet garni is used very commonly in French cooking. It consists of 3 or 4 sprigs of parsley, a sprig of thyme, and a small bay leaf. The thyme should be surrounded by the parsley so that the little leaves will not float into the sauce. Tie the herbs together with string so that they may be removed before the dish which they are flavoring is served. ¼ teaspoon of powdered thyme and 1 teaspoon parsley flakes may be substituted, but in that case the sauce must be carefully strained before serving.

Mieux vaut bon repas que bel habit.

HORS-D'ŒUVRE are not to be confused with the canapés served with cocktails or tea. In France, the hors-d'œuvre are served at table in place of soup. They consist chiefly of meat, fish, and vegetables served in the form of salad, and an occasional hot spicy cheese dish. The hors-d'œuvre should be decorative as well as delicious. At a family meal, one or two kinds are served; at dinner parties, a greater variety. French or Italian bread should be served with the hors-d'œuvre.

43. Radishes   *Radis*

Wash the radishes carefully. Cut the red peel into petals, leaving it attached to the base, so that the radish resembles a rosebud. Arrange in a silver or glass dish. Serve with butter.

44. Butter   *Beurre*

Although butter is not served with an ordinary meal in France, it is usually served with the hors-d'œuvre. Make butter balls or curls and sprinkle with chopped parsley.

45. Anchovies   *Anchois*

Alternate filets of anchovies with slices of hard-boiled egg.
Sprinkle with finely chopped parsley.

46. Sardines

Arrange the sardines on a small platter. Decorate with slivers
of lemon peel and sprigs of parsley.

47. Russian Caviar   *Caviar*

Season the caviar with a little finely chopped onion or shallot
and a dash of lemon juice. Arrange on a small, round serving
dish. Boil 2 eggs 10 minutes. When they are cool, separate the
yolks from the whites. Force the yolks through a fine strainer
and sprinkle over the caviar. Chop the egg whites fairly
coarsely and place around the caviar. Cover it all with a little
chopped parsley. Serve with triangles of hot buttered toast.

48. Red Caviar

Place the caviar in a strainer and let cold water run over it
for several moments. This will remove the excess salt and will
improve the flavor. Season and serve like Russian Caviar (47).

49. Tuna Fish   *Thon*

Put the contents of a can of tuna fish and 2 hard-boiled eggs
through a meat chopper. Add 2 tablespoons of softened butter
and 1 teaspoon of chopped herbs (parsley, chives, and tarragon). Mix well and shape into a small pyramid. Place on small
serving dish and decorate with sprigs of parsley and a little
mayonnaise.

50. Salmon Salad   *Saumon*

Use either smoked, canned, or fresh cold boiled salmon. Cut
into small pieces. Cut 2 cold boiled potatoes into pieces of the
same size. Blend with ½ cup Mayonnaise (17). Place in a
shallow dish and surround with thin slices of cold beet or
tomato.

51. Shrimp Butter   *Beurre de crevettes*

Pound canned or boiled clean shrimps to a smooth paste. Mix
with ⅓ the amount of butter. Place on small platter. Sprinkle
with chopped parsley and serve with triangles of hot buttered
toast.

To clean shrimps: When the shrimps have been boiled 10
minutes in salted water, remove and let them cool. Remove the
shell and the thin black strip that runs down the middle of the
tail. Wash in cool water.

52. Lobster Butter   *Beurre de langoustes*

Substitute lobster meat for shrimp in the preceding recipe.

53. Shrimp Salad   *Crevettes*

Arrange fresh or canned shrimp (see 51) on a thin layer of
Mayonnaise (17). Decorate with sprigs of parsley.

54. Cucumber Salad   *Concombres en salade*

Peel firm, green cucumbers. Split lengthwise and remove the
seeds. Cut into paper-thin slices. Sprinkle generously with salt
and allow them to stand 45 minutes. Drain the cucumbers dry
and wipe with a dish towel. Cover with French Dressing (32).

55. Celeriac Salad   *Céleri-rave rémoulade*

Celeriac is a variety of celery grown for its turnip-like root. It is not very common in America, but well worth growing.

Slice raw celeriac root very thin. Marinate at least 8 hours in 2 tablespoons oil, 1 teaspoon vinegar, ½ teaspoon salt, and a dash of white pepper. Drain and mix with a Rémoulade Sauce (23).

56. Red Cabbage Salad   *Chou rouge*

Shred a firm red cabbage. Cover with salt and let it stand 45 minutes. This will draw the water from the cabbage. Drain, wipe with a towel, and mix with Mayonnaise (17) or French Dressing (31).

57. Lobster and Vegetable Salad   *Macédoine de langouste*

Combine 2 cups of mixed cooked vegetables with 2 cups of lobster meat. Add 1 cup of Mayonnaise (17). Arrange the salad on a platter in the form of a pyramid. Decorate with the feelers of the lobster and with sprigs of parsley.

58. Tongue Salad   *Langue de bœuf en salade*

Cut cold boiled beef tongue in very thin slices. Cover with French Dressing (31) and sprinkle with chopped parsley.

59. Russian Salad   *Salade russe*

Combine cold boiled potatoes, cold beef, fresh tomatoes, and boiled beets, all cut into small pieces, with Mayonnaise (17).

Add 1 teaspoon chopped parsley, 1 teaspoon chopped chives, and ¾ teaspoon chopped tarragon. Mound on a platter and frost with a thin layer of mayonnaise. Powder with chopped herbs (tarragon, parsley, and chives).

60. Tomato Salad   *Salade de tomates*

Choose small ripe tomatoes. Peel them or not as you wish. To peel easily, drop the tomatoes into boiling water for a moment, plunge into cold water, and then peel. Cut the tomatoes in thin slices, taking care not to cut through completely. Each person will be served a whole tomato. Cover with salt and let the tomatoes stand 45 minutes. Drain thoroughly and cover with French Dressing (31). Powder with chopped herbs (tarragon, parsley, and chives).

61. Fried Anchovies   *Anchois frits*

Dip anchovy fillets into beaten egg. Roll in flour and fry 2 minutes in deep fat (375°F.). Sprinkle with chopped parsley and serve on heated platter.

62. Stuffed Artichoke Bottoms
Fonds d'artichauts aux champignons

Remove all the leaves from boiled artichokes, being careful not to break the artichoke bottom. Except in regions where artichokes are grown, it is more economical to buy the canned artichoke bottoms. Fry the bottoms in butter and keep in warm place while frying ½ cup chopped mushrooms in the same butter. Fill the bottoms with the mushrooms. Cover with grated gruyère and put under the broiler until the cheese melts.

63. Leek Salad   *Poireaux à la vinaigrette*

Remove most of the green leaves from medium-sized leeks. Boil 25 minutes in salted water. Drain and cool. Cover with French Dressing (31).

64. Lentil Salad   *Lentilles à la vinaigrette*

Soak 1 cup lentils overnight. Drain and boil in salted water until soft but not mushy. Drain, cool, and cover with French Dressing (31).

65. Cheese Soufflé   *Soufflé au fromage*

4 tablespoons butter	½ teaspoon salt
½ cup flour	4 eggs
2 cups milk, scalded	⅔ cup freshly grated cheese

Melt butter and stir in flour. When it is blended, add milk and salt. Stir until sauce thickens. Remove from the flame and cool. Separate the egg yolks from the whites. Beat the yolks for 1 minute and add to the mixture. Add cheese. Beat egg whites stiff and fold in carefully. Bake in buttered ramekins or baking dish 20 minutes in 350°F. oven.

66. Cheese Sticks   *Allumettes au fromage*

See recipe 590.

67. Garlic Eggs   *Œufs à l'ail*

See recipe 143.

THE most delicious soups are made from the simplest ingredients. France is justly famous for the subtle art of soup making. In most French country homes the soup pot is constantly simmering on the back of the stove, and anything in the way of left-overs, spare morsels of meat and poultry and vegetables, are thrown into the soup pot. The result is a soup worthy of the finest chef. In most American homes constant cooking heat is no longer available and soup must be made according to definite recipes, such as these offered by Tante Marie to capture the subtle flavor and rich goodness of French soup.

NECESSARY UTENSILS: Chopping knife, chopping board or bowl, food mill, large soup kettle.

BREAD AND CROUTONS: Most French soups call for bread or croutons. Stale or toasted bread cut into rounds with a cookie cutter is very presentable. If croutons are called for, cut stale bread into cubes or 3-inch sticks and fry in melted butter. Turn the croutons frequently so that they will brown on all sides.

27

SUBSTITUTION FOR STOCK OR BOUILLON: Since many recipes presuppose the soup pot with a constant source of stock, it is well to have bouillon cubes, canned consommé, or bouillon on the pantry shelf. These make a satisfactory substitute.

68. *Pot-au-feu*

The famous French *pot-au-feu* provides the basis of a whole week of good meals. Many kitchens start their weekly routine by making this soup. If the dish is to be prepared for the sake of the soup only, any of the cheapest cuts of beef may be used. However, if a slightly better cut is used, the meat can be served hot or cold or in a casserole dish.

3 pounds beef (chuck, shoulder, neck, or bottom round, rolled and tied tightly)*	2 carrots
	½ parsnip
	1 turnip
6 quarts cold water	*bouquet garni* (42)
2 tablespoons salt	3 cloves
1 teaspoon black pepper	1 onion
3 leeks	

Place the meat in a large pot. Add water, salt, and pepper. Bring to a boil over a moderate fire. A white scum will form on the water. Keep skimming this off until it has all disappeared. Slice the leeks lengthwise and tie them together with string so that they may easily be removed. Add the leeks, carrots, parsnip, turnip, *bouquet garni,* and the onion stuck with the cloves. Let this simmer for at least 4 hours. Pour the broth through a strainer and skim off as much fat as possible before serving. If the color is too pale, add a little kitchen bouquet.

* A delicious chicken soup may be made by substituting a 4- to 5-pound dressed fowl for the meat.

To serve: Place several rounds of stale or toasted bread in the bottom of the soup tureen or individual soup plates. Pour the bouillon over the bread. If bottom round has been used, place on a platter, surround with the vegetables and serve with gravy made of 2 cups of the bouillon thickened with cornstarch or potato starch (page 4). The rest of the bouillon should be kept in a cool place for future use.

A large variety of soups may be made with the broth of the *pot-au-feu.* The following six recipes (69-74) are recommended. For little children or invalids scalded milk may be used in place of the stock. In this case more salt should be added.

69. Broth with Rice   *Riz au gras*

4 cups bouillon   3 tablespoons rice

When the bouillon boils, add the rice, which has been washed in warm water. Simmer 30 minutes. If any carrots are left from the *pot-au-feu,* crush them and add to the soup. This will add flavor and color and is known as *Potage Crécy au riz.*

70. Broth with Vermicelli   *Vermicelle au gras*

4 cups bouillon   4 tablespoons vermicelli

Boil the bouillon. Break the vermicelli into small pieces and add gradually, so that the broth will not cease boiling. Stir occasionally to keep vermicelli from sticking to pan. Cook 15 minutes and skim off the froth before serving.

71. Broth with Noodles or Macaroni

Pâtes d'Italie au gras

Follow directions for Broth with Vermicelli (70), using noodles or macaroni instead of vermicelli.

72. Broth with Semolina   *Potage à la semoule*

4 cups bouillon   4 tablespoons semolina

Add semolina to boiling bouillon, taking care that the semolina does not stick to the pan. Cook ½ hour.

73. Broth with Tapioca   *Potage au tapioca*

4 cups bouillon   2 tablespoons tapioca

Add tapioca gradually to the boiling bouillon. Stir constantly so that the tapioca will not stick or lump. Cook 10 minutes only so that the broth will not be too thick.

74. Thickened Broth   *Potage à la fécule*

4 cups bouillon   1½ teaspoons cornstarch or
                               potato starch

Mix the starch with a little cold bouillon. Add to the boiling bouillon. Cook 2 minutes, stirring constantly. Remove from the fire and the soup will clear.

75. Milk Soup   *Bouillie*

6 cups milk   several slices of buttered toast
3 tablespoons flour   salt and pepper

Scald the milk. Mix flour with a little cold milk and add slowly
to the milk, stirring constantly. Salt and pepper to taste. Simmer 20 minutes and pour over toast.

76. Cabbage Soup   *Soupe aux choux*

12 cups water   3 leeks
½ pound shoulder * or breast   1 turnip
   of lamb   1 tablespoon chicken fat (op-
6 strips lean bacon   tional)
2 carrots   1 cabbage
1 onion, stuck with 3 cloves   6 potatoes
½ parsnip   salt and pepper

Add lamb, bacon, salt, and pepper to the water and bring
to the boiling point over a moderate flame. A foam will form
on the top and must be carefully skimmed off. Add the carrots, onion stuck with cloves, parsnip, leeks sliced lengthwise
and tied together, turnip, and, if possible, the chicken fat. Let
this cook 2 hours. Wash and take off the outer leaves of the
cabbage. Cut in 4 parts. Peel the potatoes and add both cabbage and potatoes to the soup. Cook until the potatoes are
soft. Fresh peas or string beans may be added along with the
cabbage. Season to taste.

* If the shoulder is used, remove and serve broiled the next
day. See recipe 258.

77. Leek and Potato Soup
Soupe aux poireaux et aux pommes de terre

6 leeks	6 or 7 potatoes
2 tablespoons butter	croutons (page 27)
6 cups water	freshly ground black pepper
2 teaspoons salt	

Peel the leeks and cut into small pieces. Melt butter and fry the leeks until they are brown. Add water and salt. Peel, wash, and cut potatoes into small pieces and add to the soup pot. Cook 1 hour. Force the soup through a food mill, or crush the leeks and potatoes with a potato masher. The soup should be thick. Pour over the croutons and season with freshly ground black pepper.

78. Sorrel Soup　　　*Soupe à l'oseille*

1½ cups sorrel leaves *	several pieces of stale or toasted
2 tablespoons butter	bread
6 cups water or stock	¾ teaspoon salt
1 egg yolk	

Chop the sorrel leaves and place them in a heavy pot over a low flame until the leaves are wilted and some of the water is drawn off. Add the butter and when it is melted add liquid and salt. Simmer 10 minutes. Beat the egg yolk slightly. Add a little soup to the yolk, stirring constantly, and then add the egg mixture to the soup. Do not let the soup boil after the egg has been added. Pour over the bread and serve.

* Watercress leaves make an excellent substitute for the sorrel leaves.

79. Sorrel Soup with Rice   *Potage au riz à l'oseille*

Follow the preceding recipe for Sorrel Soup. When the soup boils, add 4 tablespoons of well-washed rice and cook 30 minutes. Finish by thickening with egg.

80. Sorrel Soup with Vermicelli   *Vermicelle à l'oseille*

Follow recipe for Sorrel Soup (78). Add 4 tablespoons of broken vermicelli and cook 15 minutes. Finish by thickening with egg.

81. Bread and Butter Soup.   *Panade*

6 cups water or stock	3 tablespoons butter
1 teaspoon salt	1 egg yolk
$\frac{1}{2}$ loaf of bread, sliced thin	1 teaspoon sugar

Place the bread in the salted water or stock. Bring to a boil and simmer for 10 minutes, stirring often. Add butter and thicken with egg (page 3). This soup is used especially for children, and the sugar is added for their benefit.

82. Pea Soup   *Potage Saint-Germain*

2 cups dried peas	salt and pepper
6 cups water or chicken stock	croutons

Cook peas in water or stock for $1\frac{1}{2}$ hours. Force them through a food mill or strainer. Reheat, season with salt and pepper, and pour over fried croutons. The soup should be thick, but if it is too thick add more liquid. Rice or vermicelli may be cooked with the peas. In this case another pint of liquid should be added, and the soup should not be strained.

83. Lentil Soup   *Potage à la conti*

Follow directions for Pea Soup (82), substituting lentils for peas. Serve with a slice of lemon.

84. Potato Soup   *Potage Parmentier*

6 to 8 potatoes
6 cups water or chicken stock
    (or 3 cups water and 3
    cups milk)

2 tablespoons butter
salt and black pepper
croutons

Boil potatoes in liquid until they are very soft. Force through a food mill or strainer. Reheat with the liquid. Add butter. Season with salt and pepper and pour over croutons.

85. Dried Bean Soup
Potage à la purée de haricots blancs

2 cups dried beans (any of the
    dried white beans are suit-
    able)
6 cups stock or water

2 tablespoons butter
salt and pepper
croutons

Boil the beans in the liquid for 2 hours. Force through a food mill or strainer. Reheat, adding more liquid if the soup is too thick. Add butter, salt, and pepper and pour over croutons.

86. Kidney Bean Soup   *Potage Condé*

Follow the preceding recipe, using red kidney beans. Serve with slices of lemon.

87. Pumpkin Soup   *Potage au potiron*

1 cup cooked or canned pump-
    kin
4 cups scalded milk
2 tablespoons butter

salt and pepper
½ teaspoon sugar
croutons

Crush the pumpkin to a paste or force through a food mill. Add to the hot milk and season with butter, salt, pepper, and sugar (optional). Reheat, stirring constantly. Pour over fried croutons and serve immediately.

88. Onion Soup   *Soupe à l'oignon*   1814605

2 tablespoons butter
2 large onions
4 cups stock or water
rounds of dried bread

freshly grated gruyère cheese
salt and freshly ground black
    pepper

Slice onions as thin as possible. Fry gently in melted butter until yellow. Add water or stock and simmer 20 minutes. Season with salt and pepper. Pour over bread that has been generously sprinkled with cheese and brown under hot flame (optional). This is another basic French soup and has the following variations (89-93).

89. Onion Milk Soup   *Soupe à l'oignon et au lait*

Substitute milk for the stock or water in Onion Soup and omit the cheese.

90. Onion Soup with Vermicelli   *Vermicelle à l'oignon*

Follow recipe for Onion Soup. Add 4 tablespoons of broken vermicelli to the soup when it begins to simmer. Stir occasionally so that the vermicelli will not stick.

91. Onion Soup with Semolina   *Semoule à l'oignon*

Follow the recipe for Onion Soup. When the soup reaches the boiling point, add 4 tablespoons of semolina and simmer 30 minutes.

92. Onion Soup with Rice   *Riz à l'oignon*

Follow directions for Onion Soup. When the soup reaches the boiling point, add 4 tablespoons of rice and simmer 30 minutes.

93. Onion Soup with Tapioca   *Tapioca à l'oignon*

Follow directions for Onion Soup. When the soup has simmered 10 minutes, add 2 tablespoons of tapioca and simmer 10 minutes more. Stir to prevent lumping of the tapioca.

94. Julienne Soup   *Julienne*

2 carrots	2 tablespoons butter
2 small turnips	8 cups rich stock
2 potatoes	¼ cup peas (or ¼ cup string
2 leeks	beans)
3 or 4 cabbage leaves	salt and pepper

Slice carrots, turnips, potatoes, leeks, and cabbage leaves into uniformly thin strips about 1½ inches long. Fry vegetables in melted butter until they are brown. Add the stock and, when it boils, add peas or beans or both. Boil until all the vegetables are cooked (about 30 minutes). Season with salt and pepper.

95. Vegetable Purée   *Potage purée de légumes*

Follow recipe for Julienne Soup (94). Use only 4 cups of stock
or water. When the vegetables are cooked, force them through
a food mill. The soup should not be very thick and can be
thinned by adding more liquid.

96. Peasant Soup   *Potage paysanne*

2 carrots	6 cups stock
2 potatoes	salt and pepper
1 turnip	several rounds of stale bread

Dice carrots, potatoes, and turnip. Cook in 2 cups of stock
until they are soft. Add the rest of the stock and boil 5 minutes.
Season with salt and pepper and pour over bread.

97. Crayfish Soup   *Potage à la bisque d'écrevisses*

This soup is expensive and will probably be served only when you have guests. Therefore we are giving you larger proportions than usual.

TANTE MARIE

The *écrevisse* (crayfish or crawdab) is a small fresh-water shell fish usually 3 to 5 inches long. It is very common in some parts of the United States, but rarely used and almost never marketed. Lobster or shrimp make excellent substitutes (4 chicken lobsters or 2 pounds shrimp).

4 cups water	50 crayfish
1½ teaspoons salt	8 slices stale bread
¼ teaspoon black pepper	8 cups rich stock
1 onion	¼ cup of Madeira (or white
1 carrot	wine)
bouquet garni (42)	3 tablespoons butter

Dice carrot and onion and add to the water with salt, pepper, and *bouquet garni*. Bring to a full rolling boil and put in fresh crayfish. Reduce heat and cook gently 15 minutes. Strain off liquid but do not throw it away. When the fish is cool enough to handle, extract the meat from the tails. Force the shells through a meat chopper, using the finest blade. Pound to a paste. Add the paste to 2 cups of the broth and simmer 5 minutes. Strain and return to the fire. Add the stock and stale bread. Stir until the bread has blended with the stock. Add the wine and the rest of the broth and bring to the boiling point, stirring constantly with a wooden spoon. Just before serving, put in the meat and add the butter. This soup must be served immediately.

98. *Bouillabaisse*

This famous southern dish may be classified as a soup or fish dish. See recipe 188.

99. Tomato Soup   *Potage aux tomates*

4 or 5 large tomatoes, uartered	1 onion, sliced thin
	6 cups water
½ bay leaf	1 teaspoon salt
1 small branch of thyme (or ¼ teaspoon powdered thyme)	2 tablespoons butter
	croutons

Crush the tomatoes slightly in the bottom of a heavy saucepan. Cook very slowly with bay leaf, thyme, and onion for 30 minutes. Take care that the tomatoes do not stick to the pan. Force the tomatoes through a food mill or strainer. Add water, salt, and butter. Bring to the boiling point. Pour over croutons. Serve immediately. If the tomatoes are acid, add ½ teaspoon sugar.

100. Tomato Tapioca Soup

Potage au tapioca à la tomate

Follow the preceding recipe for making tomato purée. Add 2 tablespoons of tapioca to 6 cups of boiling salted water. Stir so that the tapioca will not lump. Cook 5 minutes. Combine the mixtures and bring to a boil. Add 2 tablespoons of butter and more salt if necessary. Do not use croutons.

101. Barley Soup   *Potage à la crème d'orge*

2 tablespoons butter
2 tablespoons flour
5 cups hot water
1 cup barley

4 cups rich stock, preferably chicken
1 egg yolk
salt and pepper
croutons

Melt butter and stir in flour. When well blended, add water. When the surface of the water begins to whiten, add the barley. As the barley absorbs the water, add a little more from time to time until the barley is very soft (30 to 40 minutes). Force the barley through a fine strainer and add to stock. Return to the fire for 10 minutes. Bind with the egg yolk (page 3). Season with salt and pepper and serve with croutons.

102. *Julienne languedocienne*

Prepare vegetables as for Julienne Soup (94). Cook them in ½ cup olive oil 10 minutes. Drain and add to Pea Soup (82). Add 2 cups of water, salt and pepper, and simmer 1 to 2 hours. The vegetables will be thoroughly cooked at the end of 1 hour, but the longer cooking heightens the flavor. Pour over rounds of bread.

103. Russian Soup   *Potage livonien*

2 carrots
2 turnips
2 leeks
3 or 4 cabbage leaves
2 onions
4 celery stalks
1 tablespoon chopped parsley
2 tablespoons butter

4 tablespoons cooked rice
6 cups water or stock
1 cup thick cream
1 teaspoon salt
1 teaspoon sugar
2 egg yolks
fried croutons

Slice the vegetables into narrow 2-inch strips. Boil 30 minutes in salted water. Melt butter. Add the vegetables, which have been well drained, parsley, and cooked rice. Stir the vegetables carefully so that the butter will coat everything. Add liquid and cook 5 minutes. Force through a food mill or strainer. Reheat in the top of a double boiler. Add cream, salt, and sugar. Bind with 2 egg yolks (page 3). Serve with fried croutons. Sprinkle with chopped parsley.

104. Mushroom Julienne   *Julienne aux champignons*

Prepare Julienne Soup (94). 30 minutes before serving add ½ pound of mushrooms, washed and thinly sliced. Use both caps and stems. Serve with croutons.

105. Finnish Soup   *Potage finlandais*

8 eggs	¼ cup grated Parmesan cheese
½ teaspoon salt	
¼ teaspoon white pepper	¼ cup melted butter
1 tablespoon chopped parsley	2 quarts well-seasoned rich consommé
2 tablespoons cream	
rounds of stale bread	

Beat eggs and add salt, pepper, a little of the cheese, parsley, and cream. Follow directions for making omelet (125). When the omelet is thoroughly cooked so that it is quite dry, turn upside down on a floured bread board. Cut the omelet with the same cookie cutter that is used for the bread. Place the rounds of omelet on the rounds of bread. Brush with melted butter, cover with the remaining Parmesan cheese, and place in hot oven for 3 minutes. Serve on heated platter and send to the table with a tureen of good consommé.

106. Mushroom Consommé   *Bouillon de champignons*

½ pound dried mushrooms (or   *bouquet garni* (42)
    1 pound fresh mushrooms)   salt and pepper
2 carrots   6 cups water
2 leeks

Soak the dried mushrooms 3 hours in warm water. Drain and wash well. If fresh mushrooms are used, wash well and use without soaking. Dice carrots and leeks and cook with mushrooms and the *bouquet garni* in water over a low flame for 1 hour. Season with salt and pepper. Strain before using. This is a delicious consommé and may be used in place of a meat stock. The mushrooms may be extracted from the other vegetables, cut into strips, and served with the consommé.

107. Italian Cabbage Soup   *Potage aux choux à l'italienne*

6 cups water   1 onion, chopped fine
1 cup rice   salt and pepper
1 small cabbage   6 cups stock
2 tablespoons butter (or 2   ¼ cup grated Parmesan cheese
    tablespoons chicken fat)

Bring water to a boil. Add the rice and small cabbage. Salt and cook 45 minutes. Drain well. Melt fat, add onion, cabbage, rice, salt, pepper, and stock. Simmer 30 minutes, stirring occasionally. Just before serving, sprinkle with cheese.

108. Milanaise Rice Soup   *Potage au riz à la milanaise*

1 onion, chopped fine   1 tablespoon butter
3 tablespoons butter   ¼ cup Parmesan cheese
6 cups chicken or meat stock   ⅛ teaspoon nutmeg
1 cup rice   salt and pepper
a pinch of saffron

Fry onion gently in melted butter until yellow. Add stock and bring to a boil. Wash the rice thoroughly. Add rice and saffron and simmer 45 minutes. Add more stock if necessary. The rice should keep its shape and the soup should be thicker than most soups, but still liquid. Remove from the fire. Add butter, cheese, nutmeg, salt, and pepper. Serve very hot.

A bon appétit il ne faut pas de sauce.

One must be most careful that the eggs that are being prepared are fresh for there is nothing as bad as an egg which is not perfectly fresh. It can ruin the most exquisitely prepared dish.

TANTE MARIE

109. Boiled Eggs in the Shell   *Œufs à la coque*

Place eggs in boiling water and cover the pan. Leave on the fire for 3 minutes. Remove from the water and serve in individual egg cups.

110. Baked Eggs   *Œufs sur le plat*

Put 2 tablespoons of butter in a shallow oven-proof dish and place in a moderate oven (350°F.). When the butter is bubbling, break the eggs into the dish, counting 2 eggs per person. Sprinkle with salt and freshly ground black pepper and return to the oven for 10 minutes or until the whites are thoroughly cooked. Serve immediately. A pleasant variation to this dish is made by placing slices of boiled ham or salami in the butter and breaking the eggs over them.

111. Soft-Boiled Luncheon Eggs   *Œufs mollets*

Boil eggs 5 minutes and plunge into cold water. Remove the shells, leaving the eggs whole. Serve them on Purée of Peas (455), Garden Sorrel (486), or French Spinach (487), or in ramekins with a Robert Sauce (16), Piquant Sauce (12), or Cream Sauce (2).

112. Hard-Boiled Eggs   *Œufs durs*

Boil the eggs 10 minutes. Plunge into cold water and remove the shell immediately.

113. Eggs in Béchamel Sauce   *Œufs à la béchamel*

Follow the preceding recipe for boiling eggs. Serve them whole in a Béchamel Sauce (1).

114. Salad Eggs   *Œufs durs en salade*

Slice hard-boiled eggs (112). Cover with French Dressing (31).

115. Poached Eggs   *Œufs pochés*

Fill a frying pan ¾ full of water and add 1 teaspoon salt. When the water begins to simmer, break the eggs into it very carefully. Special forms may be bought to keep the eggs in a perfect shape, but these are not necessary. Do not poach more than 3 eggs at a time. They should not touch each other. Never let the water actually boil. After 5 minutes, remove the eggs with a skimmer.

116. Eggs in Black Butter Sauce   *Œufs au beurre noir*

Heat 2 tablespoons butter and let it brown without burning. When it is quite dark in color, break 4 eggs into the pan and fry until the whites are thoroughly cooked. Remove the eggs to a heated platter. Add 1 teaspoon wine vinegar to the butter, stir a moment, and pour over the eggs quickly. Serve at once.

117. Eggs en Matelote   *Œufs en matelote*

1½ cups red wine	¼ teaspoon pepper
1½ cups water	8 eggs
1 onion, sliced thin	2 tablespoons butter
1 clove garlic	1 tablespoon flour
bouquet garni (42)	croutons
½ teaspoon salt	

Put the wine, water, onion, garlic, *bouquet garni,* salt, and pepper in a large frying pan. Boil gently 15 minutes. Remove the onion, garlic, and *bouquet garni* with a skimmer. Poach the eggs in the liquid (115). When the whites are thoroughly cooked, place the eggs on a heated platter and keep them warm. Increase the heat under the frying pan and reduce the liquid to half its amount. Bind the sauce with butter and flour (page 4). Pour the sauce over the eggs and serve with croutons.

118. Scrambled Eggs   *Œufs brouillés*

6 eggs	½ teaspoon salt
1 tablespoon butter	freshly ground black pepper
1 tablespoon chopped parsley	

Break the eggs into a bowl and beat until the yolks and whites are blended. Melt butter in a frying pan. When the butter is sizzling, add parsley, salt, and pepper. Pour in the eggs and stir constantly with a fork until the eggs are cooked. Do not let the eggs overcook or become dry. If large lumps form, break them with the fork.

119. Scrambled Eggs with Cheese
Œufs brouillés au fromage

Follow the preceding recipe, but add ¼ cup grated gruyère or Parmesan to the beaten eggs before scrambling.

120. Scrambled Eggs with Truffles
Œufs brouillés aux truffes

Slice one truffle very thin. Fry gently in butter, cool, and add to beaten eggs before scrambling (118).

121. Scrambled Eggs with Pickled Herring
Œufs brouillés aux harengs saurs

Chop 2 fillets of pickled herring very fine. Mix with beaten eggs before scrambling (118).

122. Scrambled Eggs with Asparagus
Œufs brouillés aux pointes d'asperges

Cut cold cooked asparagus into small pieces and mix with beaten eggs before scrambling (118).

123. Scrambled Eggs with Mushrooms
Œufs brouillés aux champignons

Wash and slice ¼ pound mushrooms. Fry gently in butter. Cool and add to beaten eggs before scrambling (118).

124. Stuffed Eggs   *Œufs farcis*

6 hard-boiled eggs (112)   1 small clove garlic, chopped
1 tablespoon butter   fine
1 teaspoon chopped parsley   salt and pepper
1 tablespoon fine bread crumbs

Cut the eggs lengthwise. Remove the yolk and crush with a
fork. Work in butter, bread crumbs, parsley, garlic, salt, and
pepper until they are blended to a smooth paste. Put the mixture into the white halves. Place in a buttered oven-proof dish
and brown in hot oven.

125. Plain Omelet   *Omelette au naturel*

6 eggs   1 teaspoon water
½ teaspoon salt   1 tablespoon butter
⅛ teaspoon pepper

Beat the eggs thoroughly. Add salt, pepper, and water. Melt
the butter in a light frying pan. When the butter is sizzling
hot, but not brown, pour in the eggs. As the egg mixture
begins to set on the bottom, prick it with a fork and raise a
little, thus allowing the uncooked egg to seep through. Continue the pricking and raising process until almost all the
liquid has disappeared. Remove from the fire, loosen the edge
of half the omelet from the pan with a spatula, and fold one
half over the other. Turn upside down on a heated platter. A
French omelet should never be overcooked and the center
should be slightly runny. This requires practice, but it is an
art well worth mastering. An omelet may be made with any
number of eggs, but it is better to practice on a small quantity.

126. Omelet with Herbs   *Omelette aux fines herbes*

6 eggs
½ teaspoon salt
⅛ teaspoon pepper
1 teaspoon water

1 tablespoon chopped parsley
1 tablespoon chopped chives
1 tablespoon butter

Mix the finely chopped herbs into the beaten eggs along with the salt, pepper, and water. Follow the preceding recipe for making omelet

127. Mushroom Omelet   *Omelette aux champignons*

Wash and peel ¼ pound of mushrooms. Slice thin. Fry in butter 10 minutes. Season with salt and pepper and cool. Mix with the beaten eggs and proceed as in Plain Omelet (125).

128. Truffle Omelet   *Omelette aux truffes*

Substitute 1 or 2 small truffles for the mushrooms in the preceding recipe.

129. Kidney Omelet   *Omelette au rognon*

Cut 1 veal kidney in small pieces. A beef kidney or 4 lamb kidneys will do as well. Fry the kidney in 1 tablespoon butter until brown on all sides. Season with salt and pepper. Make a Plain Omelet (125) in a separate frying pan. Just before folding the omelet, spread the kidneys on it so that they will be in the center of the finished omelet.

130. Cheese Omelet   *Omelette au fromage*

Add ¼ cup grated Swiss or Parmesan cheese to the eggs and follow directions for making Plain Omelet (125).

131. Bread Omelet   *Omelette au pain*

2 slices stale white bread	½ teaspoon salt
½ cup milk	⅛ teaspoon pepper
4 eggs, well beaten	

Remove the crusts from the bread. Soak in milk. When the bread has absorbed the milk, add the eggs. Follow recipe 125 for making omelet. (The only advantage to this recipe is one of economy.)

132. Foamy Omelet   *Omelette mousseuse*

Beat the yolks and whites of 4 eggs separately. Fold the whites into the yolks. Season with salt and pepper and proceed as in Plain Omelet (125).

133. Macaroni Omelet   *Omelette au macaroni*

4 eggs	1 cup cold, cooked macaroni
4 tablespoons grated Swiss or	salt and pepper
Parmesan cheese	2 tablespoons butter

Beat the eggs thoroughly. Add the macaroni, cut in small pieces, cheese, salt, and pepper. Cook like Plain Omelet (125). Take care that it does not stick to the frying pan.

134. Salt Pork or Bacon Omelet   *Omelette au lard*

6 eggs   ¼ teaspoon white pepper
¼ pound salt pork or bacon,
   diced

Try out the bacon or salt pork. Pour off the excess fat, leaving
not more than 2 tablespoons in the frying pan. Pour in the
well-beaten eggs, seasoned with pepper, and proceed as in
Plain Omelet (125).

135. Ham Omelet   *Omelette au jambon*

¼ pound boiled ham   6 eggs
1 tablespoon butter   ⅛ teaspoon white pepper

Trim the fat off the ham. Dice ham and fry in butter. Add to
well-beaten eggs and proceed as in Plain Omelet (125).

136. Onion Omelet   *Omelette à l'oignon*

2 tablespoons butter   6 eggs
1 large onion, sliced thin   salt and pepper

Fry the onions in butter until they are a golden brown. Pour
well-beaten eggs over the onion and proceed as in Plain
Omelet (125).

137. Asparagus Omelet   *Omelette aux pointes d'asperges*

1 cup cold cooked asparagus   6 eggs
2 tablespoons butter   salt and pepper

Cut the asparagus in small pieces. Heat in the melted butter
in the omelet pan. Pour the well-beaten eggs over the asparagus
and proceed as in Plain Omelet (125).

138. Potato Omelet   *Omelette aux pommes de terre*

2 cups diced boiled potatoes
2 tablespoons butter

6 eggs
salt and pepper

Fry the potatoes in butter until they are golden. Mix with well-beaten eggs and proceed as in Plain Omelet (125).

139. Tomato Omelet   *Omelette aux tomates*

4 tomatoes
2 tablespoons olive oil

6 eggs
salt and pepper

Peel the tomatoes and remove the seeds. Cut the tomato flesh into eighths and fry gently in olive oil for 5 minutes. Cool. Mix with well-beaten eggs and proceed as in Plain Omelet (125).

140. Cheese Fondue I   *Fondue I*

6 tablespoons butter
3 tablespoons flour
3 egg yolks
½ cup milk

1½ cups freshly grated cheese
1 egg white
salt and pepper

Melt the butter in the top of a double boiler and stir in flour. Add milk and egg yolks and simmer over hot but not boiling water until the mixture begins to thicken. Stir constantly with a wooden spoon so that the eggs will not curdle. Remove from the fire. Add cheese, salt, and pepper, and egg white beaten stiff. Bake in a buttered baking dish for 25 minutes in a 350°F. oven. The fondue should not be too thick.

141. Cheese Fondue II *Fondue* II

2 tablespoons butter
4 eggs, well beaten

4 tablespoons freshly grated cheese
salt and pepper

Combine butter, eggs, cheese, salt, and pepper in the top of a double boiler. Do not let the water boil. Stir constantly until the mixture is smooth. Serve immediately with fresh French bread or crisp toast. If Parmesan cheese is used, use 4 tablespoons butter and ⅓ cup cheese.

142. Cheese Soufflé *Soufflé au fromage*

See recipe 65.

143. Garlic Eggs *Œufs à l'ail*

4 cloves garlic
2 fillets of anchovy
6 capers
3 tablespoons olive oil
1 teaspoon wine vinegar

½ teaspoon salt
⅛ teaspoon freshly ground pepper
6 hard-boiled eggs

Chop and crush the garlic. Add anchovies and capers and mash them all together to make a paste. Stir in oil, vinegar, salt, and pepper. Quarter the shelled hard-boiled eggs and cover with the sauce.

A l'œuvre on connaît l'artisan.

FISH is more appreciated and generally better prepared in France than anywhere else in the world. The variety of commonly used fish is greater and the methods of preparing it are more imaginative. Actually almost every fish caught for the French market can be found somewhere in the lakes, streams, or coastal waters of the United States, but since they do not appear in most markets, we shall try to indicate the fish that is obtainable and most nearly approximates the fish called for by Tante Marie.

FRESHNESS OF FISH: Fish must be absolutely fresh to be good. One can determine freshness by the appearance of the eyes and gills. The eyes should be bright and the gills should be red. Tante Marie warns, *Beware the merchant who colors the gills with lamb's blood.*

TO CLEAN FISH: Usually the merchant will clean and prepare the fish for cooking. Some people prefer to do it themselves. Small fish may be cleaned by inserting the finger in the opening of the gills and withdrawing the intestines. The larger fish are cleaned by making a short incision in the belly of the fish and removing the blood and intestines. The gills should be removed but the roe may be left.

TO SCALE FISH: Hold the fish by the tail and scrape the scales off with a sharp knife, running from tail to head. Hold the knife flat against the fish so that the skin will not be broken.

TO SKIN THE FISH: Rub your hands with salt to keep them from slipping. Loosen the skin at either the head or tail with the sharp point of a knife. Holding the fish with one hand, grasp the loosened skin with a dish cloth or, if possible, a pair of pliers. Jerk the skin off with a quick pull.

TO KEEP FISH: If fish is not to be used immediately, clean it and wipe it with a damp dish towel. Wrap it in wax paper and store in the cold part of the refrigerator.

144. Court-bouillon

The most common method of preparing fish in France is by simmering it in a *court-bouillon*. The following basic recipe will be called for in many of the succeeding recipes.

In a pan large enough to cook the fish, pour equal amounts of white wine and water. There should be enough to cover the fish, which will be put in later. Add 1 teaspoon salt, $\frac{1}{4}$ teaspoon white pepper, *bouquet garni* (42), 2 cloves, 1 onion sliced thin, and 1 carrot cut in rounds. Cover the pan and simmer 45 minutes. Put in the fish and let it simmer until cooked. The *court-bouillon* should never boil. This keeps the flesh from breaking. When the fish is cooked, remove from the fire but keep in the *court-bouillon* until it is ready to be served.

145. Salt-Water Cooking   *A la bonne eau*

When the recipe calls for cooking *à la bonne eau*, put enough water in the kettle to cover the fish, which will be put in later. Add a large amount of salt—1 tablespoon to a quart of water —and bring water to the boiling point. Place the fish in the water carefully and let it simmer—not boil—until the fish is cooked. It will then be removed and served with the appropriate sauce.

146. Boiled Salmon   *Saumon au court-bouillon*

3 pounds salmon, whole or chunk	choice of:
court-bouillon (144)	Hollandaise Sauce (10)
parsley	Cream Sauce (2)
	Italian Sauce (26)

Prepare the *court-bouillon.* Wipe the fish and tie it in a piece of cheese cloth or dish towel. When the *court-bouillon* is ready, lower the fish into it carefully. Let the fish simmer 45 minutes. Do not let it boil. Lift the cloth from the kettle. Drain off all the water and place fish on a platter. Decorate with sprigs of parsley and serve with a bowl of sauce.

147. Cold Salmon with Green Mayonnaise
Saumon froid à la mayonnaise verte

A small salmon or large pink-fleshed trout is perfect for this attractive dish. If a whole fish is used, leave the head and tail on and remove the eyes only. A chunk of salmon is equally delicious although not so decorative.

Prepare the salmon as in the preceding recipe. Let the fish cool in the *court-bouillon.* Drain thoroughly and place on a long platter. Remove the skin carefully. Decorate with sprigs of parsley and thin slices of lemon. A realistic eye may be made with the white end of a hard boiled egg and a round of truffle or black olive. Serve with a bowl of Green Mayonnaise (18).

148. Trout with Herb Sauce

Truites de rivière à la genevoise

4 large trout	2 tablespoons chopped parsley
court-bouillon (144)	2 tablespoons chopped onions
2 tablespoons butter	2 pieces stale bread
3 tablespoons chopped mush-	salt and pepper
rooms	

Prepare a *court-bouillon*. Clean the trout. When the *court-bouillon* is ready, let the trout simmer in it 15 to 20 minutes, depending on the size of the trout. Meanwhile, lightly fry the mushrooms, parsley, and onion in the melted butter. Soak the bread in a little of the *court-bouillon*. Squeeze the liquid from the bread and add the bread and ¼ cup of the *court-bouillon* to the herbs. Blend thoroughly. Season and spread the sauce on a heated platter. Place the trout on the sauce and serve very hot.

149. Fried Trout   *Truites frites*

8 small trout	salt
salad oil or butter	slices of lemon
flour	

Heat enough oil or butter so that it measures ¼ inch in the frying pan. Roll each cleaned fish in flour. When the fat is sizzling hot, fry the fish 5 minutes on each side. Salt them and serve on a heated platter with slices of lemon.

150. Tuna Fish   *Thon*

Fresh tuna caught on the Pacific Coast is prepared like salmon.
Follow recipes 146 and 147. Canned tuna is served as an
hors-d'œuvre (48).

151. Striped Bass   *Bar au court-bouillon*

Prepare either the *court-bouillon* (144) or the salted water
(145). Simmer the bass, allowing 15 minutes per pound.
Drain and place on heated platter. Cover with White Sauce
(3) and decorate with sprigs of parsley.

152. Broiled Perch   *Les petits bars grillés*

6 perch   Maître d'hôtel Sauce (9)

Clean and scale the fish (page 54). Preheat the broiler on
which the fish are to be broiled. This will keep them from
sticking. Broil the fish 20 minutes, turning them only once.
Place the fish on a hot platter and cover with Maître d'hôtel
Sauce.

153. Mullet with Cream Sauce   *Mulet à la sauce blanche*

1 mullet weighing about   *court-bouillon* (144)
    3 pounds   Cream Sauce (2)

Clean the fish (page 54), leaving the head and tail on. Prepare the *court-bouillon* and, when it is ready, allow the fish
to simmer 45 minutes. Remove from the *court-bouillon*, drain,
place on a warm platter, and serve with a bowl of Cream
Sauce.

154. Broiled Mullet   *Mulet grillé*

2 mullets, weighing 1 to 1½ pounds	mullet liver
	Cream Sauce (2)

When the fish is cleaned, preserve the liver carefully. Preheat the broiling rack so that the fish will not stick. Broil the fish under a moderate flame, turning only once. Crush the liver and add to the sauce. This will give it a very pretty color. Place the fish on a heated platter. Cover with Cream Sauce and garnish with sprigs of parsley.

155. Turbot with Caper Sauce

Turbot, sauce aux câpres

Turbot is a member of the flounder family. It is sometimes called 'halibut,' but it is actually much smaller than the common halibut. It is fished in the Atlantic waters from Maine to the Carolinas.

2 2-pound turbots	parsley
court-bouillon (144)	Caper Sauce (4)
½ lemon	

Clean the turbots by cutting off the heads and withdrawing the intestines from that end. Tante Marie suggests sewing the heads back on. This may seem a little excessive. Prepare the *court-bouillon*. Rub the white side of the fish with the lemon, and when the *court-bouillon* is ready, place the fish white side up in the kettle. Simmer the fish 30 minutes. Remove from the *court-bouillon*, drain, and place on a heated platter. Serve with Caper Sauce.

156. Baked Turbot   *Turbot au gratin*

2 chicken turbots (or 2 sole or
   8 fillets of sole)
3 tablespoons butter
2 tablespoons finely chopped
   onion
2 tablespoons chopped parsley

salt
black pepper
fine bread crumbs
⅓ cup dry white wine
sprigs of parsley and slices of
   lemon

Clean and scale the fish (page 54). Dot the bottom of an oven-proof dish with half the butter and spread half the chopped onion and parsley over it. Sprinkle generously with salt and pepper. Place the fish, white side up, or arrange the fillets of sole on this mixture. Cover with the remaining butter, onion, and parsley. Salt and pepper. Moisten with white wine and bake 30 minutes in 350°F. oven. Cover with bread crumbs and moisten with melted butter. Place under a broiler until the crumbs are golden brown. Garnish with the parsley and lemon slices.

157. Skate in Black Butter Sauce   *Raie au beurre noir*

1 1½- to 2-pound skate
bouquet garni (42)
1 teaspoon salt
¼ teaspoon pepper

½ pound butter
parsley
1 tablespoon wine vinegar

Clean the fish (page 54). Put enough water in a kettle so that the fish will be completely covered. Add a *bouquet garni*, salt, and pepper. Boil 5 minutes. Reduce the heat and put in the fish. Simmer 25 minutes. Meanwhile, melt butter over a moderate flame, letting it brown but not burn. When the butter is very hot, throw in several sprigs of parsley and fry them. As soon as the fish is done, remove from the water, drain, and take off the black skin. Place on a very hot platter.

Pour the butter and parsley over the fish and return the frying pan to the flame. Put in the vinegar. This will boil in a matter of seconds. Pour it over the fish and serve immediately with a side dish of boiled potatoes. Whitefish fillets may be substituted for the skate.

158. Skate with White Butter Sauce

Raie au beurre blanc

Follow the preceding recipe but, instead of browning the butter, simply melt it. When it is very hot, add 2 tablespoons chopped parsley, salt, and freshly ground black pepper. Pour over the cooked skate and serve very hot.

159. Fried Skate   *Raie frite*

1 2-pound skate	parsley
flour	salt
salad oil	

Cut the skate into strips. Roll each strip in flour and fry in $\frac{1}{2}$ inch very hot oil. Fry sprigs of parsley at the same time. Drain on absorbent paper, salt, and serve immediately.

160. Salt Cod   *Morue*

To freshen: Good salt cod may be prepared in many delicious ways. It must be properly freshened before using. Soak in cool water 8 to 10 hours, changing the water twice. If there is no time for freshening, bring the cod to a boil, starting from cold water. Throw the water away and wash the cod in cool water before using. Take care to taste before salting.

161. Salt Cod with Parsley Creamed Potatoes
Morue aux pommes de terre

1¼ pounds salt cod, in one piece	salt
2 tablespoons butter	freshly ground black pepper
2 tablespoons flour	2 tablespoons chopped parsley
2 cups milk, scalded	5 or 6 medium-sized boiled potatoes

Freshen the cod (160). Start the cod in cold water and bring to the boiling point. Remove from the fire. Skim the water and let the cod stand in the covered saucepan on the back of the stove for at least 15 minutes before using. Melt the butter and stir in flour. Add the milk and stir until smooth. If the sauce is too thick, add more milk. Season with salt, pepper, and parsley. Go lightly with the salt. Add the potatoes, which have been previously boiled. Place the cod in the center of a warm platter and surround with creamed potatoes.

162. Salt Cod au Gratin   *Morue au fromage*

Follow the preceding recipe, but instead of leaving the cod in one piece, cut it in small pieces, after it has been freshened, and add it with the potatoes to the sauce. Put in an oven-proof dish, cover with grated cheese and fine bread crumbs. Place under the broiler until the top is golden brown. Serve in the same dish and decorate with sprigs of parsley.

163. Salt Cod in Black Butter Sauce
Morue au beurre noir

1½ pounds salt cod, in one piece	Black Butter Sauce (14)

Freshen the salt cod (160). Start the freshened cod in cold water and bring to the boiling point. Skim the water and re-

move the pan from the fire. Cover and place on the back of
the stove for 15 minutes. Place the fish on a very hot platter
and cover with Black Butter Sauce. Serve immediately.

164. Burgundian Cod   *Morue à la bourguignonne*

1½ pounds salt cod, in one piece	12 small onions
	bouquet garni (42)
3 tablespoons butter	salt
2 tablespoons flour	freshly ground black pepper
2 cups hot water	dash of mace

Freshen the cod (160). Start the freshened cod in cold water
and bring to the boiling point. Skim the water, cover and set
the pan on the back of the stove. Melt butter and stir in flour.
When the flour is blended with the butter, stir in water. The
sauce should be thin. Add more water if necessary. Cook the
onions in the sauce along with the *bouquet garni*, salt, pepper,
and mace. When the onions are tender (approximately 20
minutes), remove the *bouquet garni*. Reheat the cod, drain
well, and serve on a warm platter with the sauce poured over
the fish.

165. Fresh Cod, Hollandaise Sauce

Cabillaud, sauce hollandaise

1 small cod (4 to 5 pounds), or 3- to 4-pound chunk of cod	8 to 10 small potatoes
	Hollandaise Sauce (10)

Fill a kettle with enough water to cover the fish. Add a generous amount of salt. Bring to a boil. Tie the fish, which has
been wiped clean, in a piece of cheesecloth, and place in the
water. Add the peeled potatoes at the same time. Simmer 30
to 40 minutes. Drain the fish. Place on heated platter. Surround with the potatoes and serve with a bowl of Hollandaise
Sauce.

166. Salt Cod Mousse   *Brandade de morue*

1 pound salt cod	¾ cup olive oil
2 tablespoons olive oil	salt
½ cup warm milk	freshly ground black pepper
2 truffles	

Freshen the cod (160). Bring the fish to the boiling point, starting it in cold water. Skim the water and set the fish aside to cool in the covered pan. When the cod is cool, remove the skin and bones.

Heat 2 tablespoons of olive oil in the top of a double boiler. Break the cod into small pieces and add to the oil. Stir until the mixture is smooth. Continue cooking 30 minutes and stir frequently. The cod must become a soft mass, but it must not be too thick. To prevent this, add the warm milk a little bit at a time. It may be necessary to add more than ½ cup. Chop the truffles very fine and add to the fish. At the end of 30 minutes, remove from the fire and add the rest of the olive oil, drop by drop, beating constantly as in the making of Mayonnaise (17). An electric beater is a great help. Season highly with salt and pepper. Contrary to other authorities, Tante Marie says, 'Do not add garlic or parsley.'

167. Broiled Mackerel, Maître d'hôtel
                   Maquereau à la maître d'hôtel

1 large or 2 medium-sized mackerel	2 tablespoons chopped parsley
	salt and pepper
3 tablespoons butter	½ lemon

Remove the head and split fish down the back. Wash and wipe dry. Heat the broiling rack so that the fish will not stick. Broil the fish under a low flame 25 to 30 minutes. Heat the serving platter. Spread the butter on the platter. Sprinkle with parsley, salt and pepper, and lemon juice. Place the fish over this mixture and serve immediately.

168. Mackerel with Black Butter Sauce
Maquereau au beurre noir

1 2- to 3-pound mackerel, or 2 1-pound mackerel	Black Butter Sauce (14) boiled potatoes

Cook the whole mackerel in salted water (145). The head and tail should be kept on, but the fish should be cleaned (page 54). Simmer the fish 30 to 40 minutes, depending on the size of the mackerel. Remove from the water, drain thoroughly, split open, and remove the backbone. Place the fish on a very hot platter. Serve with the Black Butter Sauce poured over the fish and surround with small new potatoes, which have been boiled in their jackets and peeled.

169. Flemish Mackerel   *Maquereau à la flamande*

1 2½- to 3-pound mackerel	2 teaspoons chopped onion
2 tablespoons butter	juice of ½ lemon
2 tablespoons chopped parsley	salt and pepper
1 tablespoon chopped chives	

Clean a fresh mackerel carefully, taking care not to remove the head or tail. Make an incision along the belly of the fish. Soften (not melt) the butter and work into it the parsley, chives, onion, salt, pepper, and 1 teaspoon lemon juice. When the mixture is well blended, place it in the fish. Roll the fish in oiled brown paper and tie at both ends. Cook 45 minutes in 350°F. oven. Remove the fish carefully from the paper onto a warm platter, and pour the butter that will be in the brown paper over the fish. Sprinkle with remaining lemon juice. Garnish with sprigs of fresh parsley.

170. Italian Mackerel   *Maquereau à l'italienne*

2 1½-pound mackerel   Italian Herb Sauce (26)
court-bouillon (144)

Prepare the *court-bouillon*. When it is ready, simmer the
mackerel 30 minutes. Drain the fish well and serve with
Italian Herb Sauce.

171. Broiled Fresh Herring   *Harengs frais sur le gril*

3 fresh herring, weighing ap-   1 tablespoon prepared mustard
   proximately 1 pound each   salt
Cream Sauce (2)

Clean and scale the herring. Make 3 incisions on each side
of the fish. Preheat the grill so that the fish will not stick.
Broil 3 to 4 minutes on each side. Salt and serve with Cream
Sauce, highly seasoned with mustard.

172. Fresh Herring, Maître d'hôtel
Harengs frais à la maître d'hôtel

3 herring, weighing approx-   lemon juice
   imately 1 pound each   salt
4 tablespoons butter   freshly ground black pepper
2 tablespoons chopped parsley

Prepare and cook the herring as in the preceding recipe. Arrange on an oven-proof platter. Garnish each herring with
butter, parsley, salt, and pepper. Place under broiler 2 minutes, sprinkle with lemon juice, and serve very hot.

173. Marinated Herring *Harengs de Dieppe marinés*

12 small herring	2 small carrots, cut in rounds
2 cups water	2 cloves garlic
2 cups dry white wine	5 peppercorns
1 cup wine vinegar	*bouquet garni* (42)
1 large onion, chopped fine	

Combine water, wine, vinegar, onion, carrots, garlic, peppercorns, and *bouquet garni*. Boil 15 minutes. Scale and clean the herring. Cook in the *court-bouillon* 6 minutes. Remove from the fire and let the fish cool in the liquor. Serve cold. This makes an excellent hors d'œuvre.

174. Sole *Soles*

The famous sole of England and France is not to be found in American coastal waters. However, species of flounder, variously called Lemon Sole, Sand Dab, Limande, and Common Flatfish, are sold as sole and make excellent substitutes. Packaged fillets of whitefish, common in American markets, can be used in recipes calling for fillets of sole.

To Prepare Sole: The black skin of the sole (or flounder) is removed before cooking. To do this, follow directions on page 55 for skinning fish. The white underskin may be removed in the same way, but usually it is sufficient just to scrape off the scales with a blunt knife. If the fish is to be filleted, remove both the black and the white skins. Cut off the head and tail and lift the fillets from either side of the backbone. The fish should be rinsed and wiped dry before cooking. A little lemon juice in the water helps to whiten the flesh.

175. Fried Sole   *Soles frites*

4 sole   salt
flour   several sprigs of parsley
oil (vegetable or peanut)

Prepare the sole, removing the black skin only (174). Roll each fish in flour and fry in ½ inch hot oil (375°F.). Turn the fish only once; 3 minutes on each side should be enough. Prick the fish with a sharp knife. If the flesh falls apart readily, it is cooked. Drain on absorbent paper and serve with fried parsley.

176. Sole in White Wine and Herbs
Soles aux fines herbes et au vin blanc

4 small sole (or 1 2-pound   salt
    flounder)   freshly ground black pepper
3 tablespoons butter   ½ cup dry white wine
3 tablespoons chopped parsley   fine bread crumbs
1 tablespoon chopped shallots
    or onion

Prepare the sole (174). Put half the butter, parsley, and shallots in the bottom of a large, shallow oven-proof dish. Sprinkle with salt and pepper. Place the sole on the mixture and cover with the rest of the butter and herbs. Salt and pepper generously. Pour the white wine over the fish, cover with bread crumbs, and dot with butter. Cook 30 minutes in a 350°F. oven. Just before serving, place under broiler until the crumbs are golden brown. Serve in the same dish. Garnish with parsley.

177. Baked Sole   *Soles au gratin*

4 small sole
2 tablespoons butter
1 tablespoon chopped shallots
    or onion
2 tablespoons chopped parsley
salt

freshly ground black pepper
½ cup dry white wine
¼ pound small mushrooms
fine bread crumbs
slices of lemon

Prepare the sole, removing the black skin only (174). Put the butter in a large shallow oven-proof platter. Place the sole in the platter and spread with shallots and parsley. Sprinkle with salt and pepper. Moisten with wine and place the mushroom caps, which have been thoroughly washed, on the fish. Cover with bread crumbs, dot with butter, and cook in moderate oven (350°F.) 30 minutes. Serve with slices of lemon.

178. Baked Fillets of Sole   *Filets de soles au gratin*

Follow the preceding recipe, substituting 6 to 8 fillets for the whole fish. This is an excellent way to prepare fish when only the packaged or frozen fillets are available.

179. Fried Fillets of Sole   *Filets de soles à la Colbert*

6 sole fillets
flour
salt

Maître d'hôtel Sauce (9) or
    Mayonnaise (17)

Split each fillet in two. Roll each piece up and place on a spit. Four pieces to each spit does very well. Dredge with flour and fry in hot (375°F.) deep fat (41) 4 to 5 minutes. Serve with Maître d'hôtel Sauce or Mayonnaise.

180. Sole Filling for Patty Shells or Vol-au-vent
Filets de soles pour garniture

6 fillets of sole
2 tablespoons butter
¼ cup dry white wine
½ cup water

½ teaspoon salt
⅛ teaspoon pepper
Béchamel Sauce (1)

Combine water, wine, butter, salt, and pepper. Bring to a boil and simmer the fillets in it for 20 minutes. Drain well and mix with a fairly thick Béchamel Sauce. This is used to fill a large Vol-au-vent (372) or individual patty shells.

181. Normandy Sole   *Soles normandes*

2 1½-pound sole
2 tablespoons butter
1 cup water
1 cup dry white wine
12 mussels or clams
12 large mushroom caps
10 oysters

10 shrimps
2 tablespoons butter
2 tablespoons flour
1 egg yolk
fried croutons
several sprigs of parsley

Prepare the sole, removing both skins (174). Combine water, wine, and butter in a large pan. Bring to the boiling point and add the sole, mushrooms, mussels or clams, and oysters. Simmer 20 minutes. Remove the sole carefully and place in an oven-proof platter. Drain the rest, but save the liquor. In another pan, melt the butter and stir in flour, allowing it to cook until light brown in color. Stir constantly with a wooden spoon to prevent burning. Add ¾ cup of the liquor in which the fish has been cooked. If the sauce is too thick, add more liquor. Thicken with egg yolk (page 3), and pour the sauce over the fish. Place the mushrooms, oysters, and clams or mussels on the fish and bake 15 minutes in a 350°F. oven. Meanwhile fry shrimps and croutons in butter and use as a garnish. Decorate with sprigs of parsley.

182. Fried Whiting *Merlans frits*

4 small whiting (approximately 1 pound each)	salad or peanut oil
flour	salt

Clean and scale the whiting (page 54). Leave the heads on. Roll in flour and fry in ½ inch hot oil (375°F.). Sprinkle with salt and serve.

183. Baked Whiting. *Merlans au gratin*

Follow the recipe for Baked Sole (177), substituting 4 whiting for sole.

184. Whiting in White Wine and Herbs
Merlans aux fines herbes et au vin blanc

Follow recipe 176, substituting 4 whiting for the sole.

185. Whiting Fillets in Tomato Sauce
Filets de merlans à l'Orly

8 whiting fillets	2 tablespoons chopped parsley
juice of ½ lemon	flour
salt	Tomato Sauce (21)
freshly ground black pepper	

Place the fillets in a shallow dish. Sprinkle with lemon juice, salt, pepper, and parsley. Let them stand for at least 1 hour. Put a generous amount of flour in a dish towel. Drain and wipe the fillets and roll them in the dish towel. Each fillet should be well coated. Fry 4 to 5 minutes in 375°F. fat or oil (41). There should be enough fat to cover the fish. Serve with Tomato Sauce, which has been prepared during the marinating of the fish.

186. Fried Smelts   *Eperlans frits*

8 large smelts	flour
milk	lemon wedges

Clean the fish through the gills, if possible (page 54). Otherwise, make as small a slit as possible in the belly and remove the intestines. Do not remove heads or tails. It is important to keep the fish whole. Place smelts on skewers, allowing 2 to each skewer. Dip in milk and then in flour. Plunge into deep fat (375°F.) and fry 4 minutes. Drain on absorbent paper, salt, and serve immediately. Garnish with lemon wedges.

187. Mixed Fish in Red Wine   *Matelote bourgeoise*

2 pounds mixed fish (haddock, whiting, eel, fresh cod, perch, carp)	salt and pepper
	2 cloves garlic
	3 tablespoons butter
1 bottle red wine	2 tablespoons flour
several sprigs of parsley	20 small onions
1 large onion, chopped fine	½ pound mushrooms
1 carrot, cut in rounds	10 shrimps
1 sprig thyme	croutons

Combine red wine, parsley, carrot, onion, thyme, garlic, salt, and pepper and simmer 1 hour. Cut the fish in 3-inch strips and simmer in this *court-bouillon* for 15 minutes. Melt butter in a large saucepan and stir in flour. Add gradually 2 cups of the strained *court-bouillon* and stir with a wooden spoon until the sauce is smooth. If the sauce is thick, add more *court-bouillon*. Add the fish strips, the mushrooms, which have been thoroughly washed, and the onions, which have been peeled and fried lightly in butter. Continue cooking the sauce over a low flame until the onions are tender—approximately 20 minutes. Meanwhile fry the croutons and shrimps. Serve in a deep platter, using the shrimps and croutons as a garnish.

188. Bouillabaisse *Bouillabaisse*

This is a home version of the famous Marseillaise bouillabaisse.

2 pounds mixed fish (haddock, carp, eel, whiting, sole)
1 cup lobster meat (optional)
6 onions, cut in quarters
1 bay leaf
3 cloves
2 cloves garlic
1 teaspoon salt
½ teaspoon pepper
generous pinch of saffron
2 cups white wine
4 cups water
1 teaspoon chopped parsley
¼ cup olive oil
several slices of stale bread

Tie the fish, lobster meat, onions, bay leaf, cloves, and garlic in a piece of cheesecloth. Suspend this in a *court-bouillon* made of white wine, water, parsley, olive oil, salt, pepper, and saffron. Cook gently 45 minutes. Drain the fish. Remove the onions, bay leaf, cloves, and garlic and place the fish in the *court-bouillon*. Add the stale bread and serve in a large tureen.

189. Fried Carp *Carpe frite*

1 small carp, weighing 2½ to 3 pounds
1 large onion, chopped fine
½ bay leaf
¼ teaspoon powdered thyme
1 tablespoon chopped parsley
1 tablespoon wine vinegar
flour
salad or peanut oil

Clean, scale, and wash the carp (page 54). Split open. If there is roe, save it carefully. Put the fish in a shallow dish (not metal). Cover with chopped onion, herbs, and vinegar. Let the fish marinate 1 to 2 hours. Drain and roll in flour. Heat enough oil in a large frying pan so that the fish will be covered. Fry 6 minutes or until tender at 390°F. During the last 3 minutes of cooking, add the roe, which has been rolled in flour. Salt the fish and serve on a heated platter with a garnish of lemon slices and sprigs of parsley.

190. Broiled Carp   *Carpe grillée*

2- to 3-pound carp
⅓ cup salad oil

slices of lemon
sprigs of parsley

Clean, scale, and wash the carp (page 54). Split open and marinate in oil 15 minutes. Preheat the grill to prevent sticking. Broil 20 minutes, turning only once. Salt and serve with lemon slices and sprigs of parsley.

191. Carp in Mushroom Herb Sauce   *Carpe à la provençale*

2- to 3-pound carp
½ bottle red wine (burgundy type)
2 tablespoons oil
1 tablespoon butter, creamed with 1 tablespoon flour

2 tablespoons chopped parsley
1 small onion, chopped fine
1 clove garlic, chopped fine
¼ pound mushrooms, chopped fine
salt and pepper

Heat wine, oil, butter and flour. Add parsley, onion, garlic, mushrooms, salt, and pepper. Cook 5 minutes. Add the carp and cook slowly 1 hour in the sauce. Place the carp on a hot platter and pour the sauce over it. If it is too liquid, boil it down quickly.

192. Eel with Tartar Sauce   *Anguille tartare*

[It may sound exotic but do not be afraid to try this dish. I have tried it on unwilling skeptics and have proved its fame is well deserved. C. T.]

Eel is apt to have a very strong fishy flavor that is not pleasant. The French method of cooking eel in a *court-bouillon* eliminates this. If the fish merchant will not skin the eel, do it yourself. Rub your hands in salt. Loosen the skin around the neck with the sharp point of a knife. Hold the head with the left hand and strip off the skin with a pair of pliers. Cut off the head. Clean the eel by making a split in the belly and removing the entrails. Wipe well before cooking.

1 eel	2 tablespoons flour
½ bottle dry white wine	1 egg yolk
2 cups stock or water	fine bread crumbs
3 small onions	4 tablespoons chopped parsley,
2 carrots, cut in rounds	onion, and chives, mixed
bouquet garni (42)	1 whole egg beaten with 2
2 cloves	tablespoons oil
2 cloves garlic	peanut or salad oil
salt and pepper	Tartar Sauce (20)
2 tablespoons butter	

Prepare a *court-bouillon* of the water or stock, wine, onions, carrots, *bouquet garni*, cloves, garlic, salt, and pepper. Simmer 30 minutes. Roll the cleaned and skinned eel into a circle, placing the tail in the slit in the belly. Tie securely so that the eel will keep its shape. Place the eel in the *court-bouillon* and simmer 30 minutes. Remove it carefully and place on a platter to cool. Melt butter and stir in flour. Keep stirring with a wooden spoon until the flour is pale brown. Add 1 cup of the *court-bouillon*, which has been carefully strained. Continue stirring until the sauce is smooth. Remove from the flame and add the egg yolk. Cool the sauce and smear the eel with it. Roll the eel in bread crumbs and then in the chopped herbs. Dip in the oil and egg mixture and then again in the bread crumbs. Heat 1 inch of salad or peanut oil in a large frying pan. Fry at 390°F. until the eel is golden brown. Place on a hot platter and fill the center with Tartar Sauce.

193. Eel with Wine and Mushroom Sauce
Anguille à la poulette

1 eel
½ bottle dry white wine
2 bay leaves
several sprigs of parsley
1 onion, chopped fine
salt and pepper
2 tablespoons butter

2 tablespoons flour
12 very small onions
¼ pound mushrooms
1 egg yolk
12 shrimps
fried croutons

Clean and skin the eel according to the preceding recipe. Cut in 3-inch pieces and place in a pan with wine, bay leaves, parsley, onion, salt, and pepper. Boil briskly 30 minutes. In another saucepan, melt the butter and stir in flour. Moisten with 1 cup of the *court-bouillon* in which the eel has been cooked. Season with salt and pepper according to taste, and stir until the sauce is smooth. Add the onions and mushrooms. Cook until the onions are tender. Add more of the *court-bouillon* if sauce is too thick. Just before serving, bind the sauce with the egg yolk (page 3). Place the eel on a warm platter, cover with the sauce, and garnish with shrimps and croutons, which have been lightly fried in butter.

194. Fried Eel   *Anguille frite*

1 eel
2 beaten eggs

fine bread crumbs
Tomato Sauce (21)

Follow recipe 192 for skinning and cleaning the eel. Cut the eel in 3-inch pieces and cook in *court-bouillon* as in the preceding recipe. When the eel is cooked, drain and dry the pieces. Dip in egg and roll in bread crumbs. Heat 1 inch of salad or peanut oil to 390°F. and fry until the pieces are golden brown. Serve with Tomato Sauce.

195. Crayfish   *Ecrevisses*

The *écrevisse* (crayfish or crawdab) is better known and more appreciated in France than in the United States. It has a very delicate flavor. Although it is rarely marketed except on the West Coast, it abounds in lakes, rivers, and swamps, particularly in the South and Midwest. It is found, although rarely, in New England ponds. The average crawdab measures 4 to 5 inches and looks like a small lobster. It takes a great many crawdabs to make a respectable meal.

196. Crayfish in *Court-bouillon*

Ecrevisses au court-bouillon

40 crayfish	1 bay leaf
½ bottle white wine	2 small cloves garlic
2 cups water	several sprigs of parsley
1 onion, finely chopped	salt
1 carrot, sliced in rounds	freshly ground black pepper

Prepare the *court-bouillon* of wine, water, onion, carrot, bay leaf, garlic, parsley, salt, and a generous amount of black pepper. Simmer 30 minutes. Wash the crayfish in several waters. Add to the *court-bouillon* and simmer (not boil) 12 minutes. Serve very hot, piled in a pyramid shape on a hot platter. Garnish with sprigs of fresh parsley. The crayfish are eaten like lobsters. Most of the meat is in the tail. Take care to remove the black strip in the center of the tail.

L'hôte et le poisson en trois jours sont poison.

197. Crayfish in Paprika Butter Sauce

Ecrevisses à la marinière

40 crayfish	¼ pound butter
court-bouillon (196)	¼ teaspoon paprika

Prepare the crayfish as in the preceding recipe. Melt butter in the top of a double boiler. Add paprika, and salt. When the butter is piping hot it is ready to be served with the crayfish.

198. Crayfish in Herb Sauce

Ecrevisses à la bordelaise

40 crayfish	1 clove garlic
court-bouillon (196)	4 tablespoons butter
6 scallions	¼ cup dry white wine
4 tablespoons finely chopped parsley	salt and pepper

Follow recipe 196 for cooking crayfish. Melt the butter. Add finely chopped scallions, parsley, garlic, and white wine. Season highly with salt and pepper. Pour the sauce over the crayfish, which have been piled in a pyramid shape on a heated platter.

199. Frog Legs in White Wine Sauce
Grenouilles à la poulette

12 pairs frog legs
2 tablespoons butter
2 tablespoons flour
½ cup dry white wine

salt
black pepper
2 tablespoons chopped parsley
2 tablespoons chopped onion
1 egg yolk

Wash the frog legs and soak in cold water 3 hours. Drain them and wipe very dry. Melt butter in heavy saucepan. Fry the legs 2 minutes on each side. Sprinkle with flour and stir carefully so that the flour and butter are blended. Add wine, parsley, onion, and season with salt and pepper. Cook 15 minutes over a moderate flame. Put the legs on a heated platter. Thicken the sauce with the egg yolk (page 3) and pour over the legs. Serve immediately. 3 pairs of legs per person is usually enough.

200. Fried Frog Legs   *Cuisses de grenouilles frites*

12 pairs frog legs
¼ cup wine vinegar
1 bay leaf, broken into small
    pieces
2 tablespoons chopped parsley

1 small onion, chopped fine
salt
freshly ground black pepper
flour
4 tablespoons butter

Wash and dry the frog legs. Marinate in vinegar, bay leaf, parsley, onion, salt, and pepper for 1 hour. Spoon the liquid over the legs several times. Drain and wipe dry. Roll in flour and fry in butter until brown on both sides. Salt and serve very hot.

201. Snails *Escargots à la bourguignonne*

½ pound snails (approximately   1 clove garlic
  50)   ½ pound butter
3 cups water   4 tablespoons chopped parsley
1 onion, chopped fine   2 cloves garlic, chopped fine
1 carrot, cut in rounds   salt and pepper
bouquet garni (42)

To clean the snails, cook them in heavily salted water for 20
minutes, stirring often. Meanwhile prepare a *court-bouillon*
with water, onion, carrot, *bouquet garni,* and garlic. Let this
simmer 15 minutes. Change the snails from the salt water to
the *court-bouillon* and cook 15 minutes. While the snails are
cooling, soften the butter and work into it the chopped parsley
and garlic. Season highly with salt and pepper. When the
snails are cool, remove each from its shell and run water over
the shells to be sure they are clean. Place a bit of the butter
mixture at the bottom of each shell, replace the snail, and fill
to the top with the butter mixture. Divide the snails into lots
of at least 12 and bake in individual baking dishes in a hot
(400°F.) oven until they are bubbling. Serve very hot.

202. Snails in White Wine Sauce   *Escargots à la poulette*

½ pound snails   2 tablespoons flour
court-bouillon (201)   ½ cup dry white wine
2 tablespoons butter   salt and pepper

Follow the preceding recipe for cleaning and cooking the
snails. Melt butter and stir in flour. As soon as the butter and
flour are well blended, stir in the wine and ½ cup of strained
court-bouillon. Stir until the sauce is smooth. Put the snails
in the sauce and simmer 5 minutes. If the sauce is too thick
add more *court-bouillon.* Serve in individual ramekins.

203. Mussels in White Sauce   *Moules à la béchamel*

Mussels should be very fresh and not too large. If they are open they are not fit for use. Before they are cooked they should be well scrubbed and washed in several waters.

3 quarts mussels	1 cup liquor from the mussels
2 tablespoons butter	3 tablespoons chopped parsley
2 tablespoons flour	1 clove garlic, chopped fine
1 cup milk	salt and black pepper

Place the mussels in a kettle with $\frac{1}{4}$ cup water. As soon as the mussels open, remove them from the kettle and take off the top shell. Melt butter in a large saucepan. Stir in flour. Add the milk and the liquor from the mussels which has been allowed to settle a few moments. Stir the sauce with a wooden spoon until it is smooth. The sauce should be thin. Add parsley, garlic, salt, and pepper and cook 5 minutes. Reheat the mussels in the sauce and serve.

204. Mussels Marinière   *Moules à la marinière*

3 quarts mussels	a sprig of thyme or $\frac{1}{4}$ teaspoon powdered thyme
$\frac{1}{2}$ cup white wine	1 clove garlic
1 carrot, cut in rounds	salt and pepper
1 onion, chopped fine	3 tablespoons butter
3 tablespoons chopped parsley	
1 bay leaf	

Scrub the mussels and wash in several waters. Place them in a large pan with wine, carrot, onion, parsley, bay leaf, thyme, garlic, salt, pepper, and butter. Cover the pan and place over a high flame. When all the mussels are open they are cooked. Remove the mussels from the pan, take the top shell off each one, and place them in a deep heated platter. Strain the *court-bouillon* and pour over the mussels.

205. Mussels in Scallop Shells   *Moules en coquilles*

Follow recipe 203. Remove both shells and mix the mussels
with the sauce, which should be quite thick. Place 5 or 6
mussels in each scallop shell or ramekin. Cover with bread
crumbs, dot with butter, and brown in a hot oven. Garnish
with fresh chopped parsley.

206. Mussels with Spanish Rice   *Paella*

1 cup rice	3 tomatoes, cut in eighths
½ cup olive oil	½ green pepper, cut in strips
2 large onions, chopped fine	salt and pepper
3 tablespoons chopped parsley	1½ quarts mussels
1 large clove garlic	

Wash rice and combine with oil, onions, parsley, garlic,
tomatoes, green pepper, salt, and pepper. Cook in a covered
pan over a slow fire until the rice is tender but not mushy.
Stir the rice from time to time to prevent crusting; 30 minutes
should be enough to cook the rice. Open the mussels, after
they have been thoroughly washed, by steaming them with
¼ cup water over a high flame. As soon as they are open,
remove the top shell and put the mussels in a deep platter.
Cover with rice and pour the liquor of the mussels, which has
been allowed to settle, over the rice. Serve very hot.

207. Oysters on the Half Shell   *Huîtres*

Open fresh oysters with special oyster knife. Serve the oyster
in the bottom shell. Place the oysters on a bed of chopped ice.
Serve with lemon wedges. Allow 6 to 9 oysters per person.

208. Oysters in Scallop Shells   *Huîtres en coquilles*

2 dozen oysters *   ½ cup dry white wine
2 tablespoons butter   2 tablespoons water
2 tablespoons flour   fine bread crumbs
¼ pound small mushrooms   salt and pepper
3 tablespoons chopped parsley

Open the oysters over a saucepan in order to catch the juice.
Set the shells aside and simmer (not boil) the oysters in the
juice for 3 minutes. Remove from the fire. Wash and stem the
mushrooms. Fry lightly with the parsley for 3 minutes. Stir
in the flour and add wine, water, and the oyster liquor. Stir
until the sauce is smooth. Reheat the oysters in the sauce. Put
2 or 3 oysters in each oyster shell, cover with bread crumbs,
dot with butter, and place in hot oven for 5 minutes. Tante
Marie recommends substituting scallop shells for the oyster
shells. In that case, 4 or 5 oysters may be put in each shell.

209. Lobster Mayonnaise   *Homard à la mayonnaise*

4 chicken lobsters   Mayonnaise (17)
court-bouillon (144)

Follow the recipe for Crayfish in *court-bouillon* (196), substituting lobsters for the crayfish. Let the lobsters cool in the
court-bouillon. Split each lobster down the middle and crack
the claws. Serve with a bowl of Mayonnaise.

* Shucked or canned oysters may be used.

210. Lobster à l'Américaine   *Homard à l'américaine*

4 chicken lobsters	¼ cup domestic brandy
¼ cup olive oil	2 tablespoons tomato paste
salt	1 teaspoon beef extract
black pepper	*bouquet garni* (42)
4 small onions, chopped fine	2 tablespoons butter
1 clove garlic, chopped fine	juice of ½ lemon
½ cup dry white wine	dash of cayenne pepper

Kill the lobsters by putting a knife through the head. Take off the claws and crack them. Take off the tail and cut into 3 or 4 pieces. Heat olive oil in a pan large enough to hold all the lobsters. Put in the lobster. Sprinkle with salt and pepper and cook 5 minutes. Meanwhile, fry the chopped onion and garlic in 1 tablespoon butter until transparent. Add to the lobster. Then add the white wine and brandy. Touch with a lighted match. It will flame for a moment. When it has died down, add tomato paste, beef extract, and *bouquet garni,* and cook 10 minutes more over a moderate flame. Put the bodies of the lobsters on a deep, heated platter. Arrange the other pieces on top. Add 1 tablespoon butter, lemon juice, and cayenne to the sauce and when it is boiling pour over the lobsters. There is no way to eat this dish delicately, but it is wonderfully delicious to taste and to smell.

211. Shrimp   *Crevettes*

The French shrimp are very tiny and high in flavor. The same shrimp are found on the Pacific Coast. They are usually boiled 10 minutes in salted water and served cold as an hors-d'œuvre. They are also delicious hot. Small eastern or southern shrimp may be substituted for the real *crevettes*.

212. Shrimp Béchamel   *Crevettes à la béchamel*

1 pound small shrimp   Béchamel Sauce (1)

Boil the shrimp 10 minutes in heavily salted water. Drain and, when they are cool enough to handle, remove the shell and the black intestine running down the tail. Reheat in a Béchamel Sauce and serve either in pastry or scallop shells. This makes a good filling for Vol-au-vent (372).

213. Scallops in the Shell   *Coquilles Saint-Jacques*

In France, scallops are always sold in the shell. They are opened by placing them in a hot oven and then detaching the white muscle which is the edible portion. In the United States, the scallops are usually sold out of the shell. The shells in which they are served can be bought or gathered at the sea shore. If one does not have the shells, individual ramekins may be used.

½ pound scallops   1 tablespoon water
½ cup dry white wine   3 tablespoons butter
1 cup water   2 tablespoons flour
bouquet garni (42)   1 egg yolk
¼ pound mushrooms   2 tablespoons cream
1 small onion, chopped fine   salt and pepper
1 teaspoon lemon juice   bread crumbs

Bring scallops to a boil in water, wine, and *bouquet garni*. Simmer 10 minutes or until tender. The scallops should not be overcooked. Remove the *bouquet garni*, strain the scallops, but reserve the liquor. Wash and chop mushrooms. Combine with onion, 1 tablespoon butter, lemon juice, and water. Cook in a covered saucepan for 10 minutes. Strain and reserve the liquor. Melt 2 tablespoons butter and stir in flour. Add the liquors saved from the mushrooms and scallops and stir with a wooden spoon until the sauce is smooth. Thicken with egg yolk and cream (page 4). Cut the scallops into small pieces and add with the mushrooms to the sauce. Put this mixture into the scallop shells or ramekins, cover with bread crumbs, dot with butter, and brown in hot oven. Garnish each shell with fresh sprigs of parsley. One of these per person makes an excellent hors-d'œuvre; two make a good main course.

La caque sent toujours le hareng.

Meat

IN FRANCE, meat is cut in a very different manner from the way it is cut in the United States. No amount of persuasion can convince the American butcher to cut meat in the French way. For the best cuts, the French butcher makes no attempt to economize. The best one can usually do is to approximate the cut called for in the French recipe. Each succeeding recipe will indicate the preferable cut.

Unless meat is to be used immediately, it should be stored in the coldest part of the refrigerator. Remove the meat from the store paper and place in a covered dish. Do not wash the meat, but wipe it off with a damp cloth so that any bit of bone will be removed.

LARDING: Many recipes call for larding the meat. This consists of inserting strips of salt pork, ¼ inch square and 3 to 4 inches long, in the meat. To do this, insert the pork in the eye end of a larding needle and pierce the meat with the sharp end. These insertions can be made in the thick part of the meat or small stitches can be taken on the top. The pork will remain in the meat. The 'stitches' should be ½ inch deep and 1 inch long and should be spaced 2 inches apart in parallel lines.

COOKING MEAT: There are many ways of cooking meat—roasting, boiling, broiling, frying, stewing, and in casseroles. In general it is best to cook meat at a moderate temperature. Each recipe will indicate the best temperature for the particular meat. It is best to have a thermometer for both oven and frying purposes.

BEEF　　*BŒUF*

214. Boiled Beef　　*Bœuf bouilli*

This is only to be served in the bosom of the family, but it is extremely good and is not to be despised for its simplicity.

TANTE MARIE

Bœuf bouilli is the 3 pounds of bottom round used in *Pot-au-feu* (68). Remove the string. Place on a platter and surround with the vegetables cooked with the meat. Serve with Robert Sauce (16), Piquant Sauce (12), Tomato Sauce (21), or Onion Sauce (34).

215. Beef Stew　　*Bœuf en miroton*

2 tablespoons butter	8 small onions
2 tablespoons flour	6 potatoes
2 cups stock or water	*bouquet garni* (42)
1 teaspoon salt	4 cups cold boiled beef,
½ teaspoon black pepper	cut in pieces

Melt butter and stir in flour. Continue stirring until flour is brown. Add liquid, salt, and pepper and stir until the sauce is smooth. Peel onions and leave them whole; peel and quarter the potatoes. Add these and the *bouquet garni* to the sauce and simmer 45 minutes. Cut the beef into small pieces and add to the sauce. Simmer 15 minutes more. Remove the *bouquet garni* before serving.

216. Cold Beef Salad   *Bœuf en vinaigrette*

Cold boiled beef, sliced thin   French Dressing (31)
3 hard-boiled eggs

Place the thin slices of cold beef on a deep platter. Cover with slices of hard boiled egg and pour French Dressing over it all. This makes a delicious luncheon dish.

217. Beef Balls   *Boulettes de hachis de bœuf frites*

1 pound lean hamburg   ¼ teaspoon pepper
¼ pound sausage meat   1 egg
2 onions, finely chopped   flour
1 teaspoon chopped parsley   1 egg, well beaten
2 slices dry bread soaked in   fine bread crumbs
¼ cup milk   parsley
1 teaspoon salt

Combine the hamburg, sausage meat, onion, and parsley. Add the bread, egg, salt, and pepper and mix thoroughly. Chill the mixture and form into small balls or into ovals. Roll in flour, dip in beaten egg and roll in bread crumbs. Fry in deep fat (375°F.). Turn the balls often so that they will brown on all sides. Serve on a platter with fried parsley (see under recipe 240).

218. Minced Beef *Bœuf en hachis*

1 pound lean hamburg	2 tablespoons flour
1/4 pound sausage meat	1/2 cup stock
2 onions, chopped fine	salt and pepper
1 teaspoon chopped parsley	croutons
2 slices dry bread, soaked in	3 hard-boiled eggs
1/4 cup milk	sprigs of parsley
2 tablespoons butter	

Combine and mix thoroughly the hamburg, sausage meat, onion, parsley, and bread. Melt butter in large frying pan and cook the mixture 10 minutes, stirring frequently. Sprinkle with flour and add stock, salt, and pepper. Cook 5 minutes longer. Place the meat in the center of a heated platter. Surround with croutons and garnish with slices of hard-boiled egg and sprigs of parsley.

219. Beef Casserole *Bœuf bouilli au gratin*

1/4 pound salt pork	3/4 teaspoon salt
1/4 pound mushrooms	1/4 teaspoon black pepper
2 onions, chopped fine	1/4 cup fine bread crumbs
1 teaspoon chopped parsley	1/2 cup white wine
1 clove garlic, chopped fine	8 slices of boiled beef (214)

Dice the pork and fry gently until most of the fat has been drawn. Place the pieces in the bottom of a casserole. Wash mushrooms and chop with onions, parsley, and garlic. Add bread crumbs, wine, salt, and pepper and mix well. Put a layer of this mixture on the bottom of the casserole, add the slices of meat and cover with the rest of the mixture. Bake 20 minutes in 375°F. oven.

Ce qui nuit à l'un sert à l'autre.

220. Beef Balls in Sauce   *Boulettes de bœuf à la sauce*

Beef Balls (217)   2 cups stock
2 tablespoons butter   *bouquet garni* (42)
2 tablespoons flour   salt and pepper

Make the beef balls but instead of frying them, cook them in
the following sauce: melt butter and stir in flour, allowing it
to brown but taking care that it does not burn. Add stock,
bouquet garni, salt and pepper to taste. Stir until the sauce
begins to thicken, and simmer 20 minutes. Place the balls in
the sauce and cook 15 minutes.

221. Minced Beef, Potato Purée
        Hachis de bœuf à la purée de pommes de terre

Minced Beef (218)   2 tablespoons butter
6 or 8 potatoes   salt and pepper

Follow directions for Minced Beef. At the same time, boil
potatoes until soft. Force through a food mill or potato ricer
or whip with an electric beater. Season with butter, salt, and
pepper. Alternate layers of beef and potato purée in a buttered
baking dish, beginning with beef and finishing with potato.
Dot with butter and bake in 400°F. oven until the potatoes
are golden brown (approximately 10 minutes). Decorate with
sprigs of fresh parsley.

222. Tenderloin Roast of Beef   *Filet de bœuf*

Ask the butcher for a tenderloin roast. This should weigh 2
to 3 pounds and should be about 4 inches in diameter. This
is an expensive cut but it is very delicious and commonly used
in France. Wrap in a paper-thin layer of salt pork and roast
in 300°F. oven. 15 minutes per pound is enough.

223. Roast Tenderloin of Beef with Madeira Sauce
Filet de bœuf au Madère

Follow the preceding recipe and serve with a Madeira Sauce
(13).

224. Roast Beef   *Aloyau rôti ou Rosbif*

Ask the butcher for a sirloin roast or face-of-the-rump roast.
A rib roast is not used in France. Rub the surface with salt
and black pepper. Roast in 300°F. oven, allowing 15 minutes
per pound. For those who do not like medium rare beef, 17-20
minutes per pound should be allowed. Prolonged cooking
lessens the flavor. Serve on a heated platter. Garnish with
parsley, watercress, or with Stuffed Mushrooms (445).

To make gravy: Pour the excess fat from the roasting pan.
Set pan on top of the stove. Add 1½ cups boiling water and
scrape off the juices that have adhered to the pan. Mix well,
strain, and serve in a heated gravy bowl with the roast.

225. Chuck Roast   *Paleron de bœuf*

Marinate a 3- to 4-pound chuck roast from 12 to 24 hours
(see recipe 32). The meat is thus made tender and may be
roasted like Roast Beef (224).

Les folles dépenses refroidissent la cuisine.

226. Burgundy Beef   *Bœuf bourguignon*

1½ pounds lean stew beef	½ cup red wine
2 tablespoons butter	½ cup stock
2 onions	salt and pepper
1 carrot	*bouquet garni* (42)
2 tablespoons flour	

Melt butter in a heavy pan. Dice carrot and onions and fry
gently with the beef in the butter. When the meat is seared
on all sides, remove the meat and vegetables and stir in flour.
Add wine, stock, *bouquet garni,* and stir until the sauce is
smooth. Put back the meat and vegetables, cover, and simmer
3 hours.

227. Steak   *Bifteck-grillade*

Order individual steaks cut from the sirloin or tenderloin or
minute steaks cut from the face of the rump. Do not salt until
after cooking, because the salt tends to draw out the juices.
Broil or pan-broil according to the following directions. Meanwhile cream softened butter with chopped parsley. Season the
butter with salt, pepper, and a dash of lemon juice. Spread
over the sizzling steaks, garnish with watercress, and serve
immediately.

TO BROIL: Place the steaks under the electric or gas broiler
or if possible over live charcoal. Broil 4 minutes on each side,
or longer if medium or well-done steaks are preferred.

TO PAN-BROIL: Heat frying pan until very hot. Rub the frying
pan with a piece of fat or melt a little butter. Fry the steaks
2 to 4 minutes on each side, depending on the thickness of
the steaks.

228. Chateaubriand Steak   *Chateaubriand*

A Chateaubriand is a thick steak—1½ to 2 inches thick, or 3 to 4 inches if the occasion is gala and the price not to be considered. Sirloin, Tenderloin, Porterhouse, or Rump steaks are all good cuts. Pan-broil or broil (227), but increase the time allowance to 10 or 12 minutes on each side according to the thickness of the steak. For medium or well-done steak allow more time. Season with butter, salt, and a generous amount of freshly ground black pepper. Garnish with parsley or fresh watercress.

229. Filets Mignons in Mushroom Sauce
Filets sautés aux champignons

4 to 6 individual steaks (1 inch thick)	1 cup beef stock
2 tablespoons butter	½ pound mushrooms
2 tablespoons flour	salt and pepper

Melt the butter in a large frying pan. When it is sizzling, put in the pan as many steaks as there are persons to be served. Sear the steaks 2 minutes on each side. Remove the steaks. Stir in flour and stock and continue stirring until the sauce is smooth. Season with salt and pepper. Add mushrooms which have been washed thoroughly and sliced. Use both caps and stems. Cook 10 minutes. Put the steaks back into the sauce and simmer 5 minutes longer. Do not let the sauce boil. Place the steaks in the center of a heated platter. Surround with the mushrooms and garnish with watercress.

230. Filets Mignons in Olive Sauce   *Filets sautés aux olives*

Follow the preceding recipe but substitute ½ cup of pitted olives for the mushrooms.

231. Braised Beef   *Entrecôte braisé*

2 to 3 pounds round steak
¼ cup diced salt pork
2 tablespoons flour
1 cup beef stock or water
1 teaspoon salt
5 peppercorns

2 cloves
bouquet garni (42)
2 onions
1 carrot
¼ cup cooking brandy

Try out the salt pork in a heavy saucepan. Sear the meat on both sides. When well browned, take out the salt pork and meat. Stir in flour and add stock. Stir until the sauce is smooth. Add onions and carrots, cut in small pieces, salt, peppercorns, cloves, *bouquet garni*, and brandy. Put the meat in the sauce and simmer 3 hours with the pan covered. Skim off the fat and strain the sauce before serving.

232. Beef à la mode   *Bœuf à la mode*

3 to 4 pounds of beef cut from the round
several larding strips 4 to 5 inches long
2 tablespoons butter or chicken fat
3 cups water
½ cup dry white wine
¼ cup cooking brandy

2 teaspoons salt
¼ teaspoon black pepper
½ calf's foot (or ½ beef or pig's knuckle)
bouquet garni (42)
2 cloves
2 carrots, cut in small pieces
12 small onions

Lard beef with strips of salt pork (page 87). Melt butter or chicken fat in a deep oven dish. Sear the meat on all sides. Add water, wine, brandy, salt, pepper, *bouquet garni*, cloves, carrots, and onions and the calf's foot or knuckle, which will add greatly to the richness of the sauce. Bring to the boiling point and place in a 300°F. oven. The dish should be covered. Cook 5 hours. Place the meat on a heated platter. Remove the *bouquet garni*, skim off the fat, and surround the meat with the sauce.

233. Beef à la mode in Aspic   *Bœuf à la mode en gelée*

Strain and save some of the sauce from Beef à la mode (232).
Chill and remove the coating of fat. Add 1 teaspoon of gelatine to 2 cups of the sauce, unless is is already quite stiff, and
bring to a boil. Arrange thin slices of cold beef on a platter.
Cover with rounds of carrot. Let the sauce cool until it is
syrupy but not stiff. Pour over the meat carefully and place
the platter in the ice box. When the aspic is stiff the dish is
ready. Garnish with sprigs of parsley and serve with mustard. This makes a delicious luncheon dish.

234. Beef Kidneys in Madeira Sauce
Rognons de bœuf au Madère

1 beef kidney	½ cup Madeira wine
2 tablespoons butter	½ cup water
2 tablespoons flour	salt and pepper

Split the kidney in two and cut out the fatty core. Cut the
kidney in small pieces. Melt butter and fry the pieces of
kidney, stirring gently so that the pieces will be browned on
all sides. Sprinkle with flour and moisten with wine and water.
Season with salt and pepper and stir until the flour is well
blended. Simmer 10 minutes but do not let the sauce boil.
Kidneys become tough if overcooked, but they should be
served very hot.

235. Kidneys and Mushrooms in Madeira Sauce
Rognons de bœuf aux champignons

Add ½ pound of well-washed mushrooms to the kidneys and
follow directions in the preceding recipe. Add 2 teaspoons of
finely chopped parsley just before serving. Serve with triangles of buttered toast.

236. Beef Tongue, Piquant or Tomato Sauce
    Langue de bœuf, sauce piquante ou sauce tomate

1 fresh tongue *	1 teaspoon salt
1 carrot, cut in rounds	¼ teaspoon pepper
2 leeks	2 cloves
bouquet garni (42)	Piquant Sauce (12) or Tomato
2 quarts of water	Sauce (21)

Cover tongue with cold water. Add carrots, leeks slit lengthwise and tied together with kitchen string, *bouquet garni,*
cloves, salt, and pepper. Simmer 3 hours. Remove tongue from
the water. Take off skin and cut out the hard roots. Split the
tongue lengthwise. Arrange in a crown around a platter and
fill the center with Piquant or Tomato Sauce.

237. Beef Tongue Casserole   *Langue de bœuf au gratin*

Cold cooked beef tongue (236)	1 teaspoon chopped parsley
4 tablespoons butter	½ teaspoon salt
¼ cup white wine	⅛ teaspoon pepper
6 small pickles	¼ cup fine bread crumbs
3 scallions or tiny onions	

Slice cold tongue as thin as possible. Chop pickles, scallions,
and parsley. Mix with bread crumbs, wine, salt, and pepper.
Dot the bottom of the casserole with butter and spread with
half the mixture. Cover with the slices of cold tongue and put
the rest of the mixture on the tongue. Bake 30 minutes in
300°F. oven.

* Corned or smoked tongue may be used. These should be
soaked in cold water several hours before using.

238. Beef Brains in Black Butter Sauce

Cervelle de bœuf au beurre noir

Beef brains are not as delicate as calf's brains, but if carefully prepared they are very delicious.

TANTE MARIE

3 pairs brains	1 clove garlic
2 tablespoons vinegar	*bouquet garni* (42)
1 teaspoon salt	6 cups water
4 peppercorns	Black Butter Sauce (14)
4 cloves	

Soak brains 2 hours in cold water, changing the water at least twice. Clean them carefully. Remove loose pieces of skin, blood, and fibers. Combine vinegar, salt, peppercorns, cloves, garlic, *bouquet garni*, and water. Add the brains and bring slowly to the boiling point. Cook gently 45 minutes. Remove the brains. Cut in two and serve on a heated platter with Black Butter Sauce poured over them.

239. Beef Brains in Mushroom and Onion Sauce

Cervelle de bœuf en matelote

3 pairs cooked beef brains	*bouquet garni* (42)
1 tablespoon butter	10 small onions
1 tablespoon flour	¼ pound mushrooms
1 cup water	salt and pepper
½ cup red wine	croutons

Follow recipe 238 for cooking brains. Melt butter and add flour, allowing it to brown but taking care that it does not burn. Add water and wine and stir until sauce begins to thicken. Add *bouquet garni*, onions, mushrooms cut in small pieces, and simmer 30 minutes. Remove *bouquet garni,* add brains, salt, and pepper, and simmer 15 minutes longer. Serve on a heated platter and garnish with long croutons.

240. Fried Beef Brains   *Cervelle de bœuf frite*

Soak and clean the brains (238). Boil gently in 1 cup water and ½ cup vinegar for 20 minutes. Drain and cut in small pieces. Dip in a thick batter (40). Fry in deep fat (360°F.), turning frequently so that the pieces will brown on all sides. Serve on a warm platter and garnish with fried parsley.

To fry parsley: Wash and dry the parsley. Throw into the hot fat and remove almost immediately with a skimmer.

241. Tripe Lyonnaise   *Tripes à la Lyonnaise*

1 to 1½ pounds tripe *	salt and pepper
2 tablespoons butter or oil	⅛ teaspoon nutmeg
4 onions, sliced very thin	

Wipe tripe very carefully. Cut in squares. Heat oil or butter in heavy saucepan and fry onion slices until they are yellow. Add tripe and brown on both sides. Add salt, pepper, and nutmeg. Cook 5 minutes. Serve very hot, because otherwise this dish is not good.

* Tripe is sold pickled and fresh. When it has been pickled it may be soaked in cold water for several hours, then drained and dried, and used exactly like fresh tripe.

242. Tripe à la mode de Caen   *Tripes à la mode de Caen*

1 to 1½ pounds tripe *	2 gloves of garlic
1 calf's foot, cut in 3 pieces	⅛ pound salt pork, diced
2 carrots, cut in rounds	6 peppercorns
bouquet garni (42), tied in 2	4 slices bacon
small bunches	½ cup water
4 cloves	½ bottle white wine

Wipe the tripe clean and cut into large pieces. At the bottom of an earthenware pot (a Boston bean pot is excellent) put a layer of carrots, 1 clove garlic, and ½ of the diced salt pork. Over this put a layer of tripe. Repeat the process. Cover the last layer of tripe with slices of bacon. Fill the jar ¾ full with white wine diluted with a little water. Put a tight cover on the pot and cook 5 hours in a 350°F. oven. Just before serving thicken the sauce with a little cornstarch (page 4).

243. Left-over Beef with Tomato or Piquant Sauce
        Restes de bœuf, sauce tomate ou sauce piquante

Slice cold roast or boiled beef very thin and heat in Tomato Sauce (21) or Piquant Sauce (12).

244. Left-over Beef in Cream Sauce
        Restes de bœuf, sauce poulette

Dice cold boiled or roast beef and heat in a Poulette Sauce (8). Garnish with sprigs of fresh parsley.

* Tripe is sold pickled and fresh. When it has been pickled it may be soaked in cold water for several hours, then drained and dried, and used exactly like fresh tripe.

245. Beef and Cabbage   *Restes de bœuf aux choux*

¼ pound diced salt pork
2 tablespoons flour
2 cups water
1 onion, chopped fine
½ teaspoon salt

¼ teaspoon pepper
bouquet garni (42)
1 cabbage, cut in eighths
1- to 2-pound chunk of cold
    roast or boiled beef

Fry the salt pork in deep saucepan. When most of the fat has been rendered, take out the pork and keep warm. Stir in the flour and let it brown. Add water, onion, *bouquet garni*, salt, and pepper. Stir until the sauce is smooth. Add cabbage and beef. Simmer 45 minutes. Place beef in center of deep platter. Surround with cabbage dotted with the salt pork. Strain the liquid and thicken with cornstarch or potato starch (page 4). Pour the sauce over the beef.

246. Croquettes   *Croquettes*

2 cups cooked meat (beef, veal,
    lamb, chicken, rabbit,
    sweetbreads, or fish)
1 teaspoon chopped parsley
½ teaspoon salt
⅛ teaspoon pepper
2 tablespoons butter

2 tablespoons flour
½ cup stock or water
½ cup chopped mushrooms
1 egg yolk
1 egg, beaten with
    2 tablespoons oil
fine bread crumbs

Chop the meat or put it through a meat grinder. Add parsley, salt, and pepper. Melt butter in a heavy saucepan. Stir in flour and add water, stirring until well blended. Add the meat and mushrooms. Simmer 20 minutes without a cover so that the mixture will be very thick. Taste for seasoning and add more salt and pepper, if necessary. Chill the mixture and add unbeaten egg yolk. Form the croquettes in balls or long ovals, using 1 tablespoon of the mixture for each. Dip in the egg beaten with oil and roll in bread crumbs. Fry in deep fat (375°F.) until golden brown (3 to 5 minutes) and serve with fried parsley.

LAMB   *AGNEAU*

Mutton is very commonly used in France and any of the recipes given below for lamb may be used for mutton, provided it is of good quality. The lamb used in the United States is taken from young sheep. 'Spring lamb' applies to the meat taken from 3- to 5-month-old lambs and is preferable to ordinary lamb or mutton. The flesh of lamb should be pink and the fat should be hard and white. The flesh of mutton is dark red and should be well 'aged' to be good.

247. Roast Lamb   *Gigot rôti*

Order a leg of lamb weighing 6 to 8 pounds. Peel 4 small cloves of garlic. Pierce the flesh with the sharp point of a knife in 4 well-separated places and insert the garlic. Place the lamb on a rack in an open pan. Place 1 cup of water, 1 tablespoon of butter, and 1 teaspoon of salt in the pan. Roast in 325°F. oven, counting 17 to 20 minutes per pound. French lamb is always served rare with the flesh still bright pink.

To make gravy: Add a little water to the pan after the meat has been placed on a heated platter. Scrape the juices from the bottom of the pan. Strain and serve with the roast. Garnish with watercress or sprigs of parsley.

248. Marinated Lamb or Mutton   *Gigot mariné*

Purchase a leg of lamb or mutton. Wipe it carefully. Make several incisions with a sharp knife and insert ¼-inch-by-1-inch pieces of salt pork in the flesh of the meat. Prepare a

Marinating Dressing (32). It is wise to double the recipe for a large piece of meat. Marinate the lamb 3 to 4 days, keeping it in a cool place. Baste the meat with the sauce several times a day. When it is ready to be cooked, place the meat on a rack in an open pan. Pour 6 tablespoons of the sauce in the bottom of the pan. Roast in a 300°F. oven, allowing 30 minutes per pound. The meat should be well done. Serve with Piquant Sauce (12) or Tomato Sauce (21). The meat will have a gamey flavor. It is delicious.

249. Braised Lamb   *Gigot d'agneau braisé*

4 pounds boned and rolled leg
  of lamb or lamb fore
several larding strips, 3 inches
  long
1 tablespoon salt
½ teaspoon black pepper
2 tablespoons butter

2 cups water
¼ cup cooking brandy
bouquet garni (42)
5 carrots
½ calf's foot or knuckle (sawed
  in small pieces)

Wipe the meat carefully. Lard the meat with the strips of salt pork (page 87). Rub with salt and pepper. Melt the butter in a deep pan that has a cover. Sear the meat on all sides. When it is browned all over, add water, brandy, *bouquet garni*, carrots cut in ½ inch pieces, and calf's foot. Cook slowly 4 hours with cover on. Remove the *bouquet garni*. Place meat on platter, surround with carrots, and pour over it all the liquid in which the meat has cooked.

⚜

Selon ta bourse gouverne ta bouche.

⚜

250. Lamb Shoulder with Turnips

Epaule d'agneau aux navets

3- to 4-pound shoulder of lamb, boned and rolled
2 tablespoons butter
2 tablespoons flour
4 cups water
1 tablespoon salt
½ teaspoon pepper
bouquet garni (42)
2 cloves
3 cups diced turnips

Melt the butter in a pan that has a cover. Brown meat on all sides in the butter. Remove the meat and add flour, allowing it to brown but taking care that it does not burn. Stir in water and when it is well blended add salt, pepper, *bouquet garni*, and cloves. Place the meat back in the pan and boil gently 2½ hours. Meanwhile, peel and dice the turnips. Fry the pieces in butter or chicken fat until they are dark yellow in color. Add the turnips to the meat 1 hour before the meat is to be served. Place meat in the center of a warm platter. Surround with a ring of turnip. Strain the sauce and pour over the meat. Garnish with parsley.

251. Stuffed Lamb Shoulder   *Epaule de mouton farcie*

4 pounds boned shoulder
½ pound sausage meat
1 teaspoon chopped onion
1 teaspoon chopped parsley
salt and pepper
2 tablespoons butter

Ask the butcher to bone but not roll a shoulder. Fill the center with a stuffing made by combining sausage meat, onion, parsley, salt, and pepper. Roll and tie securely. Brown the meat in melted butter. Add 1 cup of water, cover, and place in 300°F. oven. Cook 2½ hours, adding a little water from time to time so that the meat will not be too dry.

252. Lamb Chops   *Côtelettes d'agneau*

Order loin or rib chops. Wipe the chops and cut off excess fat. Roll the chops in fine bread crumbs (optional). Place the chops on a rack 3 inches below the flame. Sear chops on both sides with a hot flame. Lower the flame or finish cooking the chops in a moderate (350°F.) oven. Chops ¾ to 1 inch thick require 10 to 12 minutes; thicker chops require more time. Season with salt and pepper and serve with plenty of melted butter, Piquant Sauce (12), Tomato Sauce (21), or Onion Sauce (34).

253. Lamb Ragout   *Ragoût de mouton (navarin)*

1½ pounds stew lamb, cut from the shoulder or breast	6 potatoes
2 tablespoons butter or fat	1 teaspoon salt
2 tablespoons flour	⅛ teaspoon pepper
4 cups water	4 or 5 carrots
bouquet garni (42)	12 small onions
	2 tablespoons chopped parsley

Cut the lamb in small pieces and fry in melted butter. When the meat is browned, stir in flour, allowing it to brown. Add water and when it is blended add salt, pepper, carrots, *bouquet garni,* and onions. Cook slowly for 1 hour. Add the potatoes, which have been peeled and quartered, and cook 1 hour more. Remove the *bouquet garni* and place in a deep platter. Sprinkle with bright green chopped parsley.

Sans pain, sans vin, amour n'est rien.

254. Skewered Lamb Kidneys
Rognons d'agneau à la brochette

8 lamb kidneys	lemon juice
4 tablespoons butter	salt and pepper
2 teaspoons chopped parsley	

Wash the kidneys, remove the filmy skin, and split open. Cut out the hard core of fat. Thread 4 halves on a skewer and place the skewers on a rack under a hot flame. Broil 8 minutes, turning the skewers every 2 minutes. Soften the butter and add parsley, a dash of lemon juice, and season with salt and pepper. Spread the mixture on a small serving platter and place the piping hot kidneys on it. Serve immediately.

255. Lamb Kidneys with Tartar Sauce
Rognons de mouton à la tartare

8 lamb kidneys	⅛ teaspoon black pepper
¼ cup oil	¼ cup melted butter
1 teaspoon chopped parsley	fine bread crumbs
½ teaspoon salt	Tartar Sauce (20)

Wash, skin, and split the kidneys. Marinate 2 hours in combined oil, parsley, salt, and pepper. Drain the kidneys, dip in melted butter, roll in bread crumbs, skewer them, allowing 4 halves to a skewer, and broil 10 minutes. Serve with Tartar Sauce.

256. Lamb Kidneys, Madeira Sauce
Rognons d'agneau au Madère

Split the kidneys, cut out the hard core of fat, and prepare like Beef Kidneys in Madeira Sauce (234).

257. Lamb's Brains   *Cervelles d'agneau*

Lamb's brains have a more delicate flavor than beef brains.
They are prepared in the same manner as recipes 238-40.
They should be served piping hot.

258. Broiled Breast of Lamb

Poitrine de mouton sur le gril

When Cabbage Soup (76) has been made with breast of lamb,
the meat can be used for another meal. Extract the meat from
the soup, broil on both sides, and serve with Piquant Sauce
(12), Pepper Sauce (19), or Tomato Sauce (21).

259. Lamb Chops Milanaise   *Côtelettes à la milanaise*

4 to 6 thick loin chops	1 egg, well beaten
½ cup melted butter	salt and pepper
⅓ cup fine bread crumbs	Tomato Sauce (22) (or slices
⅓ cup Parmesan cheese, grated	of lemon)

Wipe the chops carefully. Dip in melted butter, roll in combined bread crumbs and cheese. Dip in egg and then again in
bread crumbs and cheese. Place on broiling rack. Brush with
melted butter, sprinkle with salt and pepper, and broil under
a low flame, turning once. 10 minutes on each side should be
enough. Serve with Tomato Sauce or lemon slices.

260. Left-over Lamb or Mutton

Restes de mouton ou d'agneau

Slice cold roast lamb very thin and serve with Mayonnaise
(17). Follow recipes 243-6, substituting lamb or mutton for
beef.

261. Left-over Lamb in White Wine Sauce
Restes de gigot à la Brissac

Cold roast lamb, sliced ¼ inch thick	2 teaspoons chopped onion
2 tablespoons butter	½ cup water
2 tablespoons flour	½ cup white wine
1 teaspoon chopped parsley	2 tablespoons olive oil
	salt and pepper

Brown the slices of lamb in melted butter, turning each slice once. Add parsley and onion and cook 5 minutes more. Stir in flour. Moisten with wine and water and cook 1 hour. Ten minutes before serving add the olive oil. Season with salt and pepper. Serve with boiled potatoes or boiled rice.

262. Kid   *Chevreau*

Kid and lamb are very similar in taste and recipes given for lamb serve equally well for kid.

VEAL   *VEAU*

Veal is more commonly used in Europe than in the United States. Most recipes in American cook books have a European origin. Veal should be grayish pink in color. The cuts used in France differ from the American cuts, but each recipe will indicate the cut most adaptable to the French recipe.

Où la chèvre est attachée il faut qu'elle broute.

263. Veal Casserole   *Veau à la bourgeoise*

3- to 4-pound veal shoulder	1/4 teaspoon pepper
3 tablespoons butter	2 cloves
3 tablespoons flour	*bouquet garni* (42)
4 cups water	7 or 8 carrots
1 teaspoon salt	12 small onions

Melt butter in heavy oven-proof dish. Brown the meat on all sides and remove from the butter. Stir in flour and water. When well blended, add salt, pepper, *bouquet garni*, cloves, carrots cut in small pieces, and onions left whole. Bring to the boiling point and add the meat. Cover and bake in 300°F. oven for 2½ hours. Place the meat on heated platter and surround with carrots and onions. Strain the sauce, thicken with cornstarch or potato starch (page 4), and pour over the meat. Garnish with sprigs of parsley.

264. Roast Veal   *Veau rôti*

Ask the butcher for a veal loin roast weighing 3 to 4 pounds. Persuade him to lard it with pork fat back or to tie strips of salt pork around it. Veal is lean and needs extra fat in cooking. The roast should be well tied. Place the roast on a rack in an open pan. Put 1 tablespoon of butter, 1 teaspoon of salt, and 1 cup of water in the bottom of the pan. Veal requires long cooking. 30 minutes per pound should be allowed.

To make gravy: Place the roast on a heated platter and keep in a warm place. Pour off excess fat, add 1 cup of boiling water, and scrape off all the juices adhering to the pan with a fork. Keep over a hot flame during this process. When the water and juices are well blended, strain and pour into a gravy bowl. If the gravy is too pale add a few drops of commercial gravy coloring.

265. Veal Ragout   *Ragoût de veau*

2 pounds shoulder or breast of veal	1 teaspoon salt
2 tablespoons butter	1/4 teaspoon pepper
2 tablespoons flour	*bouquet garni* (42)
4 cups hot water	12 small onions
	1/4 pound mushrooms

Cut the veal into small pieces. Brown it in butter in a heavy saucepan. Add flour and let it brown. Stir in water and when well blended add salt, pepper, *bouquet garni*, onions, and mushrooms which have been well washed. Use both caps and stems. Cover and cook 1 hour over a low flame. Skim off the fat floating on the top, remove the *bouquet garni*, and serve.

266. Veal Ragout with Peas   *Ragoût de veau aux pois*

Follow the preceding recipe but substitute 2 cups fresh peas for the mushrooms and use only 6 onions. If frozen or canned peas are used, add 15 minutes before serving.

267. Veal in Red Wine   *Veau en matelote*

1 1/2 pounds breast or shoulder of veal, cut in small pieces	1 teaspoon salt
2 tablespoons butter	1/4 teaspoon pepper
2 tablespoons flour	2 cloves
1 cup hot water	*bouquet garni* (42)
1 cup red wine	8 small onions
	1/4 pound mushrooms

Melt butter in heavy saucepan. Brown the pieces of meat on all sides. Remove the meat, add flour, and moisten with water and wine. Stir until well blended. Add salt, pepper, cloves, *bouquet garni*, onions, and mushrooms. Use both caps and stems. Add meat, and cover and simmer 1 1/2 hours. Remove *bouquet garni*, skim off fat, and serve.

268. Broiled Veal Chops   *Côtelettes de veau sur le gril*

8 thin loin or rib chops
salt and pepper
3 tablespoons butter

1 teaspoon lemon juice
1 teaspoon chopped parsley

Wipe the chops clean. Sprinkle with salt and pepper. Broil under slow flame, allowing 8 to 10 minutes on each side. Melt butter, add lemon juice and parsley. Pour this sauce over the chops, which are served on a heated platter.

269. Veal Chops with Herbs
Côtelettes de veau aux fines herbes

8 ¾-inch-thick veal chops
salt and pepper
3 tablespoons butter
½ cup white wine
½ cup water

2 teaspoons chopped chives (or onion tops)
2 teaspoons chopped parsley
1 teaspoon lemon juice

Melt the butter in a heavy saucepan. Brown chops on both sides. Sprinkle with salt and pepper. Add water and wine. Cover and simmer over a very low flame 30 minutes. Add the herbs and simmer 5 minutes longer. Just before serving, sprinkle with lemon juice.

270. Veal Chops in Buttered Paper

Côtelettes de veau en papillotes

8 thin veal chops	4 tablespoons chopped mush-rooms
¼ cup olive oil	
2 teaspoons chopped parsley	salt and pepper
2 teaspoons chopped onion	unglazed paper
2 teaspoons chopped chives	butter

Marinate the veal chops in the olive oil for 12 hours. Combine parsley, onion, chives, and mushrooms. Cut 8 pieces of unglazed paper—your best stationery is not too good for this—large enough to envelop the chop and have a margin for overlapping. Spread the papers with butter and sprinkle with a layer of the herb mixture. Place a chop on each paper, cover with another layer of the herb mixture. Sprinkle generously with salt and freshly ground black pepper. Fold the paper over the chop so that no steam or juice will escape. Scotch tape is not traditional but very helpful. Cook 30 minutes in 300°F. oven. Serve with the paper on.

This recipe is one of the oldest known French recipes. It has been passed down through the ages and is honored by both historians and gourmets.

271. Larded Veal   *Fricandeau*

2 to 3 pounds round steak
12 ¼″ by 3″ strips of salt pork
2 carrots
6 small onions
bouquet garni (42)

2 cloves
1 cup stock or water
1 teaspoon salt
¼ teaspoon pepper

This cut of veal, cut from the leg, is lean and needs extra fat to be good. Lard with salt pork (page 87). Place in a casserole with carrots cut in small pieces, onions, *bouquet garni,* cloves, stock, salt, and pepper. Cover and cook in 300°F. oven for 2½ hours. Just before serving, strain off the liquid into a small saucepan and boil down the sauce to half its amount. Place the meat on a layer of cooked spinach or chicory (recipe 429 or 487) and pour the sauce over the meat.

272. Veal Cutlets   *Escalopes de veau*

6 or 8 veal cutlets
3 tablespoons butter
1 cup stock

2 teaspoons chopped parsley
1 teaspoon chopped onion
salt and pepper

Order individual, well-trimmed cutlets, cut ½ inch thick. Ask the butcher to pound them. Heat butter in frying pan until it is sizzling hot. Sear cutlets 3 minutes on each side. Add stock, parsley, onion, sprinkle with salt and pepper, and cover. Simmer 20 minutes. Arrange the cutlets in a crown around a heated platter. Fill the center with the sauce left in the frying pan or with a Tomato Sauce (21).

Morceau avalé n'a plus de goût.

273. French Veal Stew   *Blanquette de veau*

2 pounds stewing veal, cut from
    breast or leg
salt and pepper
1 carrot
1 onion cut in half
bouquet garni (42)
4 cups water or stock
2 tablespoons butter

2 tablespoons flour
12 small onions
½ pound mushrooms
1 tablespoon butter
2 egg yolks
½ teaspoon lemon juice (or ½
    teaspoon vinegar)

Combine veal, carrot cut in pieces, onion, *bouquet garni,* and
water. Season with salt and pepper. Bring to a boil and simmer 20 minutes. Extract the pieces of veal and keep in a warm
place. Melt butter and stir in flour. Add gradually the strained
liquid in which the veal was cooked. When the sauce is
smooth, add onions and mushrooms which have been well
washed. Use both stems and caps. Cook until the onions are
tender. Add the meat and cook 15 minutes longer. Thicken
with egg yolks (page 3), add butter, and just before serving
add lemon juice or vinegar. Do not let the sauce boil after
the eggs have been added. Taste for seasoning. Garnish with
chopped parsley. This will serve 8 people.

274. Baked Calf's Liver   *Foie de veau à la broche*

2 to 2½ pounds calf's liver * in
    1 piece
12 small pieces of salt pork

several paper thin slices of salt
    pork
1 cup water
1 tablespoon butter

With a sharp pointed knife insert small pieces of salt pork
into the liver. Cover the whole piece of liver with a thin layer
of salt pork. Place on a rack in an open pan into which the

* Baby beef liver is an excellent substitute.

water and butter has been put. Bake 45 minutes in 350°F. oven.

To make gravy: Pour 1 cup of boiling water into the bottom of the pan. Scrape the juices with a fork, mix well, strain, and serve in a gravy bowl.

275. Calf's Liver, Family Style

Foie de veau à la bourgeoise

2 to 3 pounds of calf's liver *
    in one piece
12 small pieces of salt pork
2 tablespoons butter
2 tablespoons flour
½ cup white wine
½ cup water

bouquet garni (42)
2 cloves
½ teaspoon salt
¼ teaspoon pepper
8 carrots, cut in small pieces
12 small onions

With a sharp pointed knife insert small pieces of salt pork in the liver. Heat butter in a heavy oven-proof dish. Sear liver on both sides and remove the meat from the pan. Add flour and stir in water and wine. When the sauce is smooth add *bouquet garni,* cloves, salt, and pepper. Parboil onions and carrots 10 minutes. Add liver and vegetables to the sauce. Cover the dish and place in 300°F. oven. Bake 1 hour. Place the liver on a heated platter. Surround with onions and carrots. Strain the sauce and thicken with cornstarch or potato starch (page 4). Pour the sauce over the liver and garnish with green parsley sprigs.

* Baby beef liver is an excellent substitute.

276. Calf's Liver, Maître d'hôtel   *Foie de veau à la poêle*

1½ pounds calf's liver (or
   baby beef liver) sliced

2 tablespoons butter
Maître d'hôtel Sauce (9)

Melt butter in frying pan. When butter is sizzling hot, brown liver on both sides. Reduce the heat and continue cooking 10 minutes, turning the slices once or twice. It should remain slightly pink in the center. Place meat on hot platter and cover with Maître d'hôtel Sauce.

277. Calf's Liver en Papillotes   *Foie de veau en papillotes*

6 slices calf's liver (or baby
   beef liver)
2 tablespoons butter
6 pieces unglazed paper
salad oil

12 thin slices salt pork
2 teaspoons chopped parsley
2 teaspoons chopped chives or
   onions
salt and pepper

Brown the liver in sizzling hot butter; 2 minutes on each side should be enough. Cut pieces of unglazed paper a little more than twice the size of the pieces of liver. Oil the paper and place a paper-thin layer of salt pork on each piece. Sprinkle each piece with half the combined herbs, salt, and pepper. Place a slice of liver on each paper, sprinkle again with herbs, salt, and pepper. Cover with a slice of salt pork. Wrap each piece of paper around the liver and fold the edges carefully so that none of the juices will escape. Bake 20 minutes in 350°F. oven. Serve with the paper still on.

278. Veal Kidneys   *Rognons de veau*

Veal kidney has a finer flavor than beef kidney. It is prepared in the same way as Beef Kidneys in Madeira Sauce (234) or as Kidneys and Mushrooms in Madeira Sauce (235). It is also delicious served in an omelet (129).

279. Larded Sweetbreads   *Ris de veau en fricandeau*

2 large sweetbreads
12 small strips salt pork
2 carrots
6 small onions
bouquet garni (42)

2 cloves
1 cup stock
salt and pepper
Tomato Sauce (21)

Soak the sweetbreads in warm water for 1 hour. Drain and plunge into boiling salted water. Boil 10 minutes. Drain and plunge into cold water. Drain and wipe dry. With a sharp pointed knife make little incisions in the sweetbreads and insert the salt pork. Place the sweetbreads in a casserole. Cover with carrots and onions sliced thin, *bouquet garni*, cloves, and stock. Sprinkle with salt and pepper. Bake 1 hour in 300°F. oven. Spread the bottom of a hot platter with French Spinach (487), Garden Sorrel (486), or Tomato Sauce (21) and place the sweetbreads on top.

280. Sweetbreads à la Financière
Ris de veau à la financière

1 large or 2 small sweetbreads
3 small onions, sliced thin
2 tablespoons butter
2 tablespoons flour
1 cup chicken stock
½ cup white wine

½ cup Madeira wine
salt and pepper
¼ pound mushrooms
1 teaspoon lemon juice
croutons
parsley

Follow the directions in the preceding recipe for preparing and parboiling the sweetbreads. Fry the onions and sweetbreads in the melted butter. When they are yellow, stir in the flour. Moisten with stock and wine. Add mushrooms, which have been washed, stemmed, and fried in butter 10 minutes. Season with salt and pepper and simmer 15 minutes. Just before serving, add lemon juice. Garnish with croutons and sprigs of parsley.

281. Calf's Brains, Black Butter Sauce
Cervelles de veau au beurre noir

Calf's brains are considered the best for flavor and delicacy. In France, because of their high nutritive value and easy digestibility, brains are given very commonly to children. They are prepared in the same manner as Beef Brains in Black Butter Sauce (238).

282. Calf's Brains in Mushroom and Onion Sauce
Cervelles de veau en matelote

Follow directions given in recipe 239.

283. Fried Calf's Brains   *Cervelles de veau frites*

Follow directions given in recipe 240.

284. Calf's Brains à la Poulette
Cervelles de veau à la poulette

3 pairs calf's brains	10 small onions
2 tablespoons butter	¼ pound mushrooms
2 tablespoons flour	2 egg yolks
2 cups hot water	1 teaspoon lemon juice
salt and pepper	

Wash brains and soak 1 hour in warm water. Remove arteries and membranes. Parboil in salted water 15 minutes and drain. Melt butter in a heavy saucepan and stir in flour. Add water and when well blended add salt, pepper, onions, and mushrooms, which have been washed and stemmed. Simmer until the onions are tender (30 to 40 minutes). Add brains and simmer 15 minutes more. Place the brains on a heated platter.

Bind the sauce with 2 egg yolks (page 3). Do not let the sauce boil again, but when it is piping hot add lemon juice and pour over the brains. Serve immediately.

285. Calf's Head with French Dressing
Tête de veau à la vinaigrette

1 calf's head	*bouquet garni* (42)
½ cup flour	1 onion, stuck with
5 quarts water	2 cloves
1 teaspoon salt	¼ cup wine vinegar
10 peppercorns	

The butcher will split the head and remove the tongue and brains. Soak overnight in cold water or, if there is not time, blanch it by bringing it to a boil, starting in cold water, and then plunging it into cold water. Mix the flour and water. Add salt, peppercorns, *bouquet garni,* onion, cloves, and vinegar. Bring to the boiling point and add the calf's head, brains, and tongue. The brains and tongue should be extracted after 30 minutes, but the head requires 2 hours of slow cooking. Cut the hot meat from the calf's head. Arrange on a hot platter with slices of tongue and brains which have been reheated. Garnish with a ring of parsley and serve with French Dressing (31).

286. Calf's Feet with French Dressing
Pieds de veau à la vinaigrette

Ask the butcher to split 3 calf's feet lengthwise. Follow the preceding recipe for cooking calf's head. The feet may be left in the broth to cool and eaten cold, or may be eaten hot. In either case they should be accompanied with French Dressing (32).

287. Veal Birds   *Veau roulé*

6 to 8 individual veal cutlets	1½ cups water
½ cup minced left-over beef or chicken	½ cup wine
	salt and pepper
¼ pound sausage meat	2 teaspoons chopped onion
2 tablespoons butter	2 teaspoons chopped parsley
2 tablespoons flour	

The cutlets should be ½ inch thick and uniform in size and shape. Ask the butcher to pound them for you. Pound sausage meat and left-over meat together. Season with salt and pepper. Put a thin layer of this mixture on each cutlet. Roll and tie securely. Melt butter in pan large enough to accommodate all the 'birds.' Brown the meat on all sides in the butter. Remove the 'birds' and add flour to the butter. Add water, wine, salt, pepper, onion, and parsley. When the sauce is well blended, put back the 'birds,' cover, and simmer 45 minutes.

288. Cold Veal, Mayonnaise or Rémoulade Sauce
Salade de veau

Cut cold roast or boiled veal in thin slices. Arrange on a platter and serve with Mayonnaise (17) or Rémoulade Sauce (23).

Il n'y a si méchant pot qui ne trouve son couvercle.

289. Tarragon Veal   *Restes de veau à l'estragon*

2 tablespoons butter
2 tablespoons flour
1 cup water
½ cup dry white wine

salt and pepper
2 tablespoons chopped tara-
 gon *
sliced veal

Melt butter and stir in flour. Let the flour brown, taking care that it does not burn. Add water and wine. Season with salt and pepper. Stir until sauce is smooth. Add veal and tarragon. Reduce the heat and simmer 30 minutes.

290. Left-Over Veal, Blanquette Sauce
Restes de veau en blanquette

2 cups diced left-over veal
Blanquette Sauce (7)
½ cup mushrooms

6 small onions
bouquet garni (42)
salt and pepper

Prepare a Blanquette Sauce. Fry washed and stemmed mushrooms in butter or use canned mushrooms. Parboil the onions 15 minutes. Add the veal, mushrooms, onions, *bouquet garni,* season with salt and pepper, and simmer 30 minutes. Remove the *bouquet garni* and serve.

291. Left-over Veal à la Poulette   *Veau à la poulette*

Follow the preceding recipe but just before serving thicken the sauce with egg and cream (page 4).

* Tarragon is a very common herb in France and should be more common in the United States, where it is almost exclusively associated with vinegar. The herb can be easily grown. It may be bought canned.

292. Left-over Veal in Herb Sauce   *Veau en capilotade*

2 pounds cold roast veal, sliced
1 tablespoon butter
1 tablespoon flour
1 teaspoon chopped parsley
1 teaspoon chopped chives
1 teaspoon chopped onion

1 cup water
¼ cup brandy
salt and pepper
1 tablespoon olive oil
croutons

Melt butter and add flour and herbs. Stir until the flour is light brown. Add water and brandy and simmer gently 15 minutes. Season with salt and pepper. Add veal and cook slowly 15 minutes more. Cover the pan. Just before serving, add olive oil. Serve on a heated platter and garnish with croutons and sprigs of parsley.

293. Sweetbread Balls   *Restes de ris de veau en boulettes*

1 pair cooked sweetbreads
¼ pound mushrooms
Béchamel Sauce (1)
salt and pepper

1 egg, beaten
fine bread crumbs
parsley

Cut the cooked sweetbreads (279) in small pieces. Wash the mushrooms and cut in equally small pieces. Make a thick Béchamel Sauce and simmer sweetbreads and mushrooms in the sauce 15 minutes. Season with salt and pepper. Remove from the fire and chill. When the mixture is very cold, make small balls. Dip them in egg and then in bread crumbs. Fry in deep fat (375°F.) 2 to 3 minutes. Serve with fried or fresh parsley.

294. Veal Salad   *Restes de veau en salade*

	Sauce:
2 cups left-over veal, sliced thin	3 tablespoons oil
3 tablespoons oil	2 teaspoons wine vinegar
2 teaspoons wine vinegar	1 teaspoon sharp mustard
$\frac{1}{2}$ teaspoon salt	3 anchovy fillets
$\frac{1}{8}$ teaspoon black pepper	6 capers (optional)
2 hard-boiled eggs	salt and pepper
6 sweet pickles	

Marinate the veal in oil, vinegar, salt, and pepper for at least 2 hours. Arrange the slices of veal on a platter. Garnish with slices of hard boiled egg and pickle.

To make sauce: Chop the anchovies and add to oil, vinegar, mustard, capers, salt, and pepper. Stir well and serve in a sauce bowl.

295. Veal Croquettes   *Croquettes de veau*

See Croquettes (246).

296. Left-over Calf's Liver on Skewers
Restes de foie de veau en brochette

Left-over liver is often the allotment of the family pet, but it is delicious for human consumption when it is prepared this way:

Cut cold, cooked liver in small squares. Cut bacon in same size and shape. Alternate the liver and bacon on the skewers. Dip skewer in oil, roll in bread crumbs, and broil under very hot flame.

PORK   *PORC*

Fresh pork should be very pale pink. It should be firm and free of excess fat, since even the lean cuts have a good deal of fat running through them. Pork should never be served rare but should be thoroughly cooked. Long cooking not only heightens the flavor but safeguards the consumer from trichinosis.

297. Roast Pork   *Rôti de porc*

Order a 3- to 4-pound loin of pork. Wipe clean and place on rack in an open pan. Put ¾ cup water and 2 teaspoons salt in the bottom of the pan. Baste pork with the salted water several times during the roasting. Roast in a moderate oven (325°F.), allowing 30 minutes per pound.

To make gravy: Pour off the excess fat in roasting pan. Place over a flame. Add 1 cup boiling water and stir with a fork, scraping off any juices that adhere to the pan. Strain into a gravy bowl.

298. Broiled Pork Chops   *Côtelettes de porc grillés*

4 to 6 thick pork loin chops	Tomato Sauce (21), or Robert
salt and freshly ground black pepper	Sauce (16), or Onion Sauce (34)

Wipe the chops carefully and sprinkle with salt and pepper. Broil under hot flame 5 minutes on each side. Finish cooking in 325°F. oven for 30 minutes. Serve with the sauce of your choice.

299. Breaded Pork Tenderloins
Filets mignons de porc, panés et grillés

6 pork tenderloins	2 teaspoons chopped parsley
1 egg, beaten	Anchovy Butter (28), or Tartar
bread crumbs	Sauce (20), or Onion Sauce
salt and pepper	(34)

Order pork tenderloins cut ½ inch thick. Dip in egg and roll in bread crumbs. Sprinkle with salt, pepper, and chopped parsley. Brown under hot flame allowing 5 minutes on each side. Finish cooking in 325°F. oven for 30 minutes. Spread with the sauce of your choice.

300. Pork Chops with Chestnuts and Red Cabbage
Côtelettes de porc à la Courlandaise

6 thick loin pork chops	1 cup stock
1 egg, beaten	1 teaspoon lemon juice
2 tablespoons butter	2 teaspoons chopped parsley
2 tablespoons flour	1 large red cabbage
salt and pepper	20 chestnuts

Trim the chops and wipe them. Dip in beaten egg and brown them in melted butter, allowing 5 minutes to each side. Reduce the heat, cover, and continue cooking 20 minutes longer. Remove chops and keep in a warm place. Stir the flour into the fat, add salt and pepper. Moisten with stock and simmer 10 minutes. While the chops are cooking, combine chestnuts, which have been previously parboiled 20 minutes and peeled, with coarsely shredded red cabbage. Boil 15 minutes and drain. Arrange the chops in the center of a heated platter. Surround with a ring of cabbage and chestnuts. Add lemon juice and parsley to the sauce, strain into a gravy bowl, and serve with the chops.

301. Head Cheese   *Fromage de cochon*

small pig's head	12 peppercorns
1 onion, quartered	nutmeg
2 carrots, cut in rounds	cayenne
double *bouquet garni* (42)	1 tablespoon chopped parsley
2 teaspoons salt	salt and pepper

Ask the butcher to split the pig's head. Soak in warm water
15 minutes. Remove any blood that there may be. Place the
head in a deep kettle. Cover with water. Add onion, carrot,
bouquet garni, cloves, salt, and pepper. Boil gently 5 hours.
Cut the flesh from the bones in small strips. Season highly
with nutmeg, a little cayenne, parsley, salt, and pepper.
Place in a mold or a bread tin. Moisten with 1 cup of the
strained liquid. Cover with a board or piece of wax paper
and weight it down so that the meat will be firmly pressed.
Chill in ice box overnight and serve cold.

302. Pork Liver   *Foie de cochon*

Pig's liver is not so delicate in flavor as calf, baby beef, or
lamb's liver. It is, however, the most nutritive and can be
very delicious. Follow recipes 274-7. Allow a little more time
for cooking pig's liver, for it should be well done. Pig's
liver is more economical and should be tried by those skeptics
who have never dared.

303. Pork Kidneys   *Rognons de cochon*

Follow recipes 234-5, 254-5. Allow a little more time for
cooking pork kidneys.

304. Broiled Pig's Feet   *Pieds de cochon grillés*

Order 6 pickled pig's feet and have the butcher split them lengthwise. Wipe them carefully. Dip in oil, roll in bread crumbs, and broil under a hot flame 15 minutes. Turn from time to time so that they will brown on all sides. Serve with a Piquant Sauce (12). If only fresh pig's feet are obtainable, split them lengthwise and wrap each piece in cheese cloth and tie at both ends. Put in a deep pan. Weight them down and fill the jar with water, salt, pepper, 3 cloves of garlic, a large *bouquet garni* (42), and ¼ cup vinegar. Boil gently 5 hours. Drain, cool and unwrap each piece. They are then ready to be cooked like pickled pig's feet.

305. Boiled Ham   *Jambon au naturel*

Scrub a whole ham (weighing about 11 pounds) or half a ham if the family is small. Place in a deep kettle and cover with water. Add 2 onions and 2 carrots cut in small pieces, 1 clove of garlic, and a double *bouquet garni.* Cover and simmer very, very gently allowing 45 minutes per pound. The slower the cooking the better. When the bone is loosened from the meat, the ham is done. Let the ham cool in the liquid. It should be thoroughly chilled before slicing.

306. Ham with Spinach or Chicory
Jambon aux épinards ou à la chicorée

Serve boiled ham—in this case it should be hot—with French Spinach (487) or Braised Chicory (429). Surround with fried croutons.

307. Ham in White Wine Sauce　*Jambon à la poêle*

6 to 8 thin slices uncooked ham
2 tablespoons butter
2 tablespoons flour

1 cup dry white wine
salt and pepper

Melt butter in frying pan. When the butter is sizzling hot, brown the ham slices on both sides. Allow 5 minutes for cooking the ham. Remove the meat, stir in the flour, moisten with white wine, and stir until the sauce begins to thicken. Season with only a little salt, as the ham is quite salty. Add a dash of freshly ground black pepper. Place the slices of ham on a hot platter. Pour the sauce over the ham and garnish with sprigs of parsley.

308. Roast Suckling Pig　*Cochon de lait au four*

4- or 5-week old piglet
3 tablespoons butter
2 teaspoons chopped parsley
2 onions, stuck with
2 cloves apiece

1 tablespoon chopped shallots
1/8 pound lean salt pork
1/4 pound mushrooms
the pork liver
salt and pepper

Wash the young pig in several waters, taking care that the orifices are thoroughly cleaned. Wipe dry. Soften the butter and work in the parsley. Rub the interior of the piglet with this mixture. Place one of the onions in the cavity. Chop the shallots, salt pork, and mushrooms together. Season with salt and pepper. Fill the cavity with this mixture and put in the remaining onion. Sew up the cavity. Truss the forelegs forward and the hind legs backward, tying the pairs of legs together tightly. Place on a rack in an open pan. Brush with melted butter. Sear the piglet in 450°F. oven 15 minutes. Reduce the temperature to 325°F. and continue cooking, allowing 25 minutes per pound. Baste from time to time with salted boiling water. Five minutes before serving, brush again with melted butter. Place a bright red apple in the mouth of the piglet. Place on a large warm platter. Decorate him with a garland of parsley and serve with a bowl of Ravigote Sauce (24).

309. Sausage and Cabbage — *Saucisses aux choux*

1 pound link sausage
1 tablespoon butter or bacon fat
3 tablespoons flour

2 cups hot water
salt and pepper
bouquet garni (42)
1 medium cabbage

Prick the sausages with a fork and fry in sizzling hot fat until they are well browned. Remove the sausages and add the flour. Brown the flour and stir in the water. When the flour and water are blended, add *bouquet garni,* salt, and pepper and bring to a boil. Meanwhile quarter a cabbage and boil 15 minutes. Add the well-drained cabbage and the sausages to the sauce and simmer 30 minutes. Pile the cabbage in the center of a warm platter. Place the sausages on it. Remove the *bouquet garni* and pour the sauce around the cabbage.

310. Sausage with Pea or Potato Purée
Saucisses à la purée de pois ou de pommes de terre

1 pound link sausages
1 tablespoon fat

Pea Purée (455) or
Potato Purée (471)

Prick the sausages and fry in hot fat. Place in the center of a heated platter and surround with a crown of Pea Purée or Potato Purée. Garnish with sprigs of fresh parsley.

POULTRY includes fowl, chicken, capon, turkey, goose, domestic duck, and squab.

A *fowl* is a hen that has begun to lay eggs. It requires longer cooking—usually boiling.

A *chicken* is a young hen that has been fattened with care and has not begun to lay. It usually weighs 4 to 5 pounds.

A *capon* is a gelded rooster. It is sold weighing 8 to 10 pounds. The meat is particularly sweet and firm.

Small chickens or *broilers* are sold weighing 1½ to 2 pounds.

A *turkey* is sold weighing anywhere from 8 to 30 pounds. The smaller birds are not usually marketed in the United States, but for French recipes it is best to try to find the 10- to 12-pound turkeys.

Goose, duck, and *squab* are more gamey in flavor. They do not have as much meat per pound. Younger birds are better. Old birds run to fat.

TO TRUSS POULTRY: Order the poultry cleaned and dressed. When it comes from the butcher, wipe the inside and outside with a damp cloth. There are many ways of trussing poultry. Skewers may be used instead of string. If skewers are used, place bird on its back. Press thighs close to the body and hold in place by inserting the skewer in the middle of a thigh, running it through the body and bringing it out in the middle of the other thigh. If a string is used, run a trussing needle through the thighs in the same way and tie the string over the back. Draw neck skin out and tuck under a wing. Press the wings close to the body and skewer or tie in the same manner. Tie drumsticks together. If the bird is to be stuffed, both neck and body ends must be filled and the skin skewered or sewed.

311. Roast Chicken *Poulet rôti*

Order a 4- to 5-pound chicken. Wipe and truss according to directions in the preceding paragraph. Cover the chicken with a thin layer of salt pork, tied on with twine. Place chicken on rack in an open pan. Place 1 tablespoon of butter and ½ cup water in the pan. Roast in 375°F. oven, allowing 20 minutes to the pound. Baste every 10 minutes with the liquid in the pan. Insert a fork into the breast at the end of the cooking time. If the meat is tender and no red juices come out, the chicken is done. Take off the salt pork, remove the skewers, and place the chicken on warm platter. Garnish with watercress.

To make gravy: Pour off the excess fat in roasting pan. Place over a flame. Add 1 cup boiling water and stir with a fork, scraping off any juices that adhere to the pan. Strain into a gravy bowl.

La belle cage ne nourrit pas l'oiseau.

312. Chicken and Rice *   *Poule au riz*

5-pound fowl or chicken
water
2 teaspoons salt
¼ teaspoon pepper
bouquet garni (42)

2 cloves garlic (optional)
1 carrot, cut in rounds
1 onion, sliced
1½ cups rice

Wipe and truss the chicken (page 130). Make a *court-bouillon* by putting enough water to cover the chicken in a deep kettle. Add salt, pepper, *bouquet garni,* garlic, carrot, and onion and simmer 30 minutes before adding chicken. Let the chicken simmer—not boil—in the *court-bouillon* 2 to 3 hours or until tender. Do not overcook or the chicken will not keep its shape.

Three quarters of an hour before serving remove the *bouquet garni,* add washed rice, and continue cooking. The rice will absorb most of the liquid. Serve on deep platter. Remove string or skewers from the chicken and serve on a bed of rice. Garnish with fresh parsley.

313. Chicken Blanquette   *Blanquette de volaille*

2 cups cooked chicken or fowl
 (311 or 312)
2 tablespoons butter
2 tablespoons flour
3 cups chicken stock or water

salt and pepper
bouquet garni (42)
8 small onions
½ pound mushrooms
1 tablespoon chopped parsley

Melt butter in a saucepan. Stir in flour. Add liquid and when the sauce is blended add *bouquet garni,* salt, pepper, onions,

---

* The first paragraph of this recipe is the basic method of boiling chicken or fowl. It is the basis for other recipes. If the chicken is not to be eaten hot, allow it to cool in the broth.

and mushrooms which have been washed and stemmed. Use both caps and stems. Simmer 45 minutes. Add the chicken, which may be cubed or left in fairly large pieces. Heat the chicken but do not let the sauce boil. Serve very hot. Sprinkle with chopped parsley.

314. Chicken Mayonnaise   *Mayonnaise de volaille*

cold cooked chicken (311-12)   Mayonnaise (17)

Slice the chicken and arrange on a platter. Garnish with fresh parsley and serve with a bowl of Mayonnaise.

315. Chicken Casserole   *Poulet à la casserole*

3- to 4-pound chicken   salt and pepper
3 tablespoons butter

Wipe and truss the chicken (page 130). Melt butter in a casserole. When the butter is sizzling, brown the chicken on all sides. Sprinkle with salt and pepper. Cover and place in 300°F. oven. Cook 1½ hours. Turn the chicken once or twice, letting it rest on one thigh and then the other. Remove from the casserole and place on heated platter. Pour the juice and butter from the casserole over the chicken. Serve with new boiled potatoes and peas. This is a simple but delicious dish.

⚜

Pain tant qu'il dure, vin à mesure.

⚜

316. Truffled Chicken   *Poulet truffé*

5-pound roasting chicken (or 2 2½-pound broilers)	1½ teaspoons salt
2 truffles or 1 small can truffles	¼ teaspoon black pepper
½ pound sausage meat	2 teaspoons chopped parsley
1 cup bread crumbs	⅛ teaspoon powdered thyme
	paper-thin slices salt pork

Peel truffles. Chop the peelings and mix with the sausage meat, salt, pepper, parsley, and thyme. Cook gently 15 minutes. Remove from the fire, stir in bread crumbs, and chill. Slice the whole truffles very thin. Lift the skin of the chicken and slide the slices of truffle under the skin. Take care not to break the skin. The round black truffles, placed ½ inch apart, make a very pleasing effect.

When the stuffing is cold, fill the interior of the bird. Sew the skin over the openings. Truss the bird (page 130). Cover the chicken with a layer of salt pork and roast in 350°F. oven, allowing 25 minutes per pound.

317. Chicken Fricassee   *Fricassée de poulet*

4-pound chicken or fowl, cut in pieces for serving	¼ teaspoon pepper
2 tablespoons butter	*bouquet garni* (42)
2 tablespoons flour	10 small onions
4 cups water	½ pound mushrooms
2 teaspoons salt	1 egg yolk
	1 teaspoon lemon juice

Ask the butcher to cut the chicken in 8 pieces or, if you are to do it yourself, cut it in the following way. Remove the legs and wings. Split the body in the center. It is best to place the chicken on a wooden board and to use a sharp knife and a mallet to split the bird. Divide each side in two. Soak the pieces in warm water for 30 minutes.

Melt butter in a heavy saucepan. Mix in flour, stirring well but not allowing it to brown. Add water and stir until the sauce is smooth. Add salt, pepper, *bouquet garni,* chicken, and onions. Cook 1 hour over a moderate flame. 15 minutes before the end of the cooking, add the mushrooms, which have been washed, stemmed, plunged in boiling water, and drained. Strain off the sauce.

Place the chicken in the center of a heated platter. Surround with onions and mushrooms. Thicken the sauce with the egg yolk (page 3), add lemon juice, and pour over the chicken. Garnish with fresh parsley. See recipe 337 for using left-over fricasseed chicken.

318. Chicken in White Wine   *Poulet sauté au vin blanc*

2 small frying chickens	salt and pepper
2 tablespoons butter	8 small onions or
2 tablespoons flour	2 large onions, sliced thin
½ cup dry white wine	½ cup water
½ cup water	2 tablespoons butter

Split or quarter the chickens, depending on size. Cook the onions in ½ cup water and 2 tablespoons butter for 10 minutes. Melt butter in frying pan large enough for all the chicken. Brown the chicken on all sides. Remove the chicken, stir in flour. Add water and wine and, when the sauce is smooth, put back the chicken and the onions along with the liquid in which they have been cooking. Season with salt and pepper. Cover and cook over low flame 45 minutes. Serve on a heated platter. Garnish with parsley.

319. Tarragon Chicken   *Poulet à l'estragon*

4- to 5-pound roasting chicken
4 or 5 tarragon leaves
3 paper-thin slices salt pork
water
2 teaspoons salt
¼ teaspoon pepper
bouquet garni (42)

2 sprigs of tarragon
2 carrots, cut in rounds
1 onion, sliced thin
2 teaspoons cornstarch
2 or 3 drops yellow coloring
8 tarragon leaves

This is a wonderful summer chicken dish if you have tarragon growing in the garden.

Wipe and truss the chicken as for roasting (page 130). Mince tarragon leaves and place in the interior of the chicken. Sew up the openings. Tie a thin layer of salt pork over the breast of the chicken. Prepare the following *court-bouillon:* Put enough water in the kettle to cover the bird. Add salt, pepper, *bouquet garni,* tarragon sprigs, carrots, onion, and bring to a boil. Place the chicken in the kettle and cook until tender. Remove the chicken and drain well so that there is no liquid inside the bird. Strain the *court-bouillon.*

To make sauce: Mix the cornstarch in a little cold water and add to 1 cup of the *court-bouillon.* When it is well blended, pour into 4 cups of the broth. Add the yellow coloring to the sauce. Remove the salt pork from the chicken and place 4 tarragon leaves diagonally on each side. Fill a deep platter with the sauce and place the chicken on it. Serve with rice or new potatoes.

320. Chicken with Olives   *Poulet aux olives*

3- to 4-pound chicken
2 tablespoons butter
2 tablespoons flour
3 cups water

bouquet garni (42)
salt and pepper
½ cup pitted green olives

Clean and truss the chicken as for roasting. Melt butter in deep saucepan and brown chicken on both sides. Remove the chicken, add flour and allow it to brown, taking care that it does not burn. Add water, *bouquet garni,* salt, and pepper. Stir until the sauce is smooth. Put back the chicken and cover. Simmer 45 to 60 minutes or until tender. 15 minutes before serving add olives. Place chicken on platter. Remove the strings or skewers. Surround with olives and pour the sauce over it all. Serve with boiled potatoes or rice.

321. Chicken Marengo   *Poulet Marengo*

Tradition has it that during a quiet moment in the battle between the Austrians and Napoleon's army at Marengo in northern Italy, supplies were very low, and the chef was desperately trying to find something to give Napoleon for his dinner. He captured a straying hen, gathered wild mushrooms, and concocted this now famous dish. [c. t.]

4-pound chicken, cut in pieces for serving	2 tablespoons flour
4 tablespoons olive oil	1 tablespoon tomato paste
salt and pepper	½ cup stock or water
bouquet garni (42)	½ cup dry white wine (or ½ cup Madeira wine)
1 clove garlic, chopped fine	½ pound mushrooms

Heat the olive oil in a deep saucepan. Brown the chicken in the oil, turning each piece so that all sides are crisp. Remove the chicken. Stir in flour and moisten with stock and wine. When well blended add *bouquet garni,* tomato paste, garlic, and mushrooms, which have been washed and cut in pieces. Season with salt and pepper. Replace the chicken and cover. Simmer 1 hour. Remove the *bouquet garni* and serve.

322. Chicken Galantine   *Galantine de poulet*

Wipe clean a 4-pound chicken. Remove the wings. Make an incision the entire length of the back. With a sharp knife loosen the flesh from each side of the backbone, being careful not to pierce the skin. Lay the chicken wide open and remove the bones. The main skeleton will come out in one piece. The thigh bones have to be eased out carefully. This is not easy and takes practice. Lay the boned bird as near flat as possible on a double layer of cheese cloth. It is then ready for stuffing.

Stuffing:
- 1½ pounds finely ground veal
- 1½ pounds finely ground fresh pork
- salt and pepper
- 1 teaspoon poultry seasoning
- 1 clove garlic, finely chopped
- 1 tablespoon chopped onion
- 2 teaspoons chopped parsley
- several strips of boiled ham

Court-bouillon:
- water
- *bouquet garni* (42)
- ½ calf's foot or 2 tablespoons gelatine
- 2 carrots, cut in pieces
- 1 large onion, sliced
- 3 drops yellow coloring

Ask the butcher to grind the pork and veal together. Mix well with the seasonings and spread half of it on the chicken, making sure that all the cavities where the bones were removed are filled. Lay thin strips of boiled ham on this, and finish by filling the chicken with the rest of the stuffing. Sew the chicken up so that it resumes its original shape. Wrap it up in cheese cloth and tie securely. Meanwhile prepare the *court-bouillon* and when it has reached the boiling point, place the chicken in the kettle. The bird should be completely immersed. Cook over a moderate flame 5 to 6 hours. Remove carefully from the kettle and do not touch until it is cold.

Strain the broth, add a little coloring, and let it cool. If calf's foot is not obtainable, add the gelatine, softened in cold water at this point. The broth will jell. When it is cold, remove the fat from the top and clarify the jelly (37). This necessitates boiling the liquid again. When it is cooling for the last time, watch carefully for the moment when the jelly is thick but not firm. The process can be hastened by placing the pan in cold water. When the jelly has the consistency of egg white, pour 1 cupful carefully over the galantine, which has been unwrapped and placed on a platter. Chill in the refrigerator and allow the rest of the jelly to become firm. Just before serving, chop up the remaining jelly and place around the galantine. Forcing it through a pastry tube is a good way to do this. Chop fresh parsley and sprinkle on the jelly. This dish can be prepared a day in advance and kept in the refrigerator.

323. Roast Turkey, Sausage and Chestnut Stuffing
Dinde rôtie

Wipe clean a 12-pound turkey (page 130). Make the following stuffing:

1 pound chestnuts	2 tablespoons flour
½ pound sausage meat	salt and pepper
3 tablespoons butter	½ cup stock or water

Slash each chestnut twice and throw into boiling water. Boil 20 minutes and peel while hot. Fry sausage and chestnuts in sizzling butter 5 minutes. Stir in flour and stock. Season with salt and pepper. Cook 3 minutes longer. When the stuffing is cool—it should be thick—stuff the turkey, sew up the openings, truss, and place on a rack in an open pan. Pour 1 cup water mixed with 1 teaspoon salt in the bottom of the pan and baste with this mixture from time to time. Roast in a 350°F. oven, allowing 25 minutes per pound.

324. Truffled Turkey   *Dinde truffée*

Order an 8- to 10-pound turkey at least 2 days before serving.
Chop 2 small cans of truffle peelings and combine with 1 large
can of whole truffles. Try out ½ pound fat salt pork. Remove
the pork and add the truffles, salt, pepper, and 1 teaspoon
poultry seasoning. Fry gently 15 minutes. Remove the truffles
and cool. Place the truffles inside the turkey, sew up the
openings, and truss. Leave the turkey in a cool place for at
least 2 days so that the taste of truffles will permeate the bird.
Cover the breast with a thin layer of salt pork and roast in
350°F. oven for 2½ to 3 hours. Place on a bed of watercress and serve with a Truffle Sauce (27). *Haute cuisine* would
require slipping slices of truffle under the skin before cooking,
but Tante Marie does not demand this extra touch.

325. Roast Squab   *Pigeon rôti*

Dress and truss squabs (page 130). Place a thin layer of salt
pork over the breast of the birds and tie in place. Roast in
350°F. oven 30 to 45 minutes, depending upon the size.
Unless squabs are unusually large it is best to count on one
per person. Serve on a bed of watercress and pour over it
all a gravy made as follows: pour ½ cup boiling water into
the roasting pan. Scrape off the juices adhering to the bottom
of the pan with a fork. Add a little salt and strain.

326. Squabs with Peas   *Pigeons aux pois*

4 squabs	2 cups water
3 tablespoons butter	salt and pepper
¼ pound diced lean bacon	*bouquet garni* (42)
3 tablespoons flour	4 cups shelled peas

Wipe and truss the birds (page 130). Melt butter in a heavy large saucepan. When butter is sizzling, brown the squabs on both sides, allowing 5 minutes to each side. Do not have the flame too high. When the birds are well browned, remove them and put in the bacon. Brown this and remove it. Stir in flour and when this has browned add water, salt, pepper, and *bouquet garni*. Stir until smooth. Replace the bacon and add the fresh peas.* Cook ½ hour, add the squabs, and continue cooking 30 minutes longer or until the squabs are tender. Place squabs on heated platter, remove the *bouquet garni* and the pieces of bacon (optional), and pour the peas and sauce around the squabs.

327. Squab Casserole   *Pigeons en compote*

2 large squabs	½ teaspoon salt
2 tablespoons butter	*bouquet garni* (42)
¼ pound diced salt pork	10 small onions
2 tablespoons flour	¼ pound mushrooms
2 cups stock	10 green pitted olives
¼ teaspoon black pepper	croutons

Split the squabs in two. Heat the butter until it sizzles. Brown squabs on both sides and remove. Brown the salt pork in the same butter. Stir in flour. Add stock, salt, pepper, and *bouquet garni*. Stir until the sauce is smooth. Put back the squabs. Add onions and cook 30 minutes. Add mushrooms, which have been washed and stemmed, and, if desired, olives. Cook 15 minutes longer. One can also add Forcemeat Balls (38). Serve the squabs in a deep platter. Remove the skewers or strings. Take out the *bouquet garni* and pour the sauce around the birds. Garnish with croutons and parsley. If squabs weigh at least 1 pound apiece, this recipe will serve 4 people.

* If frozen peas are used, add them when the squabs are put back into the sauce. If canned peas are used, add them 15 minutes before serving.

328. Roast Duck   *Canard rôti*

Wipe clean and truss a 5½- to 6-pound duck (page 130). Place on rack in open pan. Rub the breast with salt and roast in 400°F. oven, allowing 15 minutes per pound.

To make gravy: Pour ½ cup boiling water in the pan. Scrape off the juices with a fork, mix well and pour over duck. See recipes 332 and 339 for using cold roast duck.

329. Duck with Peas   *Canard aux pois*

1 5- to 6-pound duck (or 2 ducklings)	2 cups water
	salt and pepper
3 tablespoons butter	*bouquet garni* (42)
¼ pound diced lean bacon	4 cups shelled peas
3 tablespoons flour	

Follow directions given in recipe 326.

330. Duck with Olives   *Canard aux olives*

1 small duck (or 2 ducklings)	*bouquet garni* (42)
2 tablespoons butter	salt and pepper
2 tablespoons flour	½ cup pitted olives
3 cups water	

Follow directions given in recipe 320.

331. Duck with Orange Sauce   *Canard à l'orange*

Fill the cavity of a 5½- to 6-pound duck with ½ peeled orange. Sew up the opening and truss (page 130). Roast according to recipe 328. When the duck is cooked, remove the fat from the pan. Scrape off the juices with ½ cup boiling water. Put in a small saucepan. Add the juice of ½ orange,

1 cup of dry white wine, and the peel of one orange which has been parboiled 10 minutes and finely chopped. Chop the orange from the cavity. Add this and, if desired, the giblet, finely chopped. Thicken with cornstarch and butter (page 4). Heat thoroughly and serve in a gravy bowl.

332. Duck Salmis   *Salmis de canard*

1 5-pound cold roast duck	½ cup red wine
(328)	1 tablespoon olive oil
duck liver	salt and pepper
¼ cup stock	½ teaspoon grated lemon peel
1 tablespoon butter	croutons

Remove the legs, wings, and breasts of duck. The breasts may be divided in two. Pick off the rest of the meat and pound it with the liver to a smooth paste, moistening it with stock. Put the paste in a saucepan with butter, wine, oil, salt, pepper, and lemon peel. Simmer 1 hour and during last 15 minutes reheat the duck in the sauce. Place the pieces of duck on large fried croutons, thicken the sauce with butter and cornstarch (page 4), and pour over the duck. This is a good recipe for left-over duck or wild bird.

333. Roast Goose   *Oie rôtie*

Goose is prepared and stuffed like a turkey (323). A 10- to 12-pound goose is very satisfactory. Roast 2½ to 3 hours in 325°F. oven. Do not let the fat collect in the pan. Remove it from time to time, leaving only the juices. It should not be too tightly stuffed. Baste frequently with salted water. Serve with Boiled Rice (387).

Goose fat should be carefully saved. It makes an excellent seasoning for vegetables and may be used in place of butter. In this case, it should be well-salted.

334. Goose Galantine   *Oie en daube*

Follow directions for Chicken Galantine (322).

335. Poultry Left-overs in Salad
Restes de volaille en salade

Slice or dice cold cooked chicken, duck, goose, or turkey.
Arrange on lettuce leaves and serve with Mayonnaise (17), or
Rémoulade Sauce (23).

336. Poultry Left-overs Fricasseed
Restes de volaille en fricassée

2 cups cooked poultry, diced	8 small onions (or 2 medium
2 tablespoons butter	onions, quartered)
2 tablespoons flour	croutons
2 cups poultry stock or water	juice of ½ lemon
¼ pound mushrooms	1 egg yolk

Melt butter and stir in flour. Add stock and stir until the
sauce is smooth. Wash the mushrooms and cut in small pieces.
Add mushrooms and onions to the sauce and simmer over a
low flame until the onions are tender—approximately 30
minutes. Add the poultry and simmer 10 minutes more.
Thicken with egg yolk (page 3) and add lemon juice. Serve
in a deep platter and garnish with croutons and parsley.

337. Fried Fricasseed Chicken
Restes de volaille en fricassée

If there remain any pieces of fricasseed chicken (317) take
each piece with the cold sauce still on it, dip in bread crumbs,

then in an egg yolk beaten with 1 tablespoon oil, and then
again in bread crumbs. Fry in deep fat (390°F.) and serve
very hot.

338. Duck in Red Wine   *Canard au vin rouge*

2 tablespoons butter	salt and pepper
2 tablespoons flour	1 teaspoon grated orange or
1 cup stock	lemon rind
½ cup red wine	*bouquet garni* (42)
1 teaspoon chopped onion	slices of cold roast duck
1 teaspoon chopped parsley	duck liver

Melt butter and stir in flour. Add wine and stock and stir
until the sauce is smooth. Add onion, parsley, salt, pepper,
grated peel, *bouquet garni,* and duck. Simmer 1 hour. Remove *bouquet garni,* add the liver which has been crushed
(raw or cooked), and serve on rounds of toasted bread.

339. Left-over Duck with Olives

Restes de canard aux olives

Make a Brown Sauce i (5). Add ½ cup pitted olives, sliced
or whole. Heat slices of left-over duck in this sauce and serve
with Boiled Rice (387).

340. Boar *Sanglier*

Boar is a wild pig, and any of the pork recipes (297-303, 308)
may be used. As with other game, it is best to marinate the
meat 4 or 5 days before cooking (see recipe 32).

341. Roast Leg of Venison *Gigot de chevreuil mariné*

In France almost all game is marinated before cooking. It
makes the meat tender and heightens the flavor.

With a sharp-pointed knife, make 1-inch incisions all over
the leg of venison and insert small pieces of salt pork. Prepare
the following marinating sauce:

½ cup red wine   *bouquet garni* (42)
½ cup wine vinegar   2 onions, sliced
1 tablespoon salt   2 carrots, sliced
½ teaspoon black pepper   ¼ cup oil

Marinate the venison in this sauce from 5 to 6 days. Turn the leg over occasionally and baste with the sauce so that the flavor will permeate the whole leg. Roast in 350°F. oven, allowing 18 minutes per pound. Venison should be rare. Serve with Piquant Sauce (12) or Pepper Sauce (19).

342. Tenderloin Roast of Venison   *Filet de chevreuil rôti*

This roast corresponds to a tenderloin roast of beef and is particularly delicious. Marinate the roast as in the preceding recipe and follow directions in recipe 222 for cooking.

343. Venison Casserole   *Civet de chevreuil*

2 pounds breast of venison	1 teaspoon salt
¼ pound diced salt pork	⅛ teaspoon black pepper
2 tablespoons butter	*bouquet garni* (42)
2 tablespoons flour	1 clove garlic
2 cups water	12 small or 3 large onions
½ cup red wine	¼ pound mushrooms

Fry the salt pork in butter until brown. Remove the pork and fry the venison, which has been cut in small pieces, in the fat. When the venison is well browned, remove it and add flour. Add water and wine and stir until well blended. Add salt, pepper, garlic, onions, *bouquet garni,* and put back the venison. Cook gently 60 minutes. Add mushrooms, which have been washed and stemmed, and simmer 30 minutes longer. Use both caps and stems. Place the venison in a deep warm platter. Cover with a layer of onions and then with a layer of mushrooms. Strain the sauce and pour it over all. If the sauce is too thin, thicken with cornstarch or potato starch (page 4).

344. Venison Chops   *Côtelettes de chevreuil*

Wipe and trim thin chops cut from the loin. Dip in bread crumbs. Melt 2 tablespoons butter in bottom of broiling pan. When the butter is sizzling, place the chops in the pan. Do not use the broiling rack. Broil 5 minutes on each side. Season with salt and freshly ground black pepper. Serve with Pepper Sauce (19).

345. Left-over Venison   *Restes de chevreuil*

Heat left-over venison in Pepper Sauce (19) or in Piquant Sauce (12).

Hare   *Lièvre*

Hare resembles rabbit in flavor but is much gamier. It is a prized dish in France. When a hare has been cleaned and skinned, it is divided in the following manner: Cut the hare in two just back of the shoulders. The breast, neck, and shoulders are used for jugged hare. The back and hind quarters are used for roasting.

346. Roast Hare   *Lièvre rôti*

Prepare the marinating sauce described in recipe 341. Marinate the part to be roasted 1 or 2 days before cooking. Cover with a layer of paper-thin slices of salt pork. Roast 1 hour in 350°F. oven.

347. Jugged Hare   *Lièvre en civet*

forequarters, breast, and neck of hare	2 cups red wine
	salt and pepper
1/4 pound diced salt pork	*bouquet garni* (42)
2 tablespoons butter	2 cloves
2 tablespoons flour	10 small onions
2 cups water	1/2 pound mushrooms

Melt butter in a deep heavy saucepan. Fry pork in the butter until it is brown. Remove the pork. Cut the forequarters, breast, and neck into small pieces and brown in the butter and pork fat. Stir in flour and when it is slightly browned add water, wine, salt, pepper, *bouquet garni,* cloves, and onions. Put back the pork, cover, and cook slowly 2½ hours. Add mushrooms, which have been washed and stemmed, and cook 30 minutes longer. Use both caps and stems. If the hare has been killed and dressed at home, save the blood carefully and bind the sauce with the blood several minutes before serving (page 4). Remove the *bouquet garni* before serving.

348. Potted Hare *Lièvre haché en terrine*

1 small hare
1 pound lean veal
1 pound lean fresh pork
¼ pound suet
¼ pound salt pork, sliced paper-thin
¼ teaspoon powdered thyme

½ bay leaf, crushed
1 teaspoon chopped parsley
2 teaspoons chopped onion
¼ teaspoon ground cloves
salt and pepper
½ cup domestic brandy

Cut the flesh from the bones of the hare. Put the hare, veal, pork, and suet through a food chopper, using the finest blade. Season with thyme, bay leaf, parsley, onion, clove, salt, and pepper. Blend well and divide the mixture in 4 parts. Line an earthenware terrine with 1 layer of salt pork. Put in a layer of the mixture and cover with a layer of salt pork. Alternate the salt pork and combined meats until the terrine is full. Over the last layer of meat mixture pour ½ cup of brandy. Cover with a final layer of salt pork. Place a cover on the terrine, making sure that it fits tightly. Seal the top with strips of pastry or a paste made of flour. Cook 4 hours in 300°F. oven. Remove from the oven and cool. Weight the cover down while it is cooling, so that the meat will hold its shape when it is unmolded. The unmolded terrine may be garnished with Aspic (37), made of broth from the bones or of other stock, or it may be served in the terrine. It makes a delicious entrée or hors-d'œuvre. It can be kept 8 to 10 days in a cool place without spoiling.

349. Hare in White Wine *Levraut au vin blanc*

1 young hare
2 tablespoons butter
salt and pepper
¼ teaspoon powdered thyme
dash of nutmeg

1 teaspoon chopped parsley
2 teaspoons chopped onion
1 cup dry white wine
1 cup stock or water

Cut a young hare, dressed and cleaned, into pieces for serving. Melt butter in large frying pan and brown the pieces well on both sides. This should take at least 20 minutes. Add the seasonings, wine, and stock or water. Cover and simmer 25 minutes. Taste for seasoning and serve in the sauce.

350. Left-over Hare with Mushrooms
Eminc̣é de lièvre aux champignons

left-over hare cut in thin strips	1 tablespoon flour
2 tablespoons butter	½ cup white wine
¼ pound mushrooms	salt and pepper
1 teaspoon chopped parsley	juice of ½ lemon
2 teaspoons chopped shallots	croutons
or onion	parsley

Place the hare, butter, mushrooms, which have been washed and stemmed, parsley, and shallots in a heavy saucepan. When the butter is melted, sprinkle with flour and stir in gently. Add wine, salt, and pepper and cover. Simmer very gently for 30 minutes. Just before serving add lemon juice. Serve on a heated platter and garnish with parsley and croutons.

Rabbit   *Lapin*

Rabbit, when properly prepared, is very delicious. It is commonly served in France and is gradually becoming more popular in the United States. It may be found in all the large city markets, and in some sections of the country rabbits are sold commonly. The butcher will usually clean and dress the rabbit. If the rabbit is to be used for roasting, it is cut through just behind the shoulders. The back and hind quarters are roasted. If a recipe calls for cutting the rabbit into serving pieces, the body should be split down the middle and each side divided into 3 pieces—foreleg, body, and hind leg. Rabbit and Hare recipes may be used interchangeably.

351. Rabbit Fricassee   *Lapin en gibelotte*

rabbit, cut in pieces for serving
3 tablespoons butter
2 tablespoons flour
2 cups dry white wine
¼ pound diced lean salt pork
bouquet garni (42)

4 cloves
12 small onions
salt and pepper
dash of nutmeg
½ pound mushrooms (or 8 small peeled potatoes)

Melt butter in heavy saucepan and when it is sizzling, brown the pieces of rabbit on both sides. Meanwhile, in another pan, fry the salt pork until it is brown. When the rabbit has been thoroughly browned, sprinkle with flour and stir gently until the flour is blended. Add wine and when that begins to boil, add the fried pork, *bouquet garni*, cloves, onions, salt, pepper, onions, and potatoes. Cover and simmer gently for 60 minutes. If mushrooms are used in place of potatoes, add them 15 minutes before serving. If sauce is too thin, thicken with a little cornstarch (page 4), or if by chance the rabbit has been killed and dressed at home save the blood and thicken the sauce with it (page 4). This gives a gamey flavor to the dish.

352. Rabbit à la Marengo   *Lapin à la Marengo*

1 young rabbit, cut in pieces for serving (page 151)
3 tablespoons olive oil
2 teaspoons chopped onion
2 teaspoons chopped parsley
1 tablespoon tomato paste

½ cup water
¼ pound small mushrooms
salt and pepper
1 teaspoon butter
juice of ½ lemon

Heat the olive oil until it is smoking. Fry the rabbit in the oil, turning the pieces often. This takes 20 to 30 minutes, depending on the thickness of the pieces. When the rabbit is tender, remove from the fire but keep in a warm place. Put half of the oil in which the rabbit has been cooked in a saucepan. Add parsley, onion, tomato paste, and water. Cook the mushrooms, which have been washed and stemmed, in this sauce until they are tender (10 to 15 minutes). Add butter and lemon juice, season with salt and pepper, and pour over the rabbit.

353. Papa Douillet's Rabbit   *Lapin au Père Douillet*

rabbit, cut in pieces for serving (page 151)
3 tablespoons butter
⅛ pound diced lean salt pork
1 cup dry white wine
1 cup water
1 tablespoon chopped parsley
1 tablespoon chopped onion
1 tablespoon chopped chives
salt and pepper
1 teaspoon cornstarch mixed with
1 teaspoon butter

Brown the rabbit and salt pork in sizzling butter. When the rabbit is well browned on both sides, add wine, water, herbs, salt, and pepper. Cover and simmer gently for 1 hour. Just before serving, thicken with cornstarch and butter (page 4).

354. Roast Rabbit   *Lapin rôti*

Rabbit is roasted like hare (346). It may or may not be marinated before roasting. The marinating gives a gamey flavor.

355. Roast Partridge   *Perdreaux rôtis*

2 partridges
paper-thin slices of salt pork
watercress
lemon slices

Clean and truss the partridges like chickens (page 130). Cover each bird with a thin layer of salt pork and tie in place with twine. Place on rack in open roasting pan. Pour ½ cup of water seasoned with ½ teaspoon salt in the pan. Roast in 375°F. oven 30 to 40 minutes. Place the birds on a bed of watercress. Pour the juices and fat from the pan over the birds and garnish the platter with slices of lemon.

356. Truffled Partridge   *Perdreaux truffés*

Procure 2 or 3 partridges and follow recipe for Truffled
Chicken (316).

357. Partridge and Cabbage   *Perdrix aux choux*

This is a good recipe to use when the birds are a little old and
tough.

2 partridges
¼ pound lean bacon, sliced
  thin
6 link sausages
2 tablespoons butter
2 tablespoons flour
1 cup stock or water

salt and pepper
¼ teaspoon powdered thyme
4 cloves
1 carrot, sliced thin
1 medium-sized cabbage, cut in
  eighths

Melt butter in heavy saucepan. Split the partridges and brown
them along with the bacon and sausages. As the various pieces
become brown take them out of the butter. Add flour and stir
until brown. Add stock, thyme, carrot, and cloves and stir until
the sauce is smooth. Meanwhile, remove the outer leaves of
the cabbage, cut it in eighths, and parboil 20 minutes. Drain
thoroughly. Put the cabbage and partridges in the sauce, cover
and simmer very gently for 2 hours. Skim off the fat. Place the
cabbage on a heated platter. Arrange the partridges in the
center and surround with sausage and bacon. Strain the sauce
and pour carefully around the cabbage.

358. Roast Pheasant   *Faisan rôti*

Rub the cleaned and dressed pheasant with softened sweet
butter. Place on a rack in open pan. Roast in 375°F. oven for

45 minutes. At the end of the first 15 minutes, add 2 table-spoons Madeira wine to the melted butter in the pan. Baste with this mixture every 10 minutes. 15 minutes before serv-ing, place 7 or 8 small rounds of stale bread in the pan. This will absorb the juices and become brown. Place the pheasant on a bed of watercress. Surround with the rounds of bread and garnish with slices of lemon.

359. Roast Quail   *Cailles rôties*

Clean, dress, and truss quails as directed for chicken (page 130). Wrap each bird in a fresh grape leaf and in thin slices of salt pork. Tie in place and place on rack in open pan. Roast 30 minutes in 375°F. oven.

360. Hunter's Quail   *Cailles au chasseur*

4 quails	$\frac{1}{4}$ teaspoon powdered thyme
3 tablespoons butter	2 tablespoons flour
2 teaspoons chopped parsley	$\frac{1}{2}$ cup water
2 teaspoons chopped scallions	$\frac{1}{2}$ cup white wine
$\frac{1}{2}$ bay leaf	1 teaspoon lemon juice
salt and pepper	croutons

Dress and truss quails as directed for chicken (page 130). Melt butter in a heavy oven-proof casserole. Put quails, parsley, scallions, salt, pepper, and thyme in the casserole and brown the birds on both sides. Add flour and stir in gently. Add water and wine and bring to the boiling point. Cover and place in a 350°F. oven for 30 minutes. Place each quail on a round crouton. Taste the sauce to be sure it is properly sea-soned. Strain and pour some over each bird. Garnish with watercress and slices of lemon.

361. Roast Woodcock   *Bécasses rôties*

It is not necessary to dress the woodcock. Remove the head
and wing tips. Place each bird on a skewer. Cover the breast
of each bird with a thin layer of salt pork. Roast on a rack in
an open pan 30 minutes in 375°F. oven. Place rounds of
toasted bread in the bottom of the pan to catch the juices.
Remove the skewers and place each bird on a round of bread.
Garnish with lemon slices and parsley.

362. Wild Duck   *Canard sauvage*

Wild duck may be prepared in the same manner as domestic
duck. Follow recipes 328-32, 338, 339.

Qui court deux lièvres n'en prendra aucun.

PÂTÉS are a combination of meats or fish, carefully prepared and highly spiced, which are cooked in either a round or oval earthenware terrine which has a cover, or in a pastry shell. They may be used as an hors-d'œuvre, an entrée, a luncheon dish, or as the main attraction at a midnight collation.

363. Chicken Pâté   *Pâté-terrine de volaille*

1 3½- to 4-pound chicken	1 bay leaf
½ pound ground veal	1 sprig of thyme
½ pound ground fresh pork	2 large paper-thin slices salt
2 slices stale bread, soaked in	pork
¼ cup milk	½ cup water
½ pound veal cutlet	1 cup domestic brandy
½ pound thin ham steak	salt and pepper

Make an incision down the back of a properly cleaned chicken. With a sharp knife loosen the flesh from each side of the skeleton, taking care not to pierce the skin. Lay the chicken wide open and remove the skeleton in one piece. Kitchen shears are very helpful. The thigh bones should be eased out. This is difficult and for the unpracticed it is better to leave them in. The wings and legs are left on. Lay the skin and flesh as flat as possible and prepare the following stuffing: Chop the liver and heart rather fine and combine with the ground veal and pork. Squeeze the excess milk from the bread and add to the meat. Season with salt and pepper. Fill the holes left by the bones with stuffing and spread a layer of stuffing over the entire surface. Cut the veal and ham in thin strips and put a layer of each over the stuffing. Continue this until the chicken is full. Make sure that there are no holes left. Sew up the back so that the chicken will resume its original shape.

Place a thin layer of salt pork in the bottom of an oval terrine. On this put ½ bay leaf and half of the branch of thyme. Add water and brandy. Place the chicken in the terrine and cover with another strip of salt pork, ½ bay leaf, and the other half of the branch of thyme. Sprinkle with salt and pepper and cover. The terrine should be absolutely filled: if there are any open spaces between the chicken and the terrine, fill them with the stuffing. Cover and seal the rim with a little flour-and-water paste. Cook 2½ hours in a 300°F. oven. Remove from the oven but do not open until it is completely cooled. Serve cold.

A vaincre sans péril, on triomphe sans gloire.

364. Rabbit Pâté   *Pâté-terrine de lapin*

1 small rabbit
½ pound veal cutlet
½- to ¾-pound sausage meat
2 small bay leaves
¼ teaspoon ground cloves
⅛ teaspoon nutmeg

sprig of thyme
two wide paper-thin slices salt
 pork
½ cup water
1 cup domestic brandy

Remove the flesh from the bones of the cleaned and dressed rabbit. Cut the flesh into strips approximately 3 inches long and ¾ inch wide. Cut the veal into strips of the same size. Chop the liver and heart and mix with the sausage meat. Season with salt and pepper, nutmeg, and cloves. Place a layer of salt pork in the bottom of a terrine. Sprinkle with some freshly ground black pepper and place a bay leaf and half of the thyme on the salt pork. Cover this with a layer of sausage meat. Over this place a layer of rabbit meat and a layer of veal. Continue this alternation until the terrine is full. Press down so that the meat is firmly packed. Cover with a layer of salt pork. Sprinkle with pepper and place another bay leaf and half a sprig of thyme on top. Pour water and brandy over it all, piercing the pâté with a fork so that the liquid will seep through. Cover tightly and seal with a flour-and-water paste. Cook 3 hours in a 300°F. oven. Cool in the terrine and do not open until it is ready to be served. It is always better to let a pâté stand at least 24 hours before eating.

365. Partridge Pâté   *Pâté-terrine de perdreaux*

Follow directions for Chicken Pâté (363).

366. Ham and Veal Pâté   *Pâté-terrine de veau et jambon*

¾ pound veal cutlets	salt and pepper
½ pound thin ham steaks	2 small bay leaves
½ pound sausage meat	1 branch of thyme
¼ cup bread crumbs, moistened with a little water	2 paper-thin slices salt pork
½ cup pistachio nuts	½ cup water
	1 cup brandy

Trim the veal cutlets and ham steaks so that they are the
approximate size and shape of the terrine. Insert small pieces
of ham fat in the veal. Chop the trimmings fine and combine
with sausage meat and bread crumbs. Season with salt and
pepper. Place a piece of salt pork in the bottom of the terrine
and on this put a small bay leaf and half a branch of thyme.
Spread a layer of the sausage mixture on this, followed by a
layer of ham and a layer of veal. Add a few nuts. Continue this
alternation until the terrine is completely full. Press the meat
down and pour the water and brandy over the top, piercing the
meat with a fork so that the liquid will seep through. Place a
layer of salt pork, a bay leaf, and the other sprig of thyme
over this. Cover tightly, seal with a little water-and-flour paste.
Cook in 300°F. oven for 3 hours. 15 minutes before the end
of the cooking pour ½ cup consommé through the hole in the
cover. This is not absolutely necessary but does render the
pâté a little more moist. Do not remove the cover until the
terrine is really cool. It is served cold.

367. Goose Liver Pâté *Pâté-terrine de foie gras*

This wonderful dish can rarely be reproduced in America since it calls for fattened goose livers, seldom obtainable in the United States. The canned *foie gras* is too expensive to warrant its use in a pâté. A passable imitation of this dish may be made by using ordinary chicken or goose livers.

1 pound calf's liver	⅛ teaspoon mace
1 pound chicken or goose livers (substituting for 1 pound *foie gras*)	2 tablespoons chopped parsley
	1 small can truffles
	1 cup fine bread crumbs moistened with
¼ pound fresh lean pork	¼ cup water
½ pound lard	2 thin slices salt pork
salt and black pepper	1 bay leaf
¼ teaspoon ground cloves	

Cut the chicken or goose livers in ½-inch pieces. Slice the truffles very thin. Chop the calf's liver, pork, and lard rather coarsely. Add bread crumbs and any trimmings of truffles. Put ½ inch of this mixture in the bottom of a small round terrine. Place a layer of chicken or goose livers on this and cover with a single layer of truffles. Continue this alternation until the terrine is tightly packed. After each layer of truffles sprinkle with salt, pepper, cloves, and mace. The pâté is not highly spiced but should have a subtle aromatic flavor. Cover with a thin layer of lard. Place a bay leaf on this and seal the cover on with a little water-and-flour paste. Place the terrine in a pan of hot water and cook 3½ hours in 300°F. oven. Cool the pâté in the terrine. When it is thoroughly chilled, it may be unmolded by plunging it in boiling water and turning upside down on a small platter. To be traditional it should be wrapped and served in tin foil.

368. Calf's Liver Pâté   *Pâté-terrine de foie de veau*

1 pound calf's liver	salt and black pepper
1 pound lean fresh pork	¼ teaspoon ground cloves
5 wide paper-thin slices salt pork	⅛ teaspoon mace
	1 bay leaf

Chop the liver and pork together. Season with salt, pepper, cloves, and mace. Mix well. Line the bottom of a round terrine with a layer of salt pork. Divide the mixture in 4 parts and alternate layers of the mixture with layers of salt pork. Finish with a layer of salt pork. Place a bay leaf on this and seal the cover of the terrine with a flour-and-water paste. Place the terrine in a pan of hot water and cook 3½ hours in a 300°F. oven. Do not remove the cover until the terrine is very cold. It may be served in the terrine or unmolded.

369. Pig's Liver Pâté   *Pâté-terrine de foie de cochon*

Follow the preceding recipe using pig's liver instead of calf's. Do not be afraid to use pig's liver; the prolonged cooking mellows the sharp taste.

370. Fish Pâté   *Pâté-terrine de poisson*

1 pound fillets of whiting or flounder	salt and pepper
½ pound butter	1 tablespoon chopped parsley
1 cup fine bread crumbs, moistened with	1 pound salmon, sword, or cod steak
¼ cup milk	mace
1 egg yolk	cayenne
	2 tablespoons butter

Chop the fillets very fine and combine with softened butter, bread crumbs, egg yolk, parsley, and chopped truffles. Mix well and season highly with salt and pepper. Free the fish steaks of skin and bones and cut in narrow strips. Put a ½-inch layer of the fish mixture on the bottom of a small round terrine. Place a layer of fish strips over this. Sprinkle with salt, pepper, a dash of mace, and cayenne. Continue this process until the terrine is tightly packed. Dot the top layer with butter and seal the cover on the terrine with a flour-and-water paste. Cook 2½ hours in a 300°F. oven. Do not take the cover off until the terrine is chilled. Unmold and garnish with parsley.

371. Pâtés in Pastry Shells   *Pâtés en croûtes*

These pâtés are prepared in the same way as those described in the preceding recipes. They are, however, served in a pastry shell, which makes them more decorative and delicious. Special oval or round metal molds are used for this. The molds may be plain or elaborate.

To line molds: Prepare Pie Pastry (553). Butter the mold carefully, making sure that all the indentations have been covered. Roll the pastry to ½-inch thickness. Cut out a round or oval large enough to form the bottom and sides, with ¾ inch to spare to take care of the shrinkage. Line a cookie sheet with a buttered piece of wax paper. Place the mold on the cookie sheet and line the mold with the pastry. Press the pastry in all the indentations. Trim the edge so that there will be an even ¼- to ½-inch border. Moisten the edge with water. Fill the mold with the desired filling. Follow recipes 363-70, but do not add the liquid. This would soften the pastry. Roll out the remaining pastry and cut a cover, allowing for shrinkage. Make a few decorative incisions and a small hole for the steam to escape. It is easy to keep this hole open by inserting the end of a pastry tube. Brush the cover with an egg yolk beaten with 1 tablespoon water. Cook 3 hours in 375°F. oven. Just before the end of the cooking pour ½ cup consommé and 2 tablespoons brandy through the hole, using the pastry tube as a funnel. The pâtés may be eaten hot or cold.

372. Vol-au-vent   *Vol-au-vent*

This large patty shell, filled with Sweetbread Financière (280), Lamb Ragout (253), Veal Ragout (265), Shrimp Béchamel (212) or Brains (239), makes a delicious entrée.

Make a double recipe of Puff Paste (555). After the last folding, roll the pastry to a thickness of ½ inch. Place the cover to a 2-quart saucepan on the pastry and cut out around it. For a large patty shell make 2. Brush the lower thickness with water and lay one on top of the other. Roll out the remaining dough ¼ inch thick and cut out 2 more circles of the same size. With a cookie cutter cut out the center of these circles so that a circular band 1½ inches wide remains. Save one of the centers for a cover. Brush the outer edge of the top whole layer with water and lay one of the bands on this, taking care that the edges are even. Moisten this band and put the remaining band on this. Prick the bottom with a fork. Let it stand 10 minutes. Scallop the edges by using a finger and a dull edge of a knife. Place top in the center. Mix 2 yolks of egg with 2 tablespoons water and brush the whole shell with this mixture. Moisten a thick cookie sheet with water and place the shell on it. Place in a 500°F. oven. At the end of 5 minutes reduce the heat to 350° F. and cook 30 minutes. Remove the center cover, scoop out the interior, garnish with the desired filling, and replace the cover.

373. Individual Patty Shells   *Petits vol-au-vent*

Follow the preceding recipe but use a large scalloped cookie cutter for the base and sides. There should be only a single layer for the base. Cut out the centers of the remaining 2 or 3 layers with a small smooth cookie cutter. Follow the same directions for baking and cooking.

374. Puff Paste Tartlets   *Petits pâtés*

Cut out rounds of Puff Paste (555) with a small cookie cutter. Moisten the edges of half of them. Fill the center with a small dab of sausage meat, a shrimp dipped in butter, or smoked oysters. Cover with the other half of rounds. Press the edges together. Paint with an egg yolk beaten with 1 tablespoon water and bake 10 minutes in 500°F. oven. These are delicious with a salad or as an hors-d'œuvre.

Pie Pastry (553).

1 cup cooked meat, poultry or fish, finely chopped	salt and pepper
1 teaspoon onion, finely chopped	¼ cup fine bread crumbs moistened with a little water

Roll out the pastry as thin as possible. Divide in 2 long strips. Brush one half with water. Combine the rest of the ingredients to form a stuffing. Season highly. Place little dabs of this mixture 2 inches apart on the moistened strip of pastry. Lift the other strip and place it carefully over the first strip. Press the pastry together around each dab. Cut out in squares with a pastry wheel. Fry in deep fat (370°F.) 3 to 5 minutes or until the *rissoles* are light brown. Sprinkle with salt and serve very hot. For the unpracticed it is easier to handle the pastry in smaller amounts. Make several small strips instead of 2 large ones.

A moitié fait qui commence bien.

376. Cabbage Pie (Russian)

Coulibac (koulibiac) aux choux

1 cup milk	6 eggs
1 yeast cake	2 tablespoons butter
2 cups flour	1 large onion, chopped fine
½ pound butter	2 white cabbages
2 cups flour	4 hard-boiled eggs
1 teaspoon salt	salt and pepper

Scald the milk and set aside to cool. When it is lukewarm dissolve the yeast cake. Stir in 2 cups of flour and when it is well blended, cover and set in a warm place until the dough is doubled in size. Wash the butter by placing it in a large bowl of cool water and squeezing it with your hands for 3 minutes to remove most of the salt. (It is not necessary with sweet butter.) Add butter, 2 cups of flour, eggs, and salt to the dough and beat with your hands until the dough is very smooth. Place on a floured board and knead until the dough no longer sticks to the fingers. Place in a covered bowl and let it stand in a warm place for 45 minutes. It is then ready to be rolled out.

Roll out the dough ¼ inch thick to form a large square. Place in the center the following filling: Shred 2 white cabbages coarsely and combine with chopped onion. Fry gently in melted butter until the cabbage is tender. Combine with the hard-boiled eggs, chopped coarsely. Season well with salt and pepper. Moisten the edges of the pastry square. Turn the edges toward the center and lap them over the filling. Turn the pie upside down on a well-floured cooking sheet so that the smooth side is visible. Let it stand 30 minutes and then cook 60 minutes in 350°F. oven. When it is cooked, brush generously with melted butter, cut into 12 squares, and serve.

377. Salmon Pie (Russian)   *Coulibac de saumon*

Coulibac pastry (376)
3 thin salmon steaks
2 cups semolina flour, cooked
   in
2 cups water
1 teaspoon salt

½ pound mushrooms
melted butter
egg yolk beaten with
   1 tablespoon water
salt and pepper

Prepare the pastry as in the preceding recipe. While the dough is rising prepare the following filling: Fry the salmon steaks in butter, allowing 5 minutes to each side. They should not be entirely cooked. Make a mush of the semolina, salt, and water, and when it is cooked, set aside to cool. Wash and stem the mushrooms. Fry 5 minutes in butter. Cool.

Roll out a large square of pastry ¼ inch thick. Put a rectangular layer of semolina in the center of the pastry. Cover with a salmon steak and over this put a layer of mushrooms. Sprinkle with salt and pepper and continue alternations until all the filling is used. Moisten the edges and lap them over the filling. Brush the pie with melted butter and egg yolk. Make a hole for the steam to escape. Cook 3 hours in 375°F. oven. Let the pie stand one or two days before using. It is eaten cold.

IT SHOULD be remembered that Tante Marie is French and not Italian. The recipes that follow may not be truly Italian but are, none the less, delicious. [C. T.]

378. Italian Macaroni   *Macaroni à l'italienne*

1 pound macaroni
6 tablespoons butter
salt and pepper

½ cup grated Parmesan cheese
Italian Tomato Sauce (22)

The macaroni may be served without the sauce, but if the sauce is to be served, it should be started well in advance of the macaroni. Boil a large quantity of water in a big kettle. Add 1 tablespoon salt. Cook the macaroni in the uncovered kettle 15 to 17 minutes or until the macaroni is tender but not pasty. Drain well and reheat with butter. Add cheese, salt, and pepper. Serve with a bowl of Parmesan cheese and a bowl of sauce, or pour the sauce over the macaroni before serving.

379. Baked Macaroni   *Macaroni au gratin*

Follow the directions in the preceding recipe for cooking macaroni. When the macaroni is well drained and seasoned, place in oven-proof dish, cover with the grated cheese, and dot with butter. Cover and place in hot oven 15 minutes.

380. Macaroni and Sweetbreads   *Macaroni à la financière*

1 pound macaroni   Sweetbreads Financière (280)

Study recipe 280 in order to judge the time for cooking the macaroni (379). Arrange the well-drained and seasoned macaroni in a ring on a heated platter. Fill the center with the sweetbread sauce.

381. Homemade Noodles   *Pâte à nouilles*

2 cups flour   1 teaspoon salt
6 egg yolks   ¼ cup water
2 egg whites

Mix the ingredients together, working them with your hand until a thick dough is formed. Let the dough rest 15 minutes and then roll out on a floured board until paper thin. Let the sheet of paste dry for 2 hours. Cut in narrow strips and store in warm place. These noodles are richer than the commercial noodles.

To cook noodles: Boil 12 minutes in a large amount of boiling salted water. Drain well and season with butter, salt, and freshly ground black pepper.

382. Milanaise Timbale   *Timbale milanaise*

Pie Pastry (553)
½ pound spaghettini
2 tablespoons butter
salt and black pepper
⅔ cup grated Parmesan cheese

½ cooked sweetbread (optional)
½ cup Italian Tomato Sauce (22)
½ pound mushrooms

Choose a smooth round mold and follow recipe 371 for lining it with pastry. Prick the bottom of the mold with a fork and line the pastry with brown paper. Fill the mold with dried peas or beans, or with flour. This will keep the crust in shape. Cut out a round of pastry for the top and place over the mold. Paint the top with egg yolk mixed with a little water. Bake 15 to 20 minutes in 450°F. oven or until the crust is light brown.

Meanwhile plunge spaghettini in briskly boiling salted water and cook 12 minutes. Drain well. Add the remaining ingredients and season with salt and pepper. Reheat. Remove the paper and dried peas from the mold and slip the shell onto a heated platter. Fill with the spaghetti mixture and replace the cover. This is a good way to serve left-over spaghetti and tomato sauce.

383. Russian Macaroni Pie
Timbale de macaroni à la Bekendorf

1 pound macaroni
¼ pound butter
salt and pepper
bread crumbs

½ pound smoked salmon
Italian Tomato Sauce (22)
grated Parmesan cheese

Cook the macaroni (378). Drain and season with butter, salt, pepper, and grated cheese. Butter a deep, smooth mold. Sprinkle with fine bread crumbs so that both the bottom and sides are covered. Put in half the macaroni. Dip slices of salmon in tomato sauce and place on the macaroni. Cover with the rest of the macaroni. Cover and bake 20 minutes in 400°F. oven. Serve in the mold, or unmold and serve with tomato sauce and grated cheese.

384. Caneloni

3 cups flour	2 egg yolks
5 eggs	salt and pepper
1 teaspoon salt	dash of nutmeg
3 or 4 tablespoons warm water	2 tablespoons grated Parmesan
1 cup left-over poultry or meat, chopped fine	cheese
	2 egg whites, beaten stiff
1 clove garlic, chopped fine	Italian Tomato Sauce (22)

If you prepare the following paste a day ahead, it will roll out much more easily. Place the flour on a pastry board or in a deep bowl. Make a depression in the center and put in the salt and unbeaten eggs. With the tips of the fingers work the flour into the eggs, adding a little water from time to time as the paste becomes too dry. Work as quickly as possible and as soon as the paste is a smooth mass, place it in the refrigerator. This can be used after 2 hours, but the longer it stands the better it is.

Make the stuffing by combining the meat, garlic, egg yolks, salt, pepper, nutmeg, and grated cheese. Any meat or combination of meats will do. When the mixture has been combined into a smooth paste, fold in the egg whites. If the mixture is too stiff add a little milk.

Roll the paste out very thin and cut in 3-inch squares. Poach the squares in salted boiling water for 8 minutes. Remove from the water with a skimmer and drain on a towel. Spread a thin layer of the stuffing on each square. Roll them up and place in a buttered oven-proof dish. Sprinkle with Parmesan cheese, cover with tomato sauce, and heat 15 minutes in a moderate oven.

385. Ravioli

2 small eggs	1 raw egg yolk
1½ to 2 cups flour	1 hard-boiled egg
1 teaspoon salt	salt and pepper
½ cup lean ground beef	⅛ teaspoon nutmeg
½ cup chopped cooked spinach	¼ cup grated Parmesan cheese
2 tablespoons butter	Italian Tomato Sauce (22)

Beat the eggs until the whites and yolks are blended. Add salt and gradually work in the flour, using the finger tips. The amount of flour used depends on the size of the eggs. As soon as the mixture no longer sticks to the fingers, it is ready. Set in the refrigerator for at least 15 minutes. Longer resting makes the paste easier to handle.

Fry the beef lightly in butter. Add the spinach, egg yolk, chopped boiled egg, salt, pepper, nutmeg, and cheese. Combine to make a smooth mixture.

Place the ravioli paste on a floured board and roll out as thin as possible. Cut into as many 3 x 1½-inch strips as possible. Moisten half of the strips with water. On the moistened strips, place two dabs of the beef and spinach mixture. This may be done with a pastry tube or from the end of a teaspoon. Place the dry strips over these and press along the edges so that the top and bottom stick together. The squares may be outlined with the pastry wheel. Let these rest 15 minutes. Boil salted water in a large shallow pan. Poach the strips 10 minutes, drain on a dish towel, and place in an oven-proof dish. Cover with tomato sauce and Parmesan cheese and reheat in the oven.

⚜

Mauvais ouvrier n'a jamais bons outils.

⚜

386. Milanaise Rice *Risotto à la milanaise*

1 onion, chopped fine
3 tablespoons butter
6 cups stock, preferably chicken
1½ cups rice

large pinch of saffron
salt and pepper
¼ cup grated Parmesan cheese

Fry the onion in butter until it is yellow. Add the rice and stir gently until the rice is transparent. Gradually add the liquid, about 1 cup at a time, and as the rice absorbs the stock, add more. Add the saffron along with the first cup of liquid. The rice should be cooked in 30 to 35 minutes. It should not be pasty but it should not be completely dry. Add more liquid if necessary. Sprinkle with cheese, season with salt and pepper, and serve very hot.

387. Boiled Rice *Riz à la créole*

Wash 2 cups of rice thoroughly. Drain and place in 6 cups boiling salted water. Boil 17 minutes, drain, and pour over it 4 cups of warm water. This will wash away the excess starch. Place in a moderate oven for 20 to 30 minutes. Each grain of rice will be separate and of just the right consistency.

VEGETABLES are often served in France as a separate course, and, if they are properly prepared, they should frequently receive such attention. Particular care should be given to the washing of the vegetables. If the vegetables are thoroughly clean it is often unnecessary to peel them; flavor as well as nutritive value is increased when they are cooked 'in their jackets.'

388. Artichokes, Hollandaise Sauce

Artichauts à la hollandaise

Select medium-sized, firm artichokes. If they are too large or the outer leaves are spiny, they will be tough. Cut off the stem and the top. Remove the very hard outer leaves. Plunge them, stem-end down, into rapidly boiling salted water and boil uncovered 25 to 30 minutes or until the outer leaves can be easily detached. Drain well. Turn upside down and press out the water. Serve hot with Hollandaise Sauce (10).

389. Artichoke Bottoms   *Fonds d'artichauts*

Canned artichokes are very satisfactory and often more economical unless one is fortunate enough to live in the artichoke country. With fresh artichokes, the leaves and choke are removed from the boiled and drained artichoke, leaving just the bottoms. These are dipped in cold water to which a little vinegar has been added. The bottoms are then dried and fried in butter or olive oil. They are usually used as a garnish for a roast.

390. Braised Artichokes   *Artichauts au jus*

4 to 6 artichokes	1 cup stock
2 tablespoons butter	salt and pepper
3 strips lean bacon, diced	*bouquet garni* (42)
2 tablespoons flour	

Remove the stems and cut off the tops of the artichokes. Spread open the center leaves and cut out the chokes. Divide the artichokes in quarters and boil in salted water 15 minutes. Drain. Melt the butter in a large saucepan. Fry the bacon in the butter and remove when it is brown. Add flour and brown. Stir in stock and when the sauce is smooth, add salt, pepper, and *bouquet garni*. Put the artichokes and bacon in the sauce. Cover and simmer 45 minutes. Place the artichoke quarters in a crown around the platter and fill the center with the sauce which has been strained.

⚜

Il n'y a pas de petites économies.

⚜

391. Stuffed Artichokes   *Artichauts à la barigoule*

4 medium-sized artichokes
¼ pound sausage meat
1 cup fine bread crumbs
½ cup stock
2 tablespoons chopped parsley
1 small onion, finely chopped

¼ pound mushrooms
2 tablespoons butter
1 tablespoon flour
1 tablespoon oil
salt and pepper
lemon slices

Boil the artichokes (388). Drain well and cut out the choke.
Moisten the bread crumbs with stock or water. Combine with
sausage meat, parsley, onion, and mushrooms which have
been washed and finely chopped. Fry the mixture in butter
until it is light brown. Sprinkle with flour and blend. This
will thicken the stuffing. Fill the centers with the stuffing and
replace top on artichoke. Brush the inside of a heated casserole with oil. Put in the artichokes and bake 30 minutes in
a 350°F. oven. Serve each artichoke with a slice of lemon.

392. Fried Artichokes   *Artichauts frits*

Remove the stems and all the very hard leaves from 2 small
artichokes. Cut each one lengthwise in 8 or 10 pieces. Remove
the pieces of choke. Boil in salted water 15 minutes. Drain
dry, dip in frying batter (40), and fry in deep fat (370°F.).
Sprinkle with salt and serve immediately.

393. Artichokes with French Dressing
                              Artichauts à la vinaigrette

Boil artichokes (388). Serve hot or cold with French Dressing
(31).

394. Asparagus in White Sauce

Asperges à la sauce blanche

Wash 2 pounds of asparagus. Cut off the hard ends and make 6 to 8 small bunches. Tie with kitchen string. Boil gently in salted water. Drain and arrange the bunches on a heated platter. Serve with a bowl of White Sauce (3).

395. Asparagus in French Dressing   *Asperges à l'huile*

Prepare asparagus as in the preceding recipe. Cool but do not chill. Serve with French Dressing (31).

396. Chopped Asparagus   *Asperges en petits pois*

1-pound bunch of asparagus	1 teaspoon cornstarch
2 tablespoons butter	1 egg yolk, beaten with 1
1 tablespoon sugar	tablespoon water
¼ cup water	

Wash the asparagus and cut off the hard ends. Cut the green part into tiny pieces, the size of a pea. Cook 5 minutes in boiling, salted water. Drain. Melt butter and add sugar and water. Add the asparagus. Cover and simmer 20 minutes. Stir in the cornstarch. Remove from the flame and add the egg yolk. Do not let the sauce boil again. Serve hot.

La vérité comme l'huile vient au dessus.

397. Asparagus with Parmesan Cheese

Asperges à la parmesane

Wash 2 bunches of asparagus and cut off the hard ends. Boil 15 minutes in salted water. Drain and cut in 1-inch pieces. Place a layer of the pieces in a well-buttered casserole. Sprinkle with salt, pepper, and Parmesan cheese and dot with butter. Repeat the process until all the asparagus has been used. Brown in a moderate oven.

398. Green Beans, Maître d'hôtel

Haricots verts à la maître d'hôtel

1½ to 2 pounds green string beans	1 tablespoon chopped parsley
	salt and pepper
3 tablespoons butter	

Try to obtain dark green beans that are quite small. These will have the highest flavor. If they are large, slice them lengthwise. Do not cut them in small pieces. Remove the ends and wash them. Boil in salted water 15 to 20 minutes. Do not cover them. This preserves the color. When they are tender, drain. Melt butter and reheat the beans in the butter. Add parsley, salt, and pepper.

399. Green Beans à la Poulette   *Haricots verts à la poulette*

Follow the preceding recipe for preparing and boiling the beans. Serve in a Poulette Sauce (8).

400. Green Beans in French Dressing

Haricots verts en salade

Follow recipe 398 for preparing and boiling the beans. Cool and cover with French Dressing (31). Hot green beans as well as cold may be served in this way.

401. Pea Beans à la Bretonne

Haricots blancs à la bretonne

2 cups dried pea beans	1 tablespoon flour
2 tablespoons butter	salt and pepper
1 large onion, sliced thin	

Soak the beans in cool water overnight. Start cooking the beans in cold water and simmer 2 hours. When they are tender, drain. Fry slices of onion in butter until they are yellow. Add flour and let it brown. Put in the beans and ½ cup of the water in which the beans have been cooked. Season with salt and pepper, cover and simmer 15 minutes.

402. Pea Beans, Maître d'hôtel

Haricots blancs à la maître d'hôtel

2 cups dried pea beans	2 tablespoons chopped parsley
3 tablespoons butter	salt and pepper

Soak the beans overnight and cook as in the preceding recipe. Drain, reheat in melted butter. Add parsley, salt and pepper.

403. Pea Beans in French Dressing

Haricots blancs à l'huile

Soak and cook 2 cups of pea beans as in recipe 401. Drain well and serve either hot or cold in French Dressing (310).

404. Purée of Pea Beans   *Haricots blancs en purée*

1 pound pea beans
3 tablespoons butter

salt and freshly ground black
pepper

Soak and cook the beans as in recipe 401. When they are
soft, force them through a food mill. Moisten with the water
in which they have been cooked. The purée should be thicker
than soup but not as thick as mashed potatoes. Reheat with
butter, salt, and pepper. Serve very hot.

405. Kidney Beans   *Haricots rouges*

Any of the recipes for Pea Beans may be applied to Kidney
Beans.

406. Beets   *Betteraves*

French beets are much larger than the American variety.
They are usually baked for hours in sweet butter. They are
also boiled and eaten cold in French Dressing (31) or combined with other vegetables or salad greens to make a salad.
Beets should be washed and boiled in salted water 35 to
60 minutes, depending on the size and age. They may be
peeled after they are cooked.

407. Broccoli   *Brocolis*

Wash the broccoli and examine for tiny green worms. Remove
the large leaves and the thickest part of the stems. The smaller

leaves and stems are edible and delicious. Many of the recipes for cauliflower may be applied to broccoli. Boil 15 to 20 minutes in salted water. It may either be served hot Creamed (417), Buttered (418), in Tomato Sauce (419), Au Gratin (420), Fried (421), or be served cold with French Dressing (422).

408. Buttered Brussels Sprouts

Choux de Bruxelles au beurre

1 quart Brussels sprouts	1 tablespoon chopped parsley
3 tablespoons butter	salt and pepper

Wash the sprouts. Remove the stems and outer leaves if they are not perfect. Cook in briskly boiling, salted water for 10 to 15 minutes. Do not cover the pan. Drain and reheat in butter. Add parsley, salt, and pepper.

409. Braised Brussels Sprouts   *Choux de Bruxelles au jus*

Follow the preceding recipe for preparing the sprouts. While they are being reheated, add 4 tablespoons of juice from a roast or 1 tablespoon of beef extract mixed with 3 tablespoons water.

410. Creamed Cabbage   *Choux à la crème*

Remove the outer leaves of the cabbage. Cut in quarters and remove the hard core. Boil 20 minutes in salted water. Do not cover the pan. Place in a warm vegetable dish and pour over it a well-seasoned Béchamel Sauce (1).

411. Stuffed Cabbage   *Chou farci*

1 large, firm cabbage	2 cups stock or water
½ pound chopped beef or veal	1 onion, sliced thin
½ pound sausage meat	1 carrot, cut in rounds
salt and pepper	soup bone or veal knuckle,
2 tablespoons butter	sawed in 2 or 3 pieces
2 tablespoons flour	

Remove the outer leaves and cut out the center core without breaking the cabbage. Pour boiling water over the cabbage. Drain well and put between each leaf a little of the stuffing made by combining the chopped meat, sausage, salt, and pepper. Tie the cabbage with string. In a pan large enough to hold the cabbage, melt butter and stir in flour. Let it brown and then add liquid. Stir until the sauce is smooth. Place cabbage in kettle and add onion, carrot, and soup bone or knuckle. Cover tightly and simmer 3 hours. Add more liquid if necessary. Place the cabbage on a deep platter. Remove the string and pour the strained sauce over it.

412. Red Cabbage with Apples   *Chou rouge aux pommes*

1 medium-sized red cabbage	3 cloves
5 large crabapples	2 tablespoons currant jelly
2 tablespoons butter	1 teaspoon cornstarch
salt and pepper	1 tablespoon cider vinegar

After removing the outer leaves, wash the cabbage and cover with water. Peel and core the apples. Add the apples, butter, salt, pepper, and cloves to the cabbage. Cover and simmer 2½ hours. Bind the sauce with the currant jelly, mixed with cornstarch and vinegar. Serve very hot. This is a Flemish dish.

413. Carrots, Burgundian Style *

Carottes à la bourguignonne

12 large carrots
2 tablespoons butter
2 onions, sliced thin

2 tablespoons flour
1 cup stock or water
salt and pepper

Scrub the carrots and, if necessary, scrape them. Boil in salted water until tender. Fry the onions in butter until they are yellow. Sprinkle with flour and stir in stock. When the sauce is smooth, season with salt and pepper and put in the carrots, cut in small pieces. Cover and simmer 15 minutes.

414. Buttered Carrots *   *Carottes au beurre*

10 carrots
1 teaspoon butter
salted water
2 tablespoons butter

2 tablespoons chopped parsley
2 tablespoons chopped chives
salt and pepper

Scrub and, if necessary, scrape 10 carrots. Cut in 1-inch pieces. Cook in rapidly boiling salted water to which 1 teaspoon butter has been added. Cook until tender—approximately 20 minutes. Drain. Melt the butter in a sauce pan. Add parsley, chives, salt and pepper, and carrots. Cover and simmer 5 minutes. Small new carrots may be left whole and prepared in the same manner.

* Recipes 413-15 may be prepared more quickly by using a pressure cooker for the first part of the process.

415. Carrots à la Poulette   *Carottes à la poulette*

Wash and scrape 10 to 12 carrots or 2 bunches of small carrots. If small carrots are used, leave them whole. Otherwise, cut in 1-inch pieces. Boil in salted water until they are tender. Drain, place in a heated vegetable dish, and cover with a Poulette Sauce (8).

416. Carrots Vichy   *Carottes Vichy*

8 to 10 carrots	1 teaspoon sugar
¼ pound butter	½ teaspoon salt
1 tablespoon water	

Scrub and, if necessary, scrape the carrots. Cut in long, very thin strips. Melt butter in heavy saucepan. Put in the carrots with water and butter. Cover tightly and cook over slow flame 1 hour. Stir occasionally and very gently. The carrots must not fry, but they must not be mashed by too vigorous stirring. Just before serving, sprinkle with sugar and salt. Carrots are at their very best served this way.

417. Creamed Cauliflower   *Choux-fleurs à la sauce blanche*

Remove the green leaves from a good, white cauliflower. Wash and carefully inspect for little green worms. Leave whole or divide into flowerets. Boil in salted water. If left whole, cook 25 to 30 minutes; if divided, 10 to 15 minutes. Drain well. Place in warm vegetable dish and cover with Cream Sauce (2).

418. Buttered Cauliflower   *Choux-fleurs au beurre*

1 cauliflower	1 tablespoon chopped parsley
2 tablespoons butter	salt and pepper

Prepare and cook the cauliflower as in the preceding recipe. Melt butter. Add parsley, salt, and pepper. Heat until the butter bubbles. Place well-drained cauliflower in heated vegetable dish and pour the butter sauce over it.

419. Cauliflower in Tomato Sauce
Choux-fleurs à la sauce tomate

Prepare and cook cauliflower as in recipe 417. Drain and place in warm vegetable dish. Cover with Tomato Sauce (21).

420. Cauliflower au Gratin *Choux-fleurs au gratin*

1 cauliflower
Cream Sauce (2)
½ cup grated Swiss cheese

¼ cup grated Parmesan cheese
fine bread crumbs

Prepare and cook the cauliflower as in recipe 417. Divide the cauliflower into flowerets. Add the cheese to the cream sauce and combine the cauliflower with the sauce. Place in a well-buttered casserole. Cover with bread crumbs. Dot with butter and brown in 375°F. oven.

421. Fried Cauliflower *Choux-fleurs frits*

Prepare the cauliflower as in recipe 417. Divide into bouquets of 2 or 3 flowerets. Boil in salted water 8 minutes. Drain thoroughly. Soak in ¼ cup white wine vinegar, seasoned with salt and pepper. Prepare a thick frying batter (40). Dip the flowerets in the batter and fry in deep fat (375°F.) 3 minutes. See recipe 41.

422. Cauliflower in French Dressing　　*Choux-fleurs à l'huile*

Follow recipe 417 for preparing and cooking cauliflower. Drain and cool. Cover with French Dressing (31). This makes a delicious hors-d'œuvre or salad.

423. Celery Rémoulade　　*Céleri en salade*

Wash a large bunch of celery. Remove the leaves and cut into thin strips, 2 inches long. Mix with a Rémoulade Sauce (23). This makes a good hors-d'œuvre.

424. Braised Celery　　*Céleri au jus*

2 bunches of celery	½ teaspoon beef extract
2 tablespoons butter	1 teaspoon brandy
1 tablespoon flour	salt and pepper
1 cup consommé	

Wash the celery and remove the leaves. Cut off the tops, leaving the bunch 7 inches long. Cut each bunch lengthwise into 4 pieces. Boil in salted water 20 minutes. Drain. Melt butter and brown the flour in it. Stir in consommé and, when the sauce is smooth, add extract, brandy, salt, and pepper. Simmer the celery in the sauce 15 minutes. The sauce should be quite thick.

425. Celery au Gratin　　*Céleri au gratin*

Follow directions in the preceding recipe, but place the boiled celery in a flat, oven-proof dish. Pour the sauce over the celery. Chopped mushrooms or thinly sliced truffles make a good addition to the sauce. Cover with bread crumbs and a layer of grated Swiss cheese. Dot with butter and brown in 375°F. oven.

426. Celeriac Salad   *Céleri-rave rémoulade*

See recipe 55.

427. Celeriac au Gratin   *Céleri-rave au gratin*

Peel the celeriac roots. Slice in ⅛-inch thick pieces. Boil 40 to 60 minutes in salted water. It is then prepared like Celery au Gratin (425).

428. Chestnut Purée   *Marrons en purée*

1 pound chestnuts	1 tablespoon butter
½ cup hot milk	salt and pepper

Cut an X on the flat side of each chestnut. Place the nuts in a pan of cold water and bring to a boil. Boil 30 minutes. Remove the outer and inner skins. This is easier to do while the chestnuts are hot. Force the chestnuts through a food mill. Season with milk, butter, salt, and pepper. Reheat, taking care that the chestnuts do not burn. Serve in place of potato with pork or turkey.

429. Braised Chicory   *Chicorée au jus*

2 large heads of chicory	½ cup stock or consommé
2 tablespoons butter	salt and pepper
1 tablespoon flour	croutons

After removing the tough outer leaves, wash the chicory well and boil in salted water for 30 minutes. Drain thoroughly and chop rather coarsely. Melt butter and stir in flour. Add liquid, salt, and pepper. When the sauce is smooth, add chicory and reheat. Serve very hot with croutons.

430. Cucumber Salad   *Concombres en salade*

See recipe 54.

431. Cooked Cucumbers   *Concombres à diverses sauces*

Select large green cucumbers. Peel and quarter them. Remove the seeds. Boil 10 minutes in salted water to which ¼ cup vinegar has been added. Drain and serve with Béchamel Sauce (1), Poulette Sauce (8), or Maître d'hôtel Sauce (9).

432. Dandelion Greens   *Pissenlit*

Use fresh small dandelion greens and cook like Braised Chicory (429).

433. Stuffed Eggplant   *Aubergines farcies*

2 small eggplants	1 clove garlic, chopped
2 tablespoons oil	¼ pound mushrooms, chopped
1 tablespoon chopped parsley	salt and pepper
2 scallions, chopped fine	fine bread crumbs

Wash the eggplants and split. Remove the centers and chop rather coarsely. Heat 1 tablespoon of oil in a small pan. Add parsley, scallion, garlic, mushrooms, and chopped center, and heat thoroughly. Fill the eggplants with this mixture and place in a flat oven-proof dish. Sprinkle with bread crumbs and moisten with the rest of the oil. Bake 30 minutes in a 375°F. oven.

434. Fried Eggplant   *Aubergines frites*

2 small eggplants   Frying Batter (40)

Wash and peel the eggplants. Slice ½ inch thick. Dip the
slices in the frying batter and fry in deep fat (370°F.) 3 to 5
minutes or until golden brown. Sprinkle with salt and serve
immediately.

435. Braised Endive   *Endives glacées au jus*

12 small, white French endive	½ cup stock or consommé
salt and pepper	1 teaspoon cornstarch mixed
dash of nutmeg	with
1 teaspoon sugar	¼ cup consommé

Wash and trim the endive. If only very large ones are obtainable they should be blanched in boiling salted water 5 minutes. The small ones do not need this. Arrange the endive in a
heavy, well-buttered frying pan. Sprinkle with salt, pepper,
nutmeg, and sugar and moisten with liquid. Cut out a piece of
brown paper that will fit the frying pan, butter it, and place
on the endive. Cover with a tight cover and cook as slowly as
possible for 1 hour. Turn the endive once at the end of 30
minutes. Place the endive on a heated platter. Thicken the
sauce with the cornstarch and pour the sauce over the endive.

436. French Endive in Béchamel Sauce
                               Endives à la béchamel

Wash and trim 12 French endive. Cook in boiling salted water
15 minutes. Drain and place in a heated vegetable dish. Cover
with a well-seasoned Béchamel Sauce (1).

Jerusalem Artichokes   *Topinambours*

Jerusalem artichokes are becoming more common but are still foreign to most American tables. They taste somewhat like hearts of artichokes but are a little sweeter. They look like and are cooked like potatoes.

437. Jerusalem Artichokes, Maître d'hôtel
                    Topinambours à la maître d'hôtel

Follow recipe for Potatoes, Maître d'hôtel (464).

438. Creamed Jerusalem Artichokes   *Topinambours au lait*

Follow recipe for Creamed Potatoes (467).

439. Fried Jerusalem Artichokes   *Topinambours frits*

Wash and boil 1 pound of Jerusalem artichokes in salted water. Peel and slice ⅛ inch thick. Dip the slices in frying batter (40) and fry in deep fat (370°F.) 2 to 3 minutes or until golden brown.

440. Leeks au Gratin   *Poireaux au gratin*

Remove the green tops and roots of a large bunch of leeks. Cut each leek in quarters lengthwise. Boil in salted water for 20 to 25 minutes. Cover with Béchamel Sauce (1), sprinkle generously with grated Swiss cheese, and dot with butter. Brown in a 350°F. oven.

441. Lentils   *Lentilles*

Lentils are prepared like dried pea beans. See recipes 401-4. They are particularly delicious served cold with French Dressing (31).

442. Braised Lettuce   *Laitue au jus*

4 firm heads of green Boston or Romaine lettuce	½ cup stock
	½ teaspoon beef extract
2 tablespoons butter	salt and pepper
1½ tablespoons flour	*bouquet garni* (42)

Remove the outer imperfect leaves and wash the heads carefully. Do not use iceberg lettuce. Boil in salted water 10 minutes. Remove and plunge the heads into cold water. Drain and dry on a cloth. Melt butter in a heavy saucepan, stir in flour, and allow it to brown. Add stock, salt, pepper, beef extract, and *bouquet garni* and stir until the sauce is smooth. Add lettuce. Cover and simmer 45 minutes. Baste the lettuce often with the sauce. Place the lettuce in a deep serving platter, remove the *bouquet garni*, and pour the sauce over the lettuce.

Mushrooms   *Champignons*

Unless one is an expert, the only safe mushrooms to use are the cultivated ones available in the markets. There are, however, six common wild mushrooms with which it is worthwhile to become acquainted. These include the *meadow mushrooms*, the *chanterelles*, the *shaggy manes*, the *morels*, the *puff balls*, and the ink *caps*. Mushrooms should always be carefully washed. Unless they are very large and tough they do not need to be peeled. Any peelings and stems that are not used should be saved for flavoring sauces and soups.

443. Mushroom Canapé   *Croûte aux champignons*

1 pound mushrooms	1 teaspoon lemon juice
Béchamel Sauce (1)	4 large slices of bread, fried in
1 egg yolk	3 tablespoons butter

Stem and wash the mushrooms. Boil the mushrooms 5 minutes in just enough water to cover them. Drain and save the liquid to replace some of the milk in the sauce. Thicken the sauce with an egg yolk and add lemon juice just before pouring the mushrooms over the fried bread. Serve very hot.

444. Mushrooms with Herbs
Champignons sautés aux fines herbes

1 pound mushrooms	2 tablespoons chopped parsley
1 tablespoon vinegar	1 tablespoon chopped chives
2 tablespoons butter or olive oil	1 clove garlic, chopped fine
	1 teaspoon lemon juice
salt and black pepper	

Boil the mushrooms in just enough salted water to cover them. Drain and reheat with butter or oil, salt, pepper, and herbs. When thoroughly hot, add lemon juice and serve immediately.

445. Stuffed Mushrooms   *Champignons farcis*

12 extra-large mushrooms	½ clove garlic, chopped fine
4 tablespoons olive oil	salt and pepper
2 tablespoons chopped parsley	fine bread crumbs
2 tablespoons chopped onion	

Wash and peel the mushrooms. Remove the stems. Place the caps upside down in a pan greased with 2 tablespoons olive oil and fry gently until they are light brown. Meanwhile, put the rest of the oil in a saucepan with the herbs and the stems of the mushrooms, finely chopped. Cook 2 minutes. Season with salt and pepper and add enough bread crumbs to make a thick stuffing. Fill each cap with the stuffing, sprinkle with bread crumbs, and bake in 375°F. oven for 20 minutes.

446. Mushrooms à la Provençale

Champignons à la provençale

1 pound mushrooms	1 large clove garlic
2 tablespoons olive oil	1½ tablespoons flour
salt and pepper	¼ cup dry white wine
2 tablespoons chopped parsley	2 tablespoons water

Wash the mushrooms. If they are large, cut in pieces. If small, leave whole. Heat the oil in a frying pan. Add mushrooms, salt, pepper, parsley, and garlic and fry gently for 10 minutes, stirring occasionally. Sprinkle with flour and stir in gently. Add water and wine and stir until well blended. Simmer 10 minutes and serve very hot.

447. Mushrooms in Scallop Shells

Champignons en coquilles

Follow the recipe for Mushroom Canapé (443). Place in large scallop shells or ramekins. Sprinkle with fine bread crumbs, dot with butter, and brown in hot oven (375°F.).

448. Morels   *Morilles*

Dried morels can often be purchased in Italian markets. Soak them several hours before using. They can then be prepared like ordinary mushrooms except that they cannot be stuffed. They are delicious fried in butter, chopped, and added to an omelet.

449. Mushrooms in Sour Cream   *Champignons à la russe*

1 pound mushrooms
2 tablespoons butter
a bouquet of parsley, green on-
    ion tops, and fennel leaves
salt and pepper

dash of nutmeg
4 tablespoons thick Béchamel
    Sauce (1)
2 tablespoons sour cream
1 teaspoon chopped fennel

Wash the mushrooms. Cut in 2 or 4 pieces, depending on the size. Place in a heavy saucepan with butter, bouquet, salt, pepper, and nutmeg. Cook gently 15 minutes. Remove the bouquet, add the sauce and sour cream. Bring to a boil, add chopped fennel, and serve very hot.

450. Mushroom and Rice Croquettes
                           Croquettes de riz aux champignons

2 cups rice
½ pound mushrooms
salt and pepper
fine bread crumbs

1 egg, beaten slightly
oil
sprigs of parsley

Wash and boil the rice in salted water 20 minutes. At the same time, wash the mushrooms and cook in just enough salted water to cover them for 15 minutes. Drain and slice them. Add to the rice. Cook 5 minutes more or until the rice is tender. The water should be completely absorbed. Season with salt and pepper and chill. Form little balls of the mixture, roll in bread crumbs, dip in beaten egg, roll again in bread crumbs, and fry in deep fat (370°F.) for 2 to 3 minutes. Arrange the balls in a pyramid on a heated platter and garnish with sprigs of parsley.

451. Glazed Onions *Oignons glacés*

12 very small onions	2 tablespoons sugar
3 tablespoons butter	½ cup consommé

Select small onions of uniform size and peel them. Melt butter and add sugar. Brown the onions in the butter, stirring gently from time to time. Add the consommé and boil over a high flame so that the liquid will quickly be reduced. Keep spooning the liquid over the onions until a thick syrup is formed. The onions must not be overcooked. These are usually used as a garnish.

452. Stuffed Onions *Oignons farcis*

4 to 6 large Bermuda onions	2 tablespoons flour
¼ pound sausage meat	1 cup consommé
¼ pound chopped beef	1 teaspoon brandy
2 tablespoons butter	salt and pepper

Peel the onions and scoop out the centers. Mix the sausage and beef and fill the centers with the mixture. Slice the centers of the onion very thin and brown in butter. Sprinkle with flour, add consommé, brandy, salt, and pepper. When the sauce is smooth, pour into a casserole. Place the onions in the casserole and bake 1½ hours in a moderate oven. Spoon the sauce over the onions several times during the cooking.

Marchand d'oignons se connaît en ciboules.

453. French Peas   *Petits pois au sucre*

4 pounds fresh peas
2 tablespoons butter
6 small white onions
bouquet garni (42)

1 head green Boston or Romaine lettuce
2 teaspoons sugar
salt
2 tablespoons water

Shell the peas, peel the onions, and wash the lettuce carefully, keeping the head whole. Do not substitute iceberg or bitter lettuce for this. Put all the ingredients in a heavy kettle with a tight-fitting cover. Bury the lettuce and onions in the peas. Cover and cook over a very slow flame for 1 hour. Remove the *bouquet garni* and serve. The sauce may be thickened with the yolk of an egg (page 3).

454. Peas with Salt Pork   *Petits pois au lard*

4 pounds peas
¼ pound lean salt pork, diced
2 tablespoons butter
2 tablespoons flour

2 cups water
salt and pepper
bouquet garni (42)
3 small onions

Fry the salt pork in butter and when it is browned remove it. Stir in flour and water. When the sauce is smooth add salt, pepper, *bouquet garni,* onions, and peas. Cover tightly and cook 1½ hours over a very slow flame. Remove *bouquet garni* and serve very hot.

455. Purée of Peas   *Purée de pois*

2 cups large peas, too hard for ordinary use (or 2 cups dried peas), soaked in water several hours

Boil the peas until they are tender. Drain and force through a food mill or strainer. Moisten with the water in which they

have been cooked. Season with butter, salt, and pepper. Reheat but take care that the purée does not burn. It should be
thicker than soup but thinner than mashed potatoes.

456. Buttered Fresh Peas   *Petits pois à l'anglaise*

4 pounds fresh peas   salt and pepper
2 tablespoons butter

Shell the peas as soon after they are gathered as possible. Boil
in salted water 20 minutes or until tender. Drain and season
with butter, salt, and pepper. Serve very hot.

457. Boiled New Potatoes
                     Pommes de terre en robe de chambre

Scrub small new potatoes with a stiff brush. Boil 30 to 40
minutes in salted water. Serve them in their skins and eat with
fresh butter.

458. Baked Potatoes   *Pommes de terre cuites au four*

Scrub large potatoes with a stiff brush. Prick with a fork and
bake in 450°F. oven for 1 hour.

459. Steamed Potatoes   *Pommes de terre cuites à la vapeur*

Wash medium-sized or small potatoes carefully. Put them in
a heavy saucepan with 1 cup of water and ½ teaspoon salt.
Lay over the pan a double thickness of cheesecloth. Cover
the pan and steam 40 minutes or until tender. Be careful that
the potatoes do not burn and have hot water ready to add if
necessary. Special steamer kettles are very common and may
be used without the cloth. The potatoes may be peeled before
bringing them to the table or may be served in their jackets.

460. Fried Potatoes   *Pommes de terre sautées*

Wash medium potatoes and boil them in salted water until
tender. Drain and peel them. Slice them ¼ inch thick. Melt
¼ pound butter in frying pan and, when it is sizzling, fry the
potatoes until they are golden. They should not brown. Sprinkle
with salt and serve.

461. French Fried Potatoes   *Pommes de terre frites*

Peel 6 large potatoes, wash and wipe dry. Cut lengthwise in
strips approximately ½ inch thick. Heat fat to 370°F. Fry
small batches of the potatoes 2 to 3 minutes, keeping the temperature as near constant as possible (41). Drain on absorbent
paper and keep in warm place. When all the potatoes have
been fried, increase the temperature to 385°F. Return the potatoes in larger batches to the fat and fry 2 minutes more or
until golden brown. Drain and sprinkle with salt.

462. Tiny New Potatoes, Sautéed in Butter
Petites pommes de terre frites

Select very small new potatoes. Scrub with a stiff brush. Rinse
and dry. Melt ¼ pound of butter in a frying pan and fry the
potatoes in the butter slowly for 30 to 40 minutes. Turn them
fairly often. The potatoes should be golden brown all over.
Do not let the butter burn.

463. Souffléed Potatoes   *Pommes de terre soufflées*

Wash, peel, and slice medium-sized potatoes ⅛ inch thick.
Dry thoroughly. Have 2 pans of deep fat. The first pan should

be heated to a temperature of 370°F. and the second to 390°F. Fry a handful of the potato slices in the first pan and as soon as they begin to brown, remove from the first pan and place in the second. If the temperatures are exact the second frying will make the slices swell. Do not try to fry too many at one time. It takes practice to master souffléed potatoes but it is worth the effort. Sprinkle generously with salt before serving. Potatoes, fried this way, cannot wait.

464. Potatoes, Maître d'hôtel
Pommes de terre à la maître d'hôtel

Scrub the required number of potatoes and boil in salted water until tender. Drain, peel, and slice them $\frac{1}{8}$ inch thick. Melt 3 tablespoons butter. Add 2 tablespoons chopped parsley, salt, and freshly ground black pepper. Put the potatoes in this sauce and stir gently so that the butter covers all the slices. Serve very hot.

465. Potatoes à la Parisienne
Pommes de terre à la parisienne

8 medium-sized potatoes	*bouquet garni* (42)
2 tablespoons butter, oil, or fat	salt
1 large onion, sliced thin	freshly ground black pepper
2 cups water	

Fry the onion lightly in the butter, oil, or fat until it is a pale yellow. Add potatoes, peeled and thinly sliced, water, *bouquet garni*, salt, and pepper. Cover and simmer until the potatoes are tender—approximately 30 minutes. Remove the *bouquet garni* and serve. This is frequently served as a separate course.

466. Potato Ragout   *Pommes de terre en ragoût*

8 medium potatoes   2 cups water
2 tablespoons butter or oil   *bouquet garni* (42)
1 tablespoon flour   salt and pepper

Wash, peel, and slice the potatoes in 1-inch pieces. Melt butter and stir in flour, allowing it to brown. Add water gradually
and stir until smooth. Add salt, pepper, and *bouquet garni.*
Add the potatoes, cover, and simmer until the potatoes are
tender. Take care that they do not burn. Remove *bouquet garni*
and serve.

467. Creamed Potatoes   *Pommes de terre au lait*

6 medium potatoes   1½ cups warm milk
2 tablespoons butter   salt and black pepper
1 tablespoon flour   dash of nutmeg (optional)

Wash, peel, and halve the potatoes. Boil in salted water until
tender. Meanwhile melt the butter and stir in flour. Do not let
the flour color. Stir in milk and, when the sauce is smooth,
season with salt, pepper, and nutmeg. Drain the potatoes, slice
them or not as you will, and add to the sauce. Serve very hot.

468. Potatoes with Bacon   *Pommes de terre au lard*

6 medium-sized potatoes   2 tablespoons flour
2 tablespoons butter   1 cup stock or water
¼ pound lean, lightly cured   salt and pepper
    bacon   *bouquet garni* (42)

Wash, peel, and quarter the potatoes. Melt butter in a heavy
saucepan. Dice the bacon and fry lightly in the butter until

golden brown. Stir in flour and when it begins to darken, add stock and *bouquet garni*. Add potatoes. Cover and simmer 1 hour.

469. Potatoes in Wine and Herbs

Pommes de terre en matelote

8 medium-sized potatoes	1 cup red wine
2 tablespoons butter	salt and pepper
2 tablespoons flour	*bouquet garni* (42)
1 cup hot water	8 small onions

Wash, peel, and quarter potatoes. Melt butter in a heavy saucepan. Stir in flour and when it is lightly browned add water, wine, salt, pepper and *bouquet garni*. Stir the sauce until it is smooth. Add the small peeled onions and the potatoes. Cover and simmer 1 hour.

470. Stuffed Potatoes   *Pommes de terre farcies*

4 to 6 large potatoes	2 tablespoons chopped parsley
¼ pound sausage meat	salt
1 tablespoon butter	freshly ground black pepper
1 small onion, finely chopped	

Wash, peel, and cut the potatoes in half lengthwise. Scoop out a large hole in each half. Cook the scooped-out centers in boiling salted water until tender. Mash them, add butter, sausage meat, onion, parsley, salt and pepper. Fill the holes in the raw potatoes with this mixture. Place in a buttered oven-proof dish and bake in a 350°F. oven for 1 hour. This makes a good luncheon dish.

471. Potato Purée   *Purée de pommes de terre*

6 medium-sized potatoes   1 cup milk
2 tablespoons butter   salt and pepper

Wash, peel, and boil potatoes in salted water until soft. Heat
butter and milk together until the butter is melted. Force the
potatoes through a food mill or strainer or beat with an electric
beater. Stir in the milk and butter and continue stirring vigorously until the potato purée is very light. French puréed
potatoes are not as thick as our mashed potatoes. More milk
may be needed to give the desired consistency. Season with
salt and pepper and reheat before serving.

472. Potato Soufflé   *Pommes de terre en soufflé*

Prepare the potato purée of the preceding recipe. Add the
well-beaten yolks of 2 large or 3 medium-sized eggs. Beat the
egg whites stiff and fold into the potatoes. Place in a well-
buttered oven-proof dish and bake in a 375°F. oven until the
potatoes are golden brown—approximately 20 minutes.

473. Cheese Potatoes   *Pommes de terre au fromage*

8 potatoes   butter
1 cup grated Swiss cheese   salt and pepper

Wash, peel, and boil potatoes. Mash them thoroughly. Butter
a casserole and place a layer of potato on the bottom. Cover
with a layer of cheese. Sprinkle with a very little salt and a
generous dash of freshly ground black pepper. Dot with butter. Cover with another layer of potato. Continue the process
until cheese and potatoes are used. Finish with a layer of

cheese and pour a little melted butter on the top. Place in 400°F. oven and bake until the top is golden brown.

474. Potato Croquettes *Croquettes de pommes de terre*

6 potatoes	1 onion, chopped fine
¾ cup finely chopped cold roast beef	1 egg salt and pepper
2 tablespoons chopped parsley	1 egg white

Purée the potatoes (471). Keep the purée quite thick. Combine with beef, parsley, onion, egg, salt, and pepper. Chill the mixture. Make small balls of the mixture, dip in egg white and fry in deep fat (375°F.) until golden brown.

475. Duchess Potatoes *Pommes de terre duchesse*

6 to 8 potatoes	1 tablespoon butter
1 egg	salt and pepper
1 tablespoon chopped parsley	

Wash, peel, and boil potatoes in salted water until tender. Force through a food mill or mash very thoroughly. Stir the potatoes over a slow flame for several moments in order to dry them completely. Add unbeaten egg, parsley, salt, and pepper. Stir quickly and remove from fire. Let the potatoes cool and make little patties ¼ inch thick. Fry in ¼ inch of sizzling hot butter until they are golden brown on both sides. Salt and serve hot, garnished with sprigs of fried parsley. These may also be browned in the oven.

Duchess potatoes may be forced through a pastry tube to form spiral shaped patties or arranged in a ring around a platter.

476. Potato Salad   *Pommes de terre en salade*

Marinate 4 cups cold, sliced, boiled potatoes in French Dressing (31) several hours before serving. Drain and arrange on
a bed of lettuce. Garnish with rounds of pickles, fillets of
anchovies, and sliced hard-boiled eggs. Serve with a bowl of
Mayonnaise (17), if desired.

477. Green Salad   *Salade*

1 large head green lettuce	4 tablespoons olive oil
1 tablespoon chopped parsley	salt
1 teaspoon chopped tarragon	freshly ground black pepper
1 tablespoon wine vinegar	

Any of the salad greens—chicory, escarole, Boston lettuce,
romaine, small dandelion leaves, watercress, or a combination of these—may be used. The important thing is that the
greens be fresh and bright-colored. Use only perfect leaves.
Wash thoroughly and dry before placing the greens in a
wooden bowl. Add the seasonings just before serving. Toss well.

478. Salad with Cream Dressing   *Salade à la crème*

Substitute 4 tablespoons of thick cream for the oil used in
the preceding recipe.

479. Vegetable Salad   *Salade jardinière*

Cook as large a variety of vegetables as possible in salted
water. Drain and cool. Marinate them in French Dressing (31)
for 1 hour. Drain and arrange on lettuce leaves. Garnish with
hard-boiled eggs and serve with Mayonnaise (17).

480. Creamed Salsify (Oyster Plant)

Salsifis à la sauce blanche

Trim the tops, wash and scrape 1 bunch of salsify. Soak in fresh water to which a little vinegar has been added. This will keep them from discoloring. Cook in boiling salted water for 20 minutes. Drain well, place in a warm vegetable dish, and cover with Cream Sauce (2).

481. Buttered Salsify   *Salsifis au beurre*

Follow recipe 414.

482. Salsify à la Poulette   *Salsifis à la poulette*

Follow recipe 415.

483. Fried Salsify   *Salsifis frits*

Prepare and boil the salsify as in recipe 480. Drain. Dip in a thick frying batter (40) and put them, one after another, in deep hot fat (370°F.). When they are golden brown, sprinkle with salt and serve on a heated platter, garnished with parsley.

484. Sauerkraut   *Choucroute*

Sauerkraut may be bought canned or in bulk at almost all markets. For those who prefer to prepare it at home, Tante Marie gives the following recipe:

Be sure that the cabbages are firm and white. Remove the imperfect outer leaves. Quarter the heads and remove the hard core. Shred the cabbage. Line the bottom of a keg or crock with salt. Put in a layer of shredded cabbage, a few juniper berries (if possible), and whole peppercorns. Press the cabbage down without breaking it and continue alternating layers of cabbage with peppercorns and salt until the vessel is ¾ full. 12 cabbages require 2 pounds of salt. Cover with several layers of cheesecloth. Place a board or plate that will fit over the cabbage in the crock. Place a heavy weight on this. When fermentation starts, the cover will go down and the brine will come over the cover. Some of this should be removed but some should be left on the cover. The sauerkraut may be used at the end of a month. As the sauerkraut is taken out of the crock, wash the cover and cloth before putting it back and place a little fresh water on the cover. The fermentation has an unpleasant odor but it disappears when the sauerkraut is washed.

485. Sauerkraut and Sausage   *Choucroute garnie*

1 quart sauerkraut	4 frankfurters
8 slices fat bacon	½ bottle white wine
salt and pepper	2 cups stock
½ pound link sausage	

Put 3 slices of bacon in the bottom of a heavy saucepan. Place a layer of sauerkraut, which has been washed in several waters and thoroughly drained, over the bacon. Sprinkle with salt and pepper. Lay half the link sausages, 2 slices of bacon, and 2 frankfurters on the sauerkraut. Cover with a layer of sauerkraut and repeat the process. Pour wine and water over it all. Cover tightly and simmer 5 hours. Skim off the fat before serving. This recipe may be doubled or tripled.

486. Garden Sorrel   *Purée d'oseille*

4 or 5 handfuls of sorrel
2 tablespoons butter

1 egg yolk, mixed with 4 table-
    spoons cold milk
salt and pepper

Wash the sorrel well and remove the hard stems. Place in a heavy saucepan. Cover and wilt over a slow flame 10 minutes. Add butter and heat 5 minutes longer. Stir in the egg yolk and milk. Season with salt and pepper. If the sorrel is large and bitter, blanch it 5 minutes in salted water, drain, and then add the butter, etc. This is usually served with hard-boiled eggs, sausage, or ham.

487. French Spinach   *Epinards au jus*

2 pounds of spinach
2 tablespoons butter
2 tablespoons flour
½ cup stock or spinach broth

salt, black pepper
2 hard-boiled eggs, sliced
croutons

Remove all the hard stems from the spinach and wash in several waters. Plunge into boiling salted water and cook 5 minutes. Drain and press out the water. Chop fine and place in saucepan with butter. When the butter has melted, add flour. When this has blended add the liquid and stir until smooth. Season with salt and pepper and, if desired, a dash of nutmeg. Serve on a heated platter. Garnish with slices of hard-boiled egg and croutons.

488. Creamed Spinach   *Epinards à la béchamel*

Follow the preceding recipe, substituting 1 cup of milk for the stock or spinach broth.

489. Sweet Spinach   *Epinards au sucre*

2 pounds of spinach
1 tablespoon sugar
2 tablespoons butter
1 tablespoon flour

1 egg yolk, mixed with
¼ cup cold milk
salt, black pepper
croutons

Follow recipe 487 for cooking spinach but instead of adding the liquid, add sugar and thicken with egg yolk and milk. Do not let the spinach boil after adding the egg.

490. Tomatoes au Gratin   *Tomates au gratin*

6 large ripe tomatoes
2 tablespoons olive oil
1 tablespoon chopped parsley
1 clove garlic, chopped fine

1 scallion, chopped fine
fine bread crumbs
salt and pepper

Choose the tomatoes with care. They should be uniform in size and should be ripe but very firm. Cut the tomatoes horizontally in half. Heat 1 tablespoon olive oil with the herbs. Spread the mixture on the bottom of a casserole. Place the tomato halves on top. Sprinkle with salt and pepper and cover with bread crumbs. Brush with the remaining olive oil and cook ¾ hour in a 350°F. oven.

Plus on se presse, moins on arrive.

491. Stuffed tomatoes   *Tomates farcies*

6 large, firm, ripe tomatoes
4 tablespoons olive oil
2 tablespoons chopped parsley
2 tablespoons chopped scallions
1 clove garlic, chopped fine

¼ pound mushrooms, chopped
salt and pepper
fine bread crumbs
4 tablespoons grated Swiss cheese

Wash the tomatoes and hollow out a large cavity in the center of each one. Heat 2 tablespoons oil with the herbs and mushrooms and cook 3 minutes. Season with salt and pepper and add enough bread crumbs to make a thick stuffing. Place the tomatoes in a large well-oiled casserole. Fill with the stuffing. Sprinkle with cheese and brush with the remaining oil. Bake 45 minutes in 350°F. oven, basting from time to time with juice that comes from the tomatoes.

492. Sweet turnips   *Navets au sucre*

2 bunches small turnips
2 tablespoons butter
1 tablespoon sugar
1 tablespoon flour

1 cup stock or water
salt
1 tablespoon sugar

Wash and peel the turnips. Melt butter in a saucepan and add 1 tablespoon sugar. Fry the turnips gently until they are yellow. Stir in flour carefully and add liquid, salt, and 1 more tablespoon sugar. Cover the pan tightly and simmer 1 hour.

493. Braised Turnips   *Navets au jus*

2 bunches small turnips
2 tablespoons butter
1 tablespoon flour

salt and pepper
bouquet garni (42)
1 cup stock or consommé

Follow the preceding recipe but do not add sugar. Add the *bouquet garni*. This is removed just before serving.

494. Mashed Turnips   *Navets en purée*

2 bunches small turnips   salt and pepper
2 tablespoons butter

Wash and peel the turnips. Boil in salted water until they are tender—approximately 40 minutes. Force through a food mill or strainer. Season with butter, salt, and pepper and reheat before serving.

495. Truffles in Wine   *Truffes au vin*

Truffles, those highly prized nuggets usually found by inquisitive pigs at the base of French oak trees, are rarely obtainable in the United States except in cans. For the sake of the record we include Tante Marie's instructions for cleaning them. They should be washed and scrubbed in several waters, using a stiff wire brush. They are then peeled and sliced or left whole, as the recipe requires. The peelings should always be saved for sauces. Truffles may be bought in cans. The peelings and chopped truffles are cheaper. The whole truffles must be saved for very special occasions. The flavor lost in the canning process can be partly revived by frying the truffles gently in butter. [C.T.]

2 large cans whole truffles   *bouquet garni* (42)
⅛ pound salt pork, diced   salt and pepper
½ bottle dry white wine

Drain the canned truffles. Combine with the remaining ingredients and simmer in a covered saucepan for ¾ hour. Place in a heated vegetable dish and pour the strained sauce over them.

496. Sweet Omelet *Omelette au sucre*

6 eggs	¼ teaspoon salt
2 tablespoons sugar	2 tablespoons butter

Separate the yolks and whites of eggs. Beat the yolks until they are lemon-colored. Beat the whites stiff but not dry. Add 1 tablespoon sugar and the salt to the egg yolks and fold in egg whites. Follow recipe 125 for cooking the omelet. When it is cooked, sprinkle generously with sugar and, if possible, press with a red-hot poker. Serve immediately.

497. Rum Omelet *Omelette au rhum*

Follow the preceding recipe for making Sweet Omelet. Place it on a heated metal platter. Pour on 2 tablespoons of hot brandy and touch a match to it as you carry the platter to the table.

498. Jelly Omelet   *Omelette aux confitures*

Follow recipe 496 for making Sweet Omelet. Make sure that the omelet is thoroughly cooked and that the center is not runny. Before folding the omelet, put a layer of jelly or jam on one half. Serve immediately.

499. Omelet Soufflé   *Omelette soufflée*

4 eggs   1 teaspoon grated lemon peel
4 teaspoons powdered sugar

Beat the egg yolks until lemon-colored. Add sugar and lemon peel. Fold in stiffly beaten egg whites. Place in a deep buttered oven-proof dish and bake 10 minutes in 450°F. oven. Sprinkle with sugar before serving.

500. Snow Pudding   *Œufs à la neige*

4 eggs   ½ teaspoon vanilla extract
2 cups milk   ¾ cup sugar

Separate the yolks from the whites. Beat the egg whites very stiff. Add sugar and vanilla to the milk and bring to a boil. Poach the egg whites in the milk in the following manner: Take a generous tablespoonful of egg whites and place in the simmering milk. When the whites swell turn them and cook for a moment longer. Remove carefully and put on a dessert platter. Three tablespoonsful can be done at once. Continue this until all the egg whites have been used. Beat the yolks and add to the milk, taking care that the milk is cool enough not to curdle the yolks. Strain into the top of a double boiler and cook, stirring constantly, until the sauce begins to thicken.

Remove and cool. When cool, pour the sauce around the islands of egg white. This makes an attractive dessert.

501. White Lady   *Dame blanche*

4 eggs	¾ cup sugar
2 cups milk	½ teaspoon vanilla extract

Separate the yolks from the whites. Beat the whites very stiff and place in a buttered mold or casserole. The dish should be only half full. Cover and bake 15 to 20 minutes in a 350°F. oven. If the whites rise too high, remove the cover. Meanwhile beat yolks until lemon-colored and combine with milk and sugar. Cook in the top of a double boiler until the sauce begins to thicken. When the egg whites are cooked, turn the mold upside down on a dessert platter. Surround with the sauce. Serve cold. The mold may be caramelized before putting in the egg whites (538) but in this case it becomes *Gâteau d'œufs à la neige* and not the traditional *Dame blanche.*

502. Chocolate Mousse   *Mousse au chocolat*

4 1-oz. squares bitter chocolate	5 eggs
¼ cup water	1 tablespoon cognac
¾ cup sugar	

Melt the chocolate in the top of a double boiler. Add water and sugar and stir until the sugar is dissolved. Separate the yolks from the whites. Add the yolks, one by one, beating vigorously. Remove from the heat and add cognac. Beat egg whites stiff and fold into the chocolate mixture. Pour into individual molds or a dessert bowl and place in the refrigerator. Let it stand for at least 12 hours. The longer it stands the better it is. It will keep well for several days.

503. French Applesauce   *Marmelade de pommes*

8 cooking apples
2 tablespoons butter
½ cup sugar

½ teaspoon vanilla extract or
    ½ teaspoon grated lemon
    peel
3 tablespoons water
candied fruits

Peel, core, and quarter the apples. Place in heavy saucepan with butter, sugar, water, and flavoring. Cook over low flame until the apples are tender. Stir often to prevent burning. Strain the apples and serve hot in a deep dessert dish. Sprinkle with powdered sugar. Decorate with candied fruits. This sauce may be served cold. If so, heat half a glass of apricot or currant jelly with a little water and pour over the sauce.

504. Apple Charlotte   *Charlotte de pommes*

several slices white bread
4 tablespoons melted butter
French Applesauce (503)

½ jar apricot jam
1 tablespoon rum

Remove the crusts from the bread. Cut 12 long triangles. Fry gently in melted butter. Line the bottom of a smooth mold with these triangles, with the points meeting in the center. Line the sides with rectangles which have been cut the height of the mold and lightly fried. Fill the mold with the applesauce. Bake 30 minutes in 375° F. oven. Turn upside down on a dessert platter and serve with a sauce made by heating apricot jam with a little water and flavoring it with rum.

505. Apple Charlotte Meringue
Charlotte de pommes meringuées

Fill a buttered casserole with hot French Applesauce (503). Beat 1 egg white very stiff and add 1 generous tablespoonful of powdered sugar. Spread this mixture over the sauce. Sprinkle with granulated sugar and cook in 375°F. oven until the egg whites have risen and are golden brown—approximately 20 minutes.

506. Apple Supreme   *Pommes au riz*

½ cup rice	½ cup sugar
2 cups milk	½ teaspoon vanilla extract
½ cup sugar	1 egg yolk
8 cooking apples	currant jelly
2 cups water, mixed with	candied fruits

Wash the rice carefully and cook in boiling milk until the rice is soft. The milk should be entirely absorbed. Sweeten with sugar and set aside to cool. Peel and core 4 apples and simmer in syrup until a fork will easily enter the apples. Do not overcook. Remove them carefully with a skimmer. Core, peel, and cut the rest of the apples in small pieces and cook in the same syrup until they have the consistency of applesauce. Add vanilla. Mix with the cooked rice and let it stand 15 minutes. Add slightly beaten egg yolk and pour into a baking dish. Bury the 4 whole apples in the rice so that only the top halves are visible. Place under the broiler a few moments to color the apples. Just before serving fill the centers of the apples with currant jelly and decorate the rice with candied fruits.

507. Buttered Apples   *Pommes au beurre*

4 to 6 medium-sized baking apples	½ cup sugar
4 to 6 thin slices white bread	4 tablespoons butter

Core and peel apples. Place the bread in a buttered baking dish and put an apple on each slice. Fill half of each center with butter and the rest with sugar. Bake 45 to 60 minutes, depending on size, in 350°F. oven. Melt the remaining butter and combine with remaining sugar. Spoon a little of this over the apples from time to time. Serve hot with the juice from the bottom of the pan poured over the apples. If the centers are filled with currant jelly just before serving, they become *Pommes portugaises*.

508. Flaming Apples   *Pommes flambantes*

12 small, tart apples	¼ teaspoon cinnamon
2 cups water	¼ cup hot rum
1 cup sugar	

Bring water, cinnamon, and sugar to a boil. Wash the apples and poach them in the syrup until they are tender. Do not overcook or they will not keep their shape. Remove from the syrup, one by one, and arrange in a pyramid on a heated platter. Quickly reduce the syrup by boiling until it is quite thick. Pour over the apples and sprinkle with sugar. Just before carrying the platter to the table, pour the rum over the pyramid and touch with a flame.

509. Buttered Peaches   *Pêches au beurre*

Follow recipe 507, substituting ½ large peach for each apple. The peach should be placed cavity side up on the bread, in order to hold the butter and sugar.

510. Apple Fritters   *Beignets de pommes*

2 cups flour
2 egg yolks
1 teaspoon brandy
½ teaspoon salt

1 cup milk
2 egg whites
4 cooking apples

Put the flour in a bowl and make a well in the center. Place the egg yolks, brandy, and salt in the well and work in the flour until it is thoroughly mixed. Add the milk gradually until the batter is smooth. Beat the egg whites stiff and fold into the batter. Peel and core the apples and cut them in ⅛-inch rounds. Dip each piece into the batter and fry 3 to 5 minutes in 375°F. deep fat. Sprinkle with powdered sugar and serve.

511. Apricot Fritters   *Beignets d'abricots*

Choose apricots that are not quite ripe. Split them but do not peel them. Follow the preceding recipe.

512. Peach Fritters   *Beignets de pêches*

Choose peaches that are not quite ripe. Peel them and cut in two. Follow recipe 510.

513. Strawberry Fritters   *Beignets de fraises*

Choose large strawberries that are not quite ripe. Leave them whole. Follow recipe 510.

514. Sweet Almond Fritters   *Beignets sucrés aux amandes*

2 cups flour
¾ cup almonds, blanched and
   peeled
⅔ cup powdered sugar

4 tablespoons butter
½ teaspoon grated lemon peel
2 eggs

Blanch almonds by dropping them into boiling water and then removing the skins. Force almonds through a food chopper, using the finest blade. Beat eggs slightly. Add flour, sugar, almonds, butter that has been softened but not melted, and lemon peel. Work the dough with your hands until it is smooth. Roll out quite thin. Cut the dough into whatever shapes you desire and fry in deep fat (370°F.) 2 to 3 minutes.

515. Cream Fritters   *Crème frite*

1 cup flour
½ cup cold water
2 cups milk
6 tablespoons sugar
¼ teaspoon salt

½ teaspoon grated lemon or
   orange peel
1 egg yolk
1 egg yolk, beaten with
2 tablespoons sugar
fine bread crumbs

Mix the flour with the water until it is a smooth paste. Bring the milk to a boil and add the flour-and-water paste, stirring until it is well blended. Add sugar, salt, and lemon peel and continue cooking very slowly 15 minutes. Remove from the heat and when it has cooled a little, stir in the egg yolk, slightly beaten. Pour into a buttered cake tin and chill thoroughly. Cut into rounds or strips, dip in the sweetened egg yolk, roll in bread crumbs, and fry 2 to 3 minutes in 370°F. deep fat.

516. Puff Paste Fritters   *Beignets soufflés dits pets de nonne*

1 cup water	1 tablespoon butter
1 teaspoon sugar	1 cup flour
¼ teaspoon salt	4 eggs
1 tablespoon grated lemon peel	granulated sugar

Bring water, sugar, salt, lemon peel, and butter to a boil. Add flour and stir vigorously until all the flour is mixed in. Continue stirring this mixture over the flame until it is thick and dry. Remove from the flame and add the unbeaten eggs, one at a time, stirring hard after each addition. The dough will become smooth and when it drops slowly from the spoon it is the right consistency. Drop teaspoons of the mixture into deep fat (370°F.) and fry until golden brown. Sprinkle with powdered sugar. Serve hot or cold; they are delicious tea cakes.

517. Crêpes   *Crêpes*

2 cups flour	1 teaspoon salt
2 cups milk	1 tablespoon salad oil
1 cup water	1 tablespoon brandy
2 eggs	

Add the milk and water to the flour gradually, beating constantly so that the batter becomes very smooth. Add eggs, salt, oil, and brandy. Beat the batter until smooth and set aside to rest for an hour or two. Heat a large frying pan and grease very slightly. Pour a serving spoonful of the batter into the frying pan and move the pan around until its entire surface is covered. Both the batter and the resulting crêpe should be thin. When it is brown, turn with a large spatula and cook a moment on the other side. Continue this process until all the batter is used. Keep the crêpes in a warm place. Fold each in quarters or roll it. Sprinkle with sugar. Apricot jam flavored with cognac may be placed on each crêpe before folding it.

518. Crêpes Suzette   *Crêpes Suzette*

4 tablespoons butter
5 tablespoons sugar
grated rind of 2 oranges
2 teaspoons curaçao or cointreau

Sauce:
   juice of 2 oranges
   2 tablespoons sugar
   2 tablespoons curaçao (or 2
      tablespoons cointreau)

Prepare the crêpes as in the preceding recipe. Cream the
butter and sugar. Add the rind and liqueur. Spread each
crêpe with this mixture and keep in a warm place. Boil the
orange juice and sugar for a few moments and add the liqueur.
Pour this hot sauce over the crêpes and touch with a flame
as the platter is carried to the table. Brandy may be substituted for the orange liqueur.

519. Rice Cake   *Gâteau de riz*

⅔ cup rice
3 cups milk
4 eggs
½ cup butter

⅓ cup almonds, ground fine
3 tablespoons sugar
½ teaspoon vanilla extract

Wash and cook the rice in the boiling milk. When the rice is
tender, add vanilla and set aside to cool. Soften the butter
by working it with a wooden spoon. Separate the yolks from
the whites and add the yolks one by one to the butter, beating
vigorously after each addition. This can be done with an
electric beater set at a low speed. If done by hand it should
be beaten 15 minutes in order to get the right consistency.
Add sugar and almonds and gradually add the rice, beating
all the time. Fold in stiffly beaten egg whites and pour into a
buttered mold. Set the mold in a pan of hot water and bake
in 350°F. oven 45 minutes. Unmold and serve plain or with
a Custard Sauce (533). Raisins may be substituted for the
almonds.

520. Chocolate Soufflé   *Soufflé au chocolat*

2 tablespoons butter	2 tablespoons water
2 tablespoons flour	6 tablespoons sugar
¾ cup milk, warmed	3 eggs
2 squares bitter chocolate	½ teaspoon vanilla extract

Melt butter and stir in flour. Add warm milk and stir until
well blended. Melt the chocolate in the top of a double boiler.
Add sugar and water and stir until smooth. Combine the
mixtures. Separate the yolks from the whites of eggs and beat
the yolks thoroughly. Add them to the chocolate mixture.
Add vanilla. Beat the egg whites stiff and fold in carefully.
Bake in a buttered casserole 20 minutes in 350°F. oven. The
casserole should be set in a pan of hot water. A French
soufflé should not be dry, but if a drier soufflé is preferred,
bake 5 to 10 minutes longer. Powder with sugar and serve
plain or with whipped cream. It cannot wait. This dessert can
easily be made even if the hostess is the cook. Prepare the
soufflé ahead of time except for beating the egg whites. Just
before dinner is served add the stiffly beaten egg whites and
bake during dinner time.

521. Quickly Done   *Tôt-fait*

3 eggs	⅔ cup sugar
½ cup flour	½ teaspoon vanilla extract
1 cup milk	

Preheat the oven to 400°F. Beat the egg yolks until lemon-
colored. Stir in flour and when well blended add milk, sugar,
and vanilla. Fold in stiffly beaten egg whites. Bake 20 minutes
in hot oven and sprinkle with powdered sugar before serving.

522. Vanilla Cream   *Fromage à la vanille*

1 cup milk
½ cup sugar
½ teaspoon vanilla
5 egg yolks

1 quart whipping cream
2 tablespoons gelatine
½ cup powdered sugar
1 cup candied fruit peel

Scald the milk. Add sugar and vanilla and cool to lukewarm. Add well-beaten egg yolks and cook in the top of a double boiler, stirring constantly with a wooden spoon until the sauce is thick but still runny. Pour into a bowl and cool. Dissolve the gelatine in a little water in the top of a double boiler. When it has dissolved, let it cool but not thicken before adding it to the cream, which has been beaten to the thickness of custard. Add sugar and most of the candied fruit peel. Combine the mixtures and when thoroughly blended pour into a mold and place in ice or in the coldest part of the refrigerator for at least 4 hours. Just before serving, place the mold for a moment in hot water and then reverse it onto a dessert platter. Garnish with fruit peel.

523. Sweet Whipped Cream   *Fromage à la Chantilly*

Beat 2 cups heavy cream until it is thick but not stiff and dry. Stir in ½ to ¾ cup of powdered sugar and store in refrigerator until ready for use. It may be flavored with vanilla, coffee extract, or the juices of crushed fruits and served as a dessert, or it may be used as a garnish for many desserts. If the cream is to be kept a long time, dissolve 1 tablespoon of gelatine in a little water and stir in the top of a double boiler until it is completely dissolved. Cool but do not let it thicken before adding to the cream.

524. Coffee Bavarian Cream   *Bavaroise au café*

2 cups heavy cream   4 eggs yolks
6 tablespoons powdered sugar   4 tablespoons coffee extract or
4 cups milk   ½ cup strong boiled coffee
1¼ cups sugar   2 tablespoons gelatine

Prepare the whipped cream as in the preceding recipe. Chill
in ice box. Scald the milk. Add sugar and coffee extract.
Cool until lukewarm. Add well-beaten egg yolks and cook in
a double boiler until the sauce thickens. Stir in gelatine,
which has been dissolved in ¼ cup water. Pour the sauce
into a bowl and cool. Combine with cream and chill in a
buttered mold for at least 4 hours. Unmold and serve.

525. Charlotte Russe

Lady Fingers (596)   variations: chopped   walnuts,
Sweet Whipped Cream (523)   pecans, almonds, candied
                                     fruits or maraschino cher-
                                     ries

Line the sides and bottom of a lightly buttered, smooth mold
with lady fingers. Cut some in half and have the ends meet
in the center of the bottom. Line the sides with the whole lady
fingers pressing close together so that the mold will be completely lined. Trim the ends off the top of the mold. Fill the
center with the cream, to which any of the suggested variations may have been added. Chill several hours. Unmold and
serve. If the cream is mixed with chopped almonds and decorated with cherries and whipped cream, it becomes *Charlotte
Malakoff.*

526. Diplomat Rum Pudding   *Diplomate au rhum*

Lady Fingers (596)
Apricot or Peach Jam (624-5)
1 cup seedless raisins
2 tablespoons finely cut citron
3 tablespoons chopped candied
    orange peel

Rum syrup:
  1 cup water
  1 cup sugar
  ¼ cup rum

Spread each lady finger with jam. Place a layer of the lady fingers in the bottom of a deep, buttered, oven-proof dessert dish. Pour a little rum syrup—made by heating sugar, water, and rum until the sugar is dissolved—over the fingers. Sprinkle raisins, citron, and orange peel over this. Continue this process until the dish is three quarters filled. Finish with a layer of lady fingers. Place the dish in a pan of hot water and bake 1½ hours in 350°F. oven.

527. Diplomat Cream Pudding   *Diplomate à la crème*

Lady Fingers (596)
Apricot or Peach Jam (624-5)
1 cup seedless raisins
2 tablespoons finely cut citron
3 tablespoons candied orange
    peel

Sauce:
  2 cups milk
  ½ teaspoon vanilla extract
  ¾ cup sugar
  4 egg yolks

Follow the preceding recipe for preparing the pudding but, instead of moistening the lady fingers with rum syrup, prepare the following sauce: Scald the milk and add sugar and vanilla. Cool to lukewarm and add well-beaten egg yolks. Pour half of the sauce over the pudding. Place the dish in a pan of hot water and bake 1 hour in 350°F. oven. Thicken the rest of the sauce by stirring in the top of a double boiler until it thickens a little. Pour into a bowl and chill. Turn the pudding out on a dessert platter. Garnish with candied fruits and pour the sauce around the pudding.

528. Plum Pudding   *Plum-Pudding*

¼ pound suet
½ cup fine bread crumbs
½ cup flour
½ cup milk
2 eggs
1 teaspoon salt
¼ teaspoon ginger
¼ teaspoon nutmeg
½ teaspoon cinnamon
4 ounces combined candied orange and lemon peel, citron, and angelica
¼ pound seeded raisins, cut in small pieces
¼ pound seedless raisins
¼ cup rum or cognac
juice of ½ lemon
¼ cup sugar

Chop the suet fine. Add bread crumbs, flour, and milk. Mix well. Beat the eggs until lemon-colored. Add ginger, nutmeg, cinnamon, and salt and combine the mixtures. Add sugar, lemon juice, and rum to the fruit and mix thoroughly. Add to the pudding and let it stand overnight. Butter a melon mold or large bowl. Fill the bowl with the pudding. Wrap the mold in a large dish towel or cheesecloth. Bring water to a boil in a large kettle. Tie the ends of the towel to the handle of the kettle so that the mold will be suspended in the water. Boil the pudding 4 hours. Replace the water as it boils away. Before serving, plunge the mold in cold water for a few moments. Turn on to a heated platter. Cover the pudding with hot cognac or rum and ignite just before bringing it to the table.

529. Bread Pudding with Rum Sauce
Pudding au pain, sauce au rhum

8 slices white bread	¼ cup butter
½ cup milk	*Sauce:*
1 teaspoon cinnamon	4 tablespoons butter
1 teaspoon salt	1 tablespoon flour
1 tablespoon flour	3 tablespoons water
3 eggs	3 tablespoons rum
1 cup seeded raisins	⅓ cup sugar
1 cup seedless raisins	¼ teaspoon salt

Soak the bread in milk for 10 minutes. Add salt, cinnamon, flour, unbeaten eggs, raisins, and butter that has been softened but not melted. Mix all this with your hands or with a heavy spoon until the dough is thick and smooth. Dip a large dish cloth or double thickness of cheesecloth in boiling water. Spread flat on a table and sprinkle with flour. Place the mixture, formed into a large ball, in the middle of the cloth and tie the ends together. Suspend the pudding in boiling water. Tie the ends of the cloth to the handle so that the pudding cannot touch the bottom of the kettle. Boil 2½ hours, taking care to replace the water as it boils away. Remove from the water and let it stand 20 minutes before taking the pudding out of the cloth.

To make sauce: Melt butter and stir in flour. Add water, rum, sugar, and salt. Simmer 10 minutes, stirring constantly. This sauce can be made ahead of time and kept warm in a covered double boiler over hot—not boiling—water. Pour the sauce over the hot pudding.

Pain dérobé réveille appétit.

530. Russian Mousse   *Mousse à la russe*

5 egg whites   granulated sugar
1 cup French Applesauce (503)   Sweet Whipped Cream (523)

Beat the egg whites very stiff. Fold in cold applesauce. Shape
this on an oven-proof dessert platter in a pyramid. Smooth
the sides with the blade of a knife. Sprinkle with granulated
sugar and bake in 300°F. oven 40 minutes. Serve with a bowl
of cream, whipped thick but not stiff.

531. Chestnut Pudding   *Gâteau de marrons*

1 pound of chestnuts   3 egg whites
2 cups milk   3 tablespoons sugar
1 cup sugar   1 tablespoon water
1 teaspoon vanilla extract

With a sharp pointed knife make an X on the flat side of each
chestnut. Plunge the chestnuts in rapidly boiling water and
boil 10 minutes. Remove from the water and, while they are
still hot, remove the shell. Scald the milk. Add sugar and
cook the chestnuts in the milk 40 minutes. Force through a
food mill or strainer. Add vanilla and cool. Put 3 tablespoons
of sugar in a mold large enough to hold the pudding. Decorative molds may be used. Melt the sugar and let it turn brown.
Add the water and move the mold around until the caramel
has reached every part of the interior. Use more sugar for
a large mold. Fold in stiffly beaten egg whites with the chestnuts. Pour into mold. Place the mold in a pan of hot water
and cook 40 minutes in 325°F. oven. Turn mold upside
down on a platter. Serve plain or with Sweet Whipped Cream
(523).

532. Mont Blanc

Follow the preceding recipe for preparing and cooking the chestnuts. When the chestnuts have been forced through the food mill or strainer, heap them on a dessert platter in the shape of a pyramid. Smooth the sides with the moistened blade of a knife and decorate with sweetened whipped cream forced through a pastry tube. Serve warm or cold.

533. Custard Sauce   *Crème à la vanille*

2 cups milk	3 egg yolks
½ cup sugar	1 teaspoon vanilla extract

Scald the milk and cool to lukewarm. Beat the egg yolks and add sugar. Add the milk gradually, stirring constantly. Place in the top of a double boiler and stir over simmering water until the sauce thickens to the consistency of heavy cream. Remove from the fire and add vanilla.

534. Baked Custard   *Pots de crème à la vanille*

4 cups milk	3 egg yolks
½ cup sugar	1 egg white
1 teaspoon vanilla extract	

Scald the milk and cool to lukewarm. Beat the yolks and egg white together. Add sugar and vanilla. Stir in the milk gradually. Pour into individual custard cups or in one large mold. Place in a pan of hot water and bake 30 to 40 minutes in 325°F. oven, or until set. This can be tested by inserting a silver knife in the custard. If it comes out clean the custard is set. Serve warm or chilled.

535. Coffee Custard   *Crème au café*

Follow the preceding recipe but add 2 tablespoons of powdered coffee or 2 tablespoons of coffee extract to the egg mixture.

536. Chocolate Custard   *Crème au chocolat*

Follow recipe 534 but add 2 squares of cooking chocolate, melted over hot water to the egg mixture.

537. Caramel Custard   *Crème au caramel*

Heat ¼ cup sugar and 3 tablespoons water in a heavy frying pan until it is dark-brown liquid. Cool this to lukewarm before adding to the lukewarm milk. Follow recipe 534 for making custard.

538. Caramelized Custard   *Crème renversée*

2 cups milk	4 eggs
½ cup sugar	3 tablespoons sugar
1 teaspoon vanilla extract	1 tablespoon water

Scald the milk with the sugar and cool to lukewarm. Add vanilla. Beat eggs and gradually add the milk to eggs. Place 3 tablespoons of sugar in the mold and place over a direct flame. Heat until it is dark brown. Add water and turn the mold around in your hands until the liquid caramel has reached every part of the mold. Pour the custard into the mold and place the mold in the pan and bake 40 to 45 minutes or until the custard is set. Chill before unmolding it on a dessert platter. It is safer to place the platter on top of the mold before turning it upside down.

539. Zabaglione   *Crème Sambaglione*

6 eggs   ¼ cup Marsala wine
½ cup sugar (scant)

Separate the yolks from the whites. Beat egg whites almost—
but not quite—stiff. Beat the yolks slightly with the sugar
and wine. Place in a double boiler over simmering water and
stir constantly and smoothly until the yolks thicken. Remove
from the flame. Stir in the egg whites quickly. Serve warm
in custard cups or small goblets. This dessert cannot wait.

540. Blancmange   *Blanc-manger*

1 cup almonds, blanched and   1 cup milk
    peeled   1 teaspoon lemon extract
1 cup cold water   1 tablespoon gelatine
1 cup sugar

Blanch almonds by dropping them into boiling water and
then removing the skins. Force them through the food chopper, using the finest blade. With a mortar and pestle or a heavy
potato masher, pound the almonds, gradually adding water. Put
this *almond milk* in a dish towel and squeeze out the excess
water. Dissolve gelatine in the top of a double boiler with
¼ cup water. Add this and the sugar, milk, and lemon extract
to the almond milk. Mix all the ingredients well until the
sugar is dissolved. Pour into a mold or dessert bowl and
chill several hours before serving.

541. Bacchus' Delight   *Crème bachique*

2 cups Sauterne wine   ¼ teaspoon cinnamon
½ cup sugar   6 egg yolks

Bring wine, sugar, and cinnamon to a boil. Beat egg yolks
well and gradually add the wine. Pour into individual cus-

tard cups and place in a pan of hot water. Bake in 325°F. oven for 30 to 40 minutes or until the custard is firm.

542. Kirsch Jelly   *Gelée au kirsch*

1 cup boiling water	1 tablespoon lemon juice
1 tablespoon gelatine, softened in	¼ teaspoon salt
¼ cup water	½ cup kirsch
¾ cup sugar	red coloring

Add the softened gelatine to boiling water and stir until the gelatine is dissolved. Add sugar, lemon juice, salt, kirsch, and coloring. Stir until the sugar is dissolved and pour into a decorative mold. Chill. Just before serving, place the mold upside down on a dessert platter. Place a hot dish cloth around the mold for a moment to loosen the jelly. Surround the jelly with whipped cream, sweetened and flavored with kirsch.

543. Rum Jelly   *Gelée au rhum*

Follow preceding recipe substituting rum for kirsch.

544. Lemon Jelly   *Gelée au citron*

2 cups boiling water	¾ cup sugar
1½ tablespoons gelatine soaked in	½ cup lemon juice
¼ cup cold water	¼ teaspoon salt

Put the dissolved gelatine in boiling water. Stir in sugar and salt. When the sugar is dissolved add lemon juice. Pour the jelly into a mold and chill for several hours. Unmold and serve with sweetened whipped cream flavored with a little curaçao or cointreau.

545. Fruit Jelly   *Gelée aux fruits*

1 pint strawberries, raspberries, currants, or a combination of these	1½ tablespoons gelatine soaked in
1 tablespoon water	¼ cup water
¾ cup sugar	1 tablespoon lemon juice
¼ teaspoon salt	2 cups boiling water
	Sweet Whipped Cream (523)

Crush the fruit in a saucepan and bring to a boil with 1 tablespoon of water. This will extract the juice. Dissolve the gelatine in the boiling water. Add sugar, salt, and lemon juice, and when the sugar has dissolved, combine with the juice, which has been strained. Pour into a decorative large mold or into individual molds and chill for several hours. Unmold and serve with cream.

546. Vanilla Ice Cream I   *Glace à la vanille*
(*to be frozen in ice-cream freezer*)

2 cups milk	¾ cup sugar
4 egg yolks	1 tablespoon vanilla extract
¼ teaspoon salt	1 cup heavy cream

Scald the milk. Add sugar and salt and stir until sugar is dissolved. Cool to lukewarm and add to slightly beaten yolks. Cook in a double boiler, stirring constantly until the mixture thickens. Cool and add to cream. Pour into the freezing can, cover, and place in freezer. Surround with 1 part salt to 4 parts chopped ice. Turn slowly until ice begins to melt and then turn rapidly until the crank is difficult to turn. Remove the cover, scrape off the dasher, plug up the hole, and replace the cover. Let the ice cream stand 4 hours.

547. Vanilla Ice Cream II   *Glace à la vanille*
(*for mechanical refrigerator*)

2 eggs	½ cup sugar
2 tablespoons brandy (or 1	1 cup milk, scalded
tablespoon vanilla extract)	1 cup heavy cream

Beat the egg yolks until they are thick and lemon-colored. Add hot milk and sugar gradually, beating constantly. Add brandy or vanilla and chill. Fold in stiffly beaten egg whites and cream whipped until it is thick but not stiff. Freeze until firm. This may be frozen in a mold. If so, unmold just before serving and add sweetened fresh or preserved fruits. This makes a festive dessert.

548. Strawberry Ice Cream I   *Glace à la fraise*
(*to be frozen in ice-cream freezer*)

1 quart strawberries, hulled	1 cup sugar
and crushed	4 cups heavy cream

Combine strawberries and sugar and chill for 30 minutes. Mix with heavy cream and pour into ice-cream can. Place in the freezer and surround with 1 part salt to 4 parts chopped ice. Turn the crank until it turns with difficulty. Let it stand at least 4 hours in the ice before serving.

Plus on a, plus on veut avoir.

549. Strawberry Ice Cream II   *Glace à la fraise*
(*for mechanical refrigerator*)

1 pint strawberries	2 egg whites, beaten stiff
1 tablespoon water	dash of salt
1 cup sugar	2 cups heavy cream
2 tablespoons lemon juice	

Wash, hull, and crush the strawberries in the bottom of a
saucepan. Add sugar and water and bring to a boil. Set aside
to cool. Add salt to the egg whites and beat stiff. Whip cream
until very thick but not stiff. Add lemon juice to the strawberries and combine all the mixtures. Place in ice trays and
freeze, or freeze in a mold.

550. Kirsch or Rum Sherbet I   *Sorbet au kirsch ou au rhum*
(*for ice-cream freezer*)

2 cups water	¼ cup lemon juice
1 cup sugar	½ cup kirsch or rum

Boil water and sugar for 5 minutes. Add lemon juice. Strain
and cool. Pour into container and place in ice-cream freezer.
Surround with 1 part salt to 4 parts chopped ice. Turn for
8 minutes. Remove cover and pour in kirsch or rum. Continue turning the crank until the ice is stiff. Keep in freezer
until ready to serve.

Contentement passe richesse.

551. Kirsch or Rum Sherbet II   *Sorbet au kirsch ou au rhum* (*for mechanical refrigerator*)

2 teaspoons gelatine soaked in	⅓ cup lemon juice
¼ cup cold water	2 egg whites
1 cup sugar	⅛ teaspoon salt
2 cups water	½ cup kirsch

Boil sugar and water 10 minutes. Add softened gelatine and when it has dissolved, remove from the fire. Add lemon juice and kirsch or rum. Freeze 1 hour in an ice tray. Remove to a chilled bowl and beat with a rotary beater until frothy. Add salt to egg whites. Beat stiff and fold into the other mixture. Return to ice tray and freeze until firm.

552. Bombe Glacée   *Bombe glacée*

2 cups sugar	*various flavors:*
1 cup water	1 tablespoon vanilla extract
6 egg yolks	1 tablespoon powdered coffee
1 quart heavy cream	2 tablespoons cocoa
	1½ tablespoons curaçao

Dissolve sugar in water. Beat egg yolks and combine mixtures. Cook in the top of a double boiler until the eggs thicken. Stir constantly. Remove and beat with a rotary beater 15 minutes. Fold in cream, beaten thick but not stiff, and add flavoring. Pour into a chilled melon mold and place in ice until frozen. It may be served this way or, if preferred, a large scoop may be taken from the center and refilled with sherbet. The extra cream may be spread on the top of the mold. This must then be refrozen until firm. Unmold on dessert platter just before serving.

It is good for the lady of the household to know how to make good pastry—or, at least, to be able to teach others how to make it. In France, the privilege of making tarts and cakes is reserved for the young ladies of the household. These young ladies are well aware of the good effect it makes when it is announced that the beautiful cake appearing on the table has been prepared by them. It indicates an interest in domestic life.

TANTE MARIE

GOOD PASTRY-MAKING is an art that can be acquired with practice. French pastry, famous for flavor and texture, uses only the best materials. This means good bread flour and sweet butter. But sweet butter is comparatively rare and expensive, so that substitutes are often necessary. Salted butter may be washed and used with good results, or vegetable shortening with butter may be used. The necessary utensils are a large smooth rolling pin, a smooth surface—preferably a marble or wooden slab—a pastry wheel, and a variety of pie plates, squares or rings, and a cookie sheet. The following 5 recipes are basic in the art of French pastry.

236

553. Pie Pastry   *Pâte brisée*

2 cups flour	½ teaspoon salt
9 tablespoons butter (generous ½ cup)	7 tablespoons cold water (scant ½ cup)

Place the flour in a bowl or in a heap on a pastry board. Make a depression in the middle of the flour. Wash the butter by holding it under running water or in a large bowl of water and squeezing it between the hands for 3 to 4 minutes. Place the butter, water, and salt in the center and, without disturbing the flour, blend these ingredients by working them with the finger tips. Gradually work in the flour until it is all one smooth mass of dough. Knead the dough 30 to 60 seconds. Better pastry is achieved if it is not handled too much. Set aside to rest for at least 15 minutes. Roll out to the desired thickness.

554. Sweet Pastry   *Pâte à tarte*

2 cups flour	⅓ cup sugar
6 tablespoons butter	½ teaspoon baking powder
1 unbeaten egg	scant ½ cup cold milk

Place flour in a mixing bowl. Wash the butter as in the preceding recipe. Place in the center of the flour and work in with finger tips until the flour and butter are blended. Add egg, sugar, baking powder, and milk. Work the dough quickly with your hands. As soon as the dough detaches itself from the sides of the bowl, stop working it and let it stand at least 15 minutes before rolling out.

555. Puff Paste   *Pâte feuilletée*

2 cups flour   1 scant cup cold water
1 teaspoon salt   1 cup washed butter

Place flour in a bowl or in a heap on a pastry board. Make a depression in the center. Place the salt and some of the water in the depression and work the dough with the ends of your fingers. Gradually add water, working the dough as quickly as possible. As soon as the dough is a soft ball, place it on a floured board and flatten it slightly with the palm of the hand. Let it stand 10 minutes. Wash the butter so that the excess salt and buttermilk is removed (see recipe 553). The butter should be soft and workable before combining it with the dough. Shape the butter so that it is approximately the same shape but half the circumference of the dough. Place it in the center of the dough. Flour the rolling pin and roll the dough into a strip three times as long as it is wide. It should be about 8 inches wide and ¼ inch thick in order to handle it easily. Use quick, deft strokes with the rolling pin and never roll over the edge of the pastry. Fold the strip in thirds, starting with the nearer end and folding it toward the center. Lap the further end over this so that a square is formed. Set the dough aside for 15 minutes. Turn the square around so that the square will be rolled transversally. Repeat the process of making a long strip and folding it in thirds and then letting it rest 15 minutes. This process should be repeated 3 to 5 times, alternating the direction of rolling every time. The more times it is rolled out the flakier the pastry. If possible, the pastry should be used immediately after the last rolling. Otherwise chill in the ice box until ready for use.

556. Pastry Custard   *Frangipane*

3 tablespoons flour
3 eggs
2 cups milk
⅓ cup sugar

1 teaspoon vanilla
½ cup finely ground almonds
    (optional)

Add flour to slightly beaten eggs. Stir in milk gradually. Add sugar and cook over simmering water in a double boiler, stirring constantly. When the custard thickens, remove from the stove and add vanilla. If the almonds are added, this becomes Almond Pastry Custard or *Frangipane aux amandes*.

557. Pie Shells

Two-crust pies: Cut the pastry dough in two, with one piece a little larger than the other. Roll out the larger half to ⅛-inch thickness. Use quick, deft strokes, rolling from the center out and taking care not to roll over the edges. Cut a circle 1½ inches larger than the pie plate. Line the plate with the pastry and trim even with the edge. Moisten the edge with cold water. Roll out and cut the top crust 1 inch larger than the circumference of the pie-plate rim. When the pie has been filled, place the top crust over the plate. Press the edges together firmly with a fork. Trim the edges or fold the margin under the bottom crust.

One-crust pie or tart: Roll out the pastry to ⅛-inch thickness and cut 1½ inches larger than the pie plate. Line the plate with the pastry. Fold the extra margin under so that the pastry is ½ inch above the rim. Flute the edges with thumb and forefinger. Prick the bottom with a fork. If a juicy filling is to be used, paint the crust with unbeaten egg white. There are various methods of keeping the crust in shape if it is to be baked before filling. A second pie plate may be placed over the first during the baking, or the crust may be lined with brown paper or heavy stationery paper and then filled with dried peas or beans or with flour. Bake the shell 15 to 20 minutes in 450°F. oven or until light brown.

Crust for tarts: French tarts have one crust with narrow, straight sides, measuring ½ to ¾ inch. They are served without benefit of pie plate. They are baked with a pie ring or square, which is placed on a moistened cookie sheet. Roll the crust out ⅛ inch thick. Cut 1 inch larger than the ring or square. Lay the pastry over the rim. Press the sides to the ring allowing ½-inch margin above the rim. The edges may be fluted or left plain. Prick the pastry with a fork. The tart is then ready to be filled. If it is to be baked before filling, follow directions in the preceding paragraph.

To glaze tarts: French fruit tarts always glisten. This is achieved by painting the fruit, while it is still hot, with a fruit syrup. Heat ½ cup apricot jam or currant jelly with 1 tablespoon of water. As soon as the tart is baked, brush the top of the fruit with this hot syrup. These two condiments are best for glazing, because of their texture and because their flavor blends well with other fruits.

558. Apple Tart I   *Tarte aux pommes* I

Pie Pastry (553)   French Applesauce (503)

Prepare the pastry and line a pie plate or a ring with the crust
(see recipe 557). Fill the unbaked crust with the sauce and
bake in 375°F. oven 45 minutes. Little strips of pastry may
be placed on the sauce in decorative shapes. These should be
moistened before the tart is baked.

559. Apple Tart II   *Tarte aux pommes* II

Pie Pastry (553)   4 to 6 tart apples
French Applesauce (503)   apricot jam

Roll out the pastry ⅛ inch thick. Line a pie ring or square
with the pastry (557). Fill the tart half full with the sauce.
Peel and core the apples and slice very thin. Arrange the pieces
of apple in a spiral on top of the sauce. Make a little rosette of
apple in the center. Sprinkle with sugar and bake in 375°F.
oven for 45 minutes. When the tart is baked, glaze with apricot jam (557). Let the tart stand in the ring until it is cool.

560. English Apple Pie　　*Pudding aux pommes*

Pie Pastry (553) (for 8-inch pie)
6 to 8 tart apples
1 cup sugar
1 teaspoon cinnamon
¼ teaspoon powdered cloves
¼ teaspoon nutmeg
1 teaspoon grated lemon peel
2 tablespoons butter

Prepare the pastry. If a larger pie is desired, or if the cook is not practiced in the art of pie making, it is wise to make a double recipe of pie pastry. Line pie plate with pastry, following directions in recipe 557 for two-crust pies. Peel, core, and slice the apples very thin. Place the apples in the pie plate. Sprinkle with sugar, cinnamon, cloves, nutmeg, and lemon rind and dot with butter. Roll out the top crust and place over the apples, making sure that the edges are firmly pressed together. The pie should be hermetically sealed. Place the pie near the bottom of a 450°F. oven. Reduce the oven to 350°F. at the end of 10 minutes and move the pie to the middle of the oven and continue cooking 40 minutes. Serve hot. The left-over pie may be reheated with a sauce consisting of 3 tablespoons water, 1 tablespoon rum, and ⅓ cup sugar.

561. Apricot Tart　　*Tarte aux abricots*

Line a pie ring or plate with Pie Pastry (553). See recipe 557 for baking unfilled crust. When the shell is cool, remove from the ring or plate and fill with Apricot Compote (610).

562. Peach Tart　　*Tarte aux pêches*

Follow the preceding recipe substituting Peach Compote (613) for the filling.

563. Plum Tart   *Tarte aux prunes*

Prepare Pie Pastry (553) and line a pie ring or circle (557).
Fill the tart with a single closely packed layer of plums. If
Italian plums are used, stone and halve them and place in
tart, cavity side down. If greengage plums are used, stone
them but do not halve them. Sprinkle with ¾ to 1 cup sugar.
Bake 45 minutes in 375°F. oven. Immediately on taking the
tart from the oven, glaze the plums with currant jelly (557).

564. Cherry Tart I   *Tarte aux cerises* I

Prepare Pie Pastry (553). Line a pie ring or plate with the
pastry (557). Prick the crust with a fork. Fill the crust
with a Cherry Compote (612) or with canned cherries. Before
the cherry syrup is poured over the cherries it should be reduced to a thick syrup by boiling. Bake the tart 45 minutes in
375°F. oven.

565. Cherry Tart II   *Tarte aux cerises* II

Prepare Pie Pastry (553). Line pie square or ring or pie plate
with the pastry (557). Prick the bottom with a fork. Stone 1
pound of cherries. Line the cherries in rows, one tightly
pressed against the other, in the pastry shell. The cut side of
the cherry should be hidden. Sprinkle with 1 cup sugar and
bake 45 minutes in 375°F. oven. As soon as the tart is baked,
glaze with red currant jelly (557).

566. Pear Tart   *Tarte aux poires*

Prepare Pie Pastry (553). Line pie ring or plate. Prepare a Pear Compote (608) or use canned pears. Place the pears, cavity side down, in the shell. Reduce the pear syrup until it is quite thick. Spread over the pears and bake the tart 45 minutes in 375°F. oven. As soon as the tart is taken from the oven, glaze with apricot jam (557).

567. Strawberry Tart   *Tarte aux fraises*

Prepare Pie Pastry (553). Line a pie ring or square or a pie plate to make a shell. Follow directions in recipe 557 for baking the shell. When the shell is baked and cooled, fill with a closely packed layer of strawberries. Glaze with red currant jelly (557). Serve cold.

568. Alsatian Tart   *Tarte alsacienne*

Sweet Pastry (554)	1 teaspoon cinnamon
1 cup fruit (sliced apples, strawberries, peaches, or apricots)	½ cup sugar
	½ cup heavy cream
	1 egg

Prepare the pastry and line a pie circle or pie plate (557). Fill with a layer of fruit not too closely packed. Sprinkle with sugar and cinnamon. Bake 30 minutes in 375°F. oven. Beat the egg slightly and add cream. Pour over the fruit. Bake 10 minutes longer.

A merle soûl cerises sont amères.

569. Custard Tart *Tarte à la frangipane*

Line a pie circle or pie plate with Pie Pastry (553) or Sweet Pastry (554). Prick with a fork and fill with cooled Pastry Custard (556). Bake 20 to 25 minutes in 375°F. oven.

570. Rhubarb Tart *Tarte à la rhubarbe*

Pie Pastry (553)
3 cups unpeeled rhubarb cut in 2-inch pieces

$1\frac{1}{4}$ cups sugar
1 teaspoon grated lemon peel

Line a pie ring or square or pie plate with pastry (557). Prick the bottom and cover with a layer of closely packed pieces of rhubarb. Sprinkle with sugar and grated lemon peel. Bake 45 minutes in 375°F. oven.

571. Apple Tarts *Dartois aux pommes*

Puff Paste (555)
French Applesauce (503)
egg yolk mixed with 1 tablespoon water

currant jelly or apricot jam
powdered sugar

Prepare the flaky pastry. Roll the pastry as thin as possible. Cut the pastry into rectangles 3 by 4 inches. Divide the number of rectangles and on half of them spread a layer of applesauce, leaving a margin on all sides. Cover with 1 teaspoonful of currant jelly or apricot jam. Moisten the margins with water and place the remaining rectangles on the filled ones. Press the edges together firmly. Paint each tart with the egg yolk. Make several small slashes in the top layer, sprinkle with powdered sugar, and bake in 400°F. oven 30 minutes. The tarts may be eaten hot or cold. They are particularly delicious hot.

572. Cheese Tart   *Tarte au fromage*

Puff Paste (555)
1 tablespoon flour
4 tablespoons grated Swiss cheese
1 cup heavy cream

½ teaspoon salt
½ teaspoon sugar
4 tablespoons butter
¼ teaspoon nutmeg
4 egg whites

Prepare the pastry and roll out to ⅛-inch thickness. Line a buttered pie plate with pastry and follow recipe 557 for baking an unfilled crust. Remove from the oven and cool before filling. Mix flour, cheese, and cream. Add salt, sugar, butter, and nutmeg and stir over a low flame until the butter is melted. Cool and fold in stiffly beaten egg whites. Fill pastry shell and bake 15 minutes in 400°F. oven. Serve immediately.

573. Cinnamon Tart   *Tarte au canelle*

1 egg
1 cup sugar
¼ teaspoon salt
2 cups flour
2 teaspoons cinnamon

6 tablespoons butter or shortening
1½ cups French Applesauce (503)

Heap flour on a pastry board. Make a depression in the center and place in it the egg, sugar, salt, cinnamon, and butter that has been softened but not melted. Work the flour in gradually with your fingers and knead until the dough is smooth. Chill 1 hour. Roll out ⅛ inch thick and line a buttered pie plate. Trim the edge with a sharp knife. There should be an ⅛-inch margin. Fill with the applesauce. Cut the remaining dough into long strips and cross them over the sauce to form a crust. The ends should be pressed to the lower crust. Bake 30 minutes in 400°F. oven.

574. Four-Part Cake   *Quatre-quarts*

This cake is so named because the traditional method of making it is to weigh the eggs and use equal weights of flour, butter, and sugar.

4 large eggs
1½ cups sugar
1¼ cups softened butter
1 tablespoon lemon juice

2⅓ cups cake flour
¼ cup finely chopped almonds
  (optional)

Separate the yolks from the whites. Beat the yolks slightly and add sugar and butter, beating constantly until the mixture is smooth. Add lemon juice and flour and continue stirring until well blended. Fold in stiffly beaten egg whites. Pour into large round, buttered cake pan, filling it only half full because the cake will rise very high. Bake 1 hour in 350°F. oven.

If desired, blanch ¼ cup of almonds by dropping them into boiling water and then removing the skins, chop finely, and sprinkle over the cake before baking.

247

575. Cream-Puff Pastry   *Pâte aux choux*

1 cup water
½ cup butter
1 cup flour

1 teaspoon sugar
¼ teaspoon salt
4 eggs

Bring water and butter to a boil. Add flour, mixed with sugar and salt. Stir vigorously until the mixture is quite dry—approximately 3 minutes. Remove from the flame and add unbeaten eggs, one by one, beating hard after each addition. The resulting paste should be smooth.

576. Tea Puffs   *Choux sans crème*

Follow the preceding recipe for making Cream-Puff Pastry. Drop small balls of the mixture from the end of a teaspoon or from a pastry tube on a buttered and lightly floured cookie sheet, leaving ½ inch between each ball. Brush with egg yolk mixed with a little water. Let them stand 20 minutes. Bake 30 minutes in 375°F. oven or until they are a delicate brown. Sprinkle with powdered sugar and finely chopped almonds and put back in the oven until the sugar has melted.

577. Cream Puffs   *Choux à la crème*

Drop small or large balls of Cream-Puff Pastry (575) on a buttered and lightly floured cookie sheet. Bake 30 to 45 minutes in 375°F. oven until a delicate brown and until there is no moisture on the outside of the puffs. Remove from the oven and cool. Make a small hole in the bottom of each puff and force Sweet Whipped Cream (523) through a pastry tube into the puff. This leaves the top unblemished. The small puffs make an attractive tea cake. The larger ones are used for dessert.

578. Profiteroles with Chocolate Sauce
Profiteroles au chocolat

Prepare small cream puffs according to directions in the preceding recipe. The little cream puffs may be filled with Sweet Whipped Cream (523) or with Pastry Custard (556). Pile the cream puffs in a pyramid on a dessert platter and cover with the following Chocolate Sauce:

1½ cups sugar	1 cup heavy cream
2 tablespoons butter	1 teaspoon vanilla (or 2 teaspoons cognac)
4 1-oz. squares of baking chocolate	

Combine sugar, butter, and chocolate in the top of a double boiler. When the chocolate is melted, add cream and flavoring. Serve hot.

Qui veut bien se porter demeure sur son appétit.

579. Saint-Honoré Birthday Cake   *Gâteau Saint-Honoré*

double recipe Cream-Puff	⅓ cup water
Pastry (575)	Sweet Whipped Cream (523)
¾ cup sugar	candied fruits

Butter and lightly flour 2 large cookie sheets. Fill a large pastry tube, fitted with a wide-mouthed dispenser, with the pastry. Describe a large circle—the size of a large saucepan cover—on one cookie sheet by forcing the pastry through the tube. The circle should be approximately 1 inch thick. Using the same pastry tube, drop about 20 small balls on the other cookie sheet. Place both sheets in 375°F. oven and bake until both the circle and small puffs are delicate brown and free of any moisture on the outside. The circle should take 5 to 10 minutes longer than the small puffs. Meanwhile, boil the sugar and water until the syrup reaches a temperature of 238°F. or until it will form a soft ball when put in cold water. When the puffs are baked, dip each one in the syrup and place on a lightly oiled surface to cool. When the puffs and ring are cool, attach the puffs to the ring using a little hot syrup to make them stick. Fill the center of the ring with the cream and decorate with candied fruits. Place a birthday candle in each small puff.

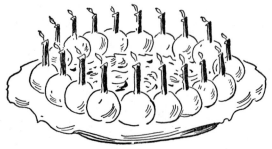

580. Brioche   *Brioche*

The famous French brioche requires time and patience. It should be started the day before it is to be used. It cannot be hurried.

½ cup flour	3 large eggs
1 yeast cake dissolved in	1 cup softened butter
¼ cup water	1 teaspoon salt
1½ cups flour	1 tablespoon sugar

Dissolve the yeast in warm water and mix with ½ cup flour. Make a gash in the top of the mass and place in a bowl of warm water to make a sponge. This will double in size. Meanwhile work the unbeaten eggs into the rest of the flour. Add a little warm water if it is too dry to beat. It should be beaten 10 minutes. Hands are the best tool for this operation. Add butter, salt, and sugar and beat 5 minutes longer. Remove the yeast from the water and combine the mixtures, but do not mix it any longer than necessary. Cover and let it rise 3 to 4 hours or until doubled. Knead it down and place in a cool place overnight. It is ready for baking the next morning. The brioche dough should then be broken down gently so that it will remain light. It may be baked in a loaf, on a buttered cookie sheet, or in a buttered ring mold. Let the brioche rest in the pan 30 minutes before baking. Bake 30 to 35 minutes in 450°F. oven. Cover with buttered unglazed paper if the brioche browns too much. Test by inserting a needle in the cake. If it comes out dry, the cake is baked.

On ne peut manier le beurre qu'on ne se graisse les doigts.

⚜

581. Large Brioche   *Brioche à tête*

Follow the preceding recipe for making Brioche. Butter a
fluted mold carefully. Take ¾ of the dough and form into a
large ball which is placed in the mold. Make a smaller ball
of the remaining dough and place on the larger one. Let it
rest 30 minutes. Brush with egg yolk mixed with a little water.
Bake 30 minutes in 450°F. oven.

582. Small Brioches   *Les petites brioches*

Place small pats of brioche dough in well-buttered, fluted or
plain muffin tins. Place a tiny ball of the dough on each pat. Let
it rest 30 minutes. Brush with egg yolk mixed with a little water.
Bake 10 to 15 minutes in 450°F. oven.

583. Brioche Tarts in Madeira   *Croûtes au Madère*

Brioche (580)   1 jar Apricot Marmalade (627)

This is a good recipe for left-over brioche dough and it is
really worthwhile saving out a little of the dough expressly
for this dessert.

Roll out the brioche dough to ⅛-inch thickness. Cut into
small diamond-shaped tarts. Melt 4 tablespoons good butter
and, when it is sizzling hot, fry the tarts until golden brown.
Cover each tart with a thin layer of Apricot Marmalade (627).
Place these tarts in a ring around the edge of an oven-proof
platter. Make a sauce by adding ¼ cup of water and ¼ cup
Madeira wine to the rest of the jar of marmalade and heating.
Stir until the sauce is smooth. Pour in the center and place the
platter in the oven for a few moments before serving.

584. Croissants *Croissants*

This recipe does not appear in the original TANTE MARIE since croissants are almost never baked at home in France. It is quite possible to make these rolls at home, however. [C. T.]

1 cup scalded skimmed milk (scant)	¼ cup warm water
	2½ to 3 cups flour
1 tablespoon butter	1 cup butter
1 teaspoon salt	1 egg yolk, mixed with
1½ tablespoons sugar	2 tablespoons milk
1 yeast cake, dissolved in	

Place butter, salt, and sugar in a bowl. Pour the scalded milk over it and cool to lukewarm. Add the dissolved yeast cake and stir a moment. Care must be taken that the milk is comfortable to touch but not cool. Add the flour and knead thoroughly. The dough should be smooth and elastic. Cover the bowl and let the dough rise in a warm place until doubled in size. Knead it a moment and chill several hours in the ice box. Wash the butter (553). Roll out the chilled dough into a strip 3 times as long as its width. Spread the butter over the dough and fold the ends of the strip in toward the center to form a three-tiered square. Turn the square side for end and roll it out transversally. Fold in the ends to form a three-tiered square and place in the refrigerator for 30 minutes. Repeat this process at intervals of 30 minutes twice more, and the final time, keep the dough in the refrigerator 1 hour. It is then ready for shaping.

Roll the dough out to ¼-inch thickness. Cut into 4-inch squares. Divide each square into 2 triangles. Beginning with the wide base, roll each triangle toward the point so that the pointed end will be in the center. Shape into crescents and place on unbuttered cookie sheet. Brush with egg yolk and bake 15 minutes in 375°F. oven. If the croissants are not to be baked immediately, return to the refrigerator.

585. Rum Baba   *Baba au rhum*

1 cup flour	⅓ cup raisins
½ yeast cake	¼ cup chopped citron
6 tablespoons warm milk	¼ cup currants
2 eggs	small pinch of saffron
1 teaspoon sugar	*syrup:*
¼ teaspoon salt	½ cup sugar
¼ cup butter	4 tablespoons water
⅓ cup sugar	2 tablespoons rum

Dissolve yeast cake in milk and add to the flour. Add unbeaten eggs and beat the dough 3 minutes. Hands are the best tools for this operation. Cover and let the dough rise until doubled. Add sugar, salt, and butter which has been softened but not melted. Beat vigorously for 5 minutes. Mix in the remaining ingredients, place the dough in a buttered angel-cake tin, and cover with a cloth. Let the dough rise until doubled. Bake 1 hour in 375°F. oven.

If the baba does not come out of the pan easily, wrap the pan completely in dish towels so that no steam may escape. At the end of 6 to 8 minutes the cake will slip out easily. Meanwhile prepare the syrup by boiling the sugar and water gently for 10 minutes and then adding the rum. Cool a little before pouring carefully over the baba and letting it permeate the cake. Serve hot or cold.

586. Small Rum Babas   *Les petits babas au rhum*

Follow the preceding recipe for making the baba dough. Fill small buttered muffin or brioche tins half full with the dough. Let them rise until doubled and bake 10 to 12 minutes in 400°F. oven. Dip in rum syrup. Serve hot or cold. These may

be garnished with Sweet Whipped Cream (523) flavored with
a little rum.

587. Savarin Cake   *Savarin*

1 cup flour
½ yeast cake dissolved in
6 tablespoons warm milk
2 eggs
1 teaspoon sugar
½ teaspoon salt
¼ cup butter

¼ cup finely chopped almonds
¼ cup sugar
2 tablespoons water
1 tablespoon rum
whole almonds and candied
    cherries

Warm the mixing bowl for a moment in the oven before
using. Sift the flour into the bowl and make a well in the
center of it. Add the yeast cake dissolved in warm milk and
the unbeaten eggs and beat with your hands for 3 minutes.
Cover the bowl and let the dough rise ¾ hour or until doubled
in size. Knead down and add the sugar, salt, and butter that
has been softened but not melted. Beat this mixture for 4 to 5
minutes. Butter an angel-cake tin or a ring mold, dust with the
finely chopped almonds, which have been blanched (514),
and fill a little less than half full with the dough. Cover and
let it rise until it reaches the top of the pan. Bake 20 minutes
in 450°F. oven. Cover with a piece of buttered paper if it gets
too brown. Meanwhile boil sugar and water for 10 minutes.
Add rum and cool to lukewarm. As soon as the cake is baked,
run a sharp knife around the sides and unmold. Spoon the
syrup over the cake and decorate with almonds and candied
cherries.

Il faut casser le noyau pour avoir l'amande.

588. Galette (Household Pastry Cake)   *Galette de ménage*

2 cups flour
¾ cup butter or shortening
½ cup warm milk
1 tablespoon sugar

½ teaspoon salt
1 egg yolk mixed with
1 tablespoon water

Heap the flour on a pastry board. Make a well in the center and place in it the sugar, salt, milk, and butter that has been softened but not melted. Work the flour into the liquid with the finger tips until a smooth ball has been formed. Let it rest 45 minutes before rolling it out to ½-inch thickness. With a sharp, pointed knife, trace vertical and horizontal lines over the cake so that it is covered with a pattern of squares or rectangles. Do not cut through the pastry. Place on a buttered and floured cookie sheet and brush with egg yolk. Bake 30 minutes in 450°F. oven.

589. Tea Tarts   *Petites galettes pour le thé*

Follow the preceding recipe. When the pastry has been rolled, cut out little tarts with a round cookie cutter. Brush each tart with the egg yolk mixture and place on greased and floured cookie sheet. Bake 20 minutes in 450°F. oven.

590. Cheese Sticks   *Allumettes au fromage*

2 cups flour
½ pound grated gruyère cheese
¾ cup butter or shortening
½ cup cold water

1 teaspoon salt
¼ cup grated gruyère
1 egg yolk mixed with
1 tablespoon water

Combine flour, cheese, butter, water, and salt to make a smooth mass. The butter or shortening should be soft and workable before adding to the flour. Roll into a strip 3 times as long as its width. Lap the ends over each other toward the center to form a three-tiered square. Turn the square side for end and roll out transversally. Sprinkle with cheese, fold into a square, and let it rest 15 minutes. Repeat this process twice at 15-minute intervals. After a final 15-minute rest, roll out the pastry 1/8 inch thick. Cut into strips 3 inches long and 3/4 inch wide. Brush with egg yolk and sprinkle with grated cheese. Bake 6 to 8 minutes in 450°F. oven.

591. Plain Tea Cakes   *Gâteaux secs*

2 cups flour	1/2 cup butter, cut in little
3/4 cup sugar	pieces
	1/2 cup milk

Combine the ingredients and knead until a smooth ball of dough has been formed. Roll out very thin on a floured board. Cut out little circles with a cookie cutter or small glass. Place on buttered cookie sheet and bake 15 minutes in 350°F. oven.

592. Madeleines   *Gâteaux de madeleine*

These traditional tea cakes are cooked in special cookie tins shaped like small scallop shells.

Follow recipe 574 for Four-Part Cake, only add the egg whites without beating them. (One half of the recipe will make 24 cakes.) Fill well-buttered madeleine tins with the batter and cook in 325°F. oven 25 minutes.

Chacun le sien n'est pas trop.

593. Strasbourg Galette   *Galette strasbourgeoise*

2 cups flour
1 cup milk
2 tablespoons butter
¼ cup sugar

¼ cup seeded raisins
½ yeast cake dissolved in
¼ cup warm milk

Heat the milk and butter until the butter is melted. Combine with flour and, when it is well mixed, add sugar, raisins, and dissolved yeast cake. Beat the mixture with your hands for several minutes. The dough should be quite liquid. Place in a deep, buttered cake tin and let it rise 2 hours. Cook ½ hour in 450°F. oven.

594. Almond Tea Cakes   *Gâteaux nantais*

4 cups flour
1¼ cups powdered sugar
½ cup butter
¾ cup almonds

grated rind of ½ lemon
4 eggs, unbeaten
¼ cup almonds

Blanch ¾ cup almonds by dropping them into boiling water and then removing the skins. Force them through a food chopper, using the finest blade. Combine with flour, sugar, butter which has been softened but not melted, lemon rind, and eggs. Mix well until a stiff dough has been formed. Roll out to ⅛-inch thickness and cut into rounds with a small cookie cutter. Sprinkle with granulated sugar and chopped or shredded almonds. Bake in 350°F. oven until pale brown—approximately 10 minutes.

595. Sponge Cake   *Biscuit de Savoie*

4 eggs
1 cup sugar

grated rind of ½ lemon
¾ cup flour

Separate the yolks from the whites. Beat the yolks until lemon-colored and gradually add sugar. Add lemon rind and continue beating until the mixture is foamy and very pale. Stir in flour and, when thoroughly blended, fold in stiffly beaten egg whites. Butter a plain or tubular cake pan and sprinkle with sugar. Place in the oven a moment before filling half full with batter. Bake 1 hour in 325°F. oven. The cake will double in size. When the cake is golden brown and firm to the touch, it is baked. Remove and let it cool before removing from the pan.

596. Lady Fingers   *Biscuits à la cuiller*

Follow the preceding recipe. Put the batter in a large pastry bag fitted with a large, plain pastry tube. Force the batter through the tube onto a buttered and floured cookie sheet or one lined with buttered, unglazed paper, forming strips 3 inches long and ½ inch wide. Sprinkle evenly with powdered sugar and bake 15 minutes in 325°F. oven.

597. Rum Cake   *Gâteau au rhum*

Sponge Cake (595)	¼ cup rum
Apricot Marmalade (627)	2 teaspoons cornstarch dissolved in a little cold water
1 cup water	candied fruits
1½ cups sugar	

Cut the cake horizontally to make 3 layers. Spread the 2 bottom layers with marmalade. Boil water and sugar together for 10 minutes and add rum. Cool to lukewarm. Spoon the syrup over the 3 layers so that the cake is well permeated. Place one layer on top of the other. Add cornstarch to the remaining syrup and spread over the cake. When this has cooled, decorate with candied fruits.

598. Pithiviers Cake   *Gâteau de Pithiviers*

Puff Pastry (555)   1 egg yolk mixed with
Pastry Custard (556)   1 tablespoon water

Prepare the pastry and divide in 2 parts. Roll out each part
to ¼-inch thickness. Using a saucepan cover as a form, cut
out 2 equal circles and moisten them both with water. Spread
one circle with the custard, which has been prepared in advance. Leave a small margin. Place the other circle, moistened
side down, on the first circle, and press the edges together
firmly. Make several decorative incisions in the top circle and
place on a moistened cookie sheet. Bake 45 minutes in 350°F.
oven.

599. Marzipan Cakes   *Massepains*

½ pound almonds   grated rind of ½ lemon
2 egg whites   2¼ cups powdered sugar

Soak almonds in hot water for 15 minutes. After removing the
skins, chop fine or force through a meat chopper, using the
finest blade. Place the almonds in a mortar or, lacking that,
in a wooden bowl. With a pestle or potato masher grind the
almonds, adding the unbeaten egg whites very gradually. When
the egg whites have been absorbed, mix in the lemon rind and
sugar. Roll tiny balls of this dough between your hands and
place on oiled, unglazed paper. Flatten each ball with a
moistened finger. Let them stand 5 hours before baking. Place
the paper on a cookie sheet and bake 15 minutes in 250°F.
oven.

600. Tea Kisses   *Petits fours au blanc d'œuf*

2 egg whites   grated rind of ½ lemon
½ cup sugar

Beat egg whites very stiff. Add sugar and lemon rind gradually and continue beating until the batter is quite stiff. Drop the mixture from the end of a teaspoon on a cookie sheet lined with oiled, unglazed paper. Bake 50 minutes in 250°F. oven. The mixture may be forced through a pastry bag fitted with a decorative tube. This makes a more attractive *petit four* and can be kept well in a tightly covered container.

601. Nougat Tart   *Nougat*

½ pound almonds   Sweet Whipped Cream (523)
1 cup sugar

Blanch (594), peel, and chop the almonds. Place in a moderate oven so they will be hot before adding to the sugar. Melt sugar in a heavy frying pan. When the sugar has melted, add nuts and remove from the stove. Have a well-oiled cake tin ready. Place some of the mixture in the pan. Press it out with a lemon. The mixture is so sticky that a knife or spatula is not satisfactory. It is necessary to work quickly because the nougat becomes brittle. If it becomes too brittle it may be reheated. Line the sides of the cake tin with a thin layer. When it is cold, remove from the mold and fill with cream.

602. Meringues   *Meringues*

4 egg whites   Sweet Whipped Cream (523)
1 cup sugar

Beat the egg whites until very stiff. Sift the sugar and add gradually, beating continually. Drop from the end of a teaspoon onto a cookie sheet, lined with unglazed paper. Sprinkle with sugar and bake 50 minutes in 250°F. oven. When they are cool, stick the bottoms of 2 meringues together with the cream.

603. Russian Rhubarb Cake   *Crakinoskis à la rhubarbe*

4 large eggs
1¼ cups softened butter
1½ cups sugar
2⅓ cups cake flour
1 tablespoon lemon juice

½ teaspoon cinnamon
dash of nutmeg
2 cups diced rhubarb
sugar

Mix all the ingredients except the rhubarb and beat vigorously until smooth. Roll out the dough on a floured board to ⅛-inch thickness. Cut with a large, round cookie cutter. Line individual molds or large muffin tins with the dough. Fill with diced rhubarb and sprinkle generously with sugar. Bake 45 minutes in 400°F. oven.

604. Plum Cake   *Plum-cake*

¾ cup sugar
¾ cup softened butter
1 cup seeded raisins, chopped
½ cup currants
½ cup mixed candied fruits, chopped

4 eggs
2¾ cups flour
2 teaspoons baking powder
2 tablespoons rum

Cream sugar and butter and beat with a wooden spoon until the mixture is very smooth. Add the fruit and add the eggs one by one, beating vigorously after each addition. Combine flour and baking powder and fold into the batter. Add rum. Beat the dough 20 minutes. Line a mold or bread tin with wax paper. Fill ¾ full with the batter and bake 45 to 50 minutes in 375°F. oven.

Dans les petits sacs sont les fines épices.

605. Steam Cake   *Dampfnoudel*

½ cup butter or shortening
¾ cup milk
1 yeast cake dissolved in
¼ cup warm milk
3 tablespoons sugar
1 teaspoon salt

4 egg yolks
4 cups flour
1½ cups scalded milk
¼ cup sugar
cinnamon and sugar

Melt butter in warm milk and, when it is cooled to lukewarm, add yeast cake dissolved in milk. Add sugar, salt, and egg yolks. Stir until the sugar is dissolved. Add flour and stir until the dough is smooth. Shape into a long roll. Cut in ¾-inch slices and place in a buttered pan. Cover and let them rise until doubled. Bake 20 minutes in 350°F. oven. Meanwhile scald milk and dissolve sugar in the milk. As soon as the cake is light brown, pour the hot milk over it. The milk will be quickly absorbed and the cake will rise very high. Sprinkle with sugar and cinnamon and serve.

606. Sand Tarts   *Pâte sablée*

2 cups flour
1 egg
1 cup sugar
¼ teaspoon salt

½ teaspoon cinnamon
6 tablespoons butter or shortening

Heap the flour on a pastry board and make a depression in the center. Place the egg, sugar, salt, cinnamon, and softened butter in the center and work in the flour. Knead the dough until it is very smooth. Chill the dough 1 hour. Roll out very thin and cut into various shapes with cookie cutters. Place the tarts on a buttered cookie sheet and bake 10 to 12 minutes in 350°F. oven.

607. Apple Compote *Compote de pommes*

8 or 10 cooking apples
⅔ cup sugar
1 cup water

½ teaspoon grated lemon peel
currant jelly (optional)

Peel, core, and quarter the apples. Heat sugar and water until the sugar is dissolved and place the apples and lemon peel in the syrup. Simmer until the fruit is soft. It is important not to overcook the fruit, which should keep its form. Place the apples in a dessert bowl. Increase the heat and boil the syrup down until it has a thick consistency. Pour the syrup over the fruit and cool. Little dots of currant jelly may be used as a garnish.

608. Pear Compote *Compote de poires*

7 or 8 medium-sized pears (or
    12 Seckel pears)
⅔ cup sugar

1 cup water
juice of ½ lemon

Peel the pears but leave the stems on. As soon as the pears are peeled, place them in cold water so that they will not turn brown. Heat sugar and water until the sugar is dissolved. Add lemon juice. Allow the fruit to simmer until it is tender. Do not let it get mushy. Stand the pears upright in a dessert bowl; if necessary, slice a little off the bottom so that they will stand erect. Boil the syrup down until it is thick, and pour it over the pears.

609. Pears in Red Wine   *Compote de poires au vin rouge*

Follow recipe 608. Just before removing the pears from the syrup, add ½ cup red wine. Substitute ½ teaspoon of cinnamon for the lemon juice.

610. Apricot Compote   *Compote d'abricots*

12 apricots   1 cup water
⅔ cup sugar

Wash and stone the apricots. The apricots may be left whole or split in two. Heat the sugar and water until the sugar has dissolved, then simmer the apricots in the syrup 15 minutes. Remove the apricots and place in a dessert bowl. Boil the syrup down until quite thick. Pour over the apricots and cool.

611. Plum Compote   *Compote de prunes*

1 pound Italian or greengage   ⅔ cup sugar
    plums   1 cup water

Boil sugar and water for 30 seconds. Simmer the plums, which have been carefully washed, 8 to 10 minutes. Remove the plums and boil down the syrup until thick. Pour over the plums and cool.

612. Cherry Compote   *Compote de cerises*

Follow the preceding recipe, but allow the cherries to simmer 5 minutes only.

613. Peach Compote   *Compote de pêches*

Follow directions in recipe 610.

614. Currant Jelly   *Gelée de groseilles*

2 quarts currants   ½ cup water
sugar

Wash and drain the currants. It is best to have at least ⅓ of the currants white. Mash a few in the bottom of a heavy saucepan. Add the water and place over a moderate flame. Continue to add the currants, mashing them as they are added. When the currants have all turned white, drain them through a strainer and then allow the juice to drip through a jelly bag or double thickness of cheesecloth. To insure clear jelly, do not squeeze the bag. Measure the juice and bring it to a boil. Add an equal number of cups of sugar. Stir over low heat until the sugar is completely dissolved. Pour into clean, hot jelly glasses and cool. Cover with paraffin and store in a cool, dry place.

615. Apple Jelly   *Gelée de pommes*

Crabapples or any tart apples make excellent jelly. Wash the apples thoroughly. Remove the stems and blossom ends. Cut in quarters and remove the core. Place in a large kettle and add enough water so that the apples are floating. Boil until the apples are soft. Place a coarse sieve over an earthenware bowl and mash the apples through it. Do not press the apples too hard, because that will make the jelly cloudy. Place the sieved apples in a jelly bag or in a double thickness of cheesecloth. Let the juice drip into a bowl. Do not try to hurry it by squeezing the bag. Measure the juice and allow ¾ cup of sugar for every cup of juice. Boil the sugar and juice until it forms a coating on a spoon. Stir every few minutes. Place a sliver of lemon peel in the bottom of clean, hot jelly glasses. Pour the jelly into the glasses and let it stand 2 days before covering with paraffin. Store in cool, dry place.

616. Quince Jelly   *Gelée de coings*

Follow the preceding recipe, substituting quinces for the apples. Instead of putting lemon peel in the glasses, add a little vanilla along with the sugar. Allow ¼ teaspoon vanilla to ¾ cup sugar.

617. Currant and Raspberry Jelly
Gelée de framboises et de groseilles

Follow recipe 614, using half currants and half raspberries.

618. Household Jam   *Confiture de ménage*

plums	apricots
peaches	sugar

Wash the fruit and remove the stones. Weigh the fruit and add half its weight in sugar. Bring slowly to a boil. Stir frequently. Continue boiling gently until the fruit falls in a lump from the spoon and is brilliant in color. This will take approximately 45 minutes. Pour into hot, clean glasses or jars and let it stand 2 days before covering with paraffin. Store in a cool, dry place.

619. Barberry Jelly   *Gelée d'épine-vinette*

Pick the berries over very carefully so that no leaves or thorns are mixed in. Place in a saucepan and add enough water so that the berries are floating. Boil slowly 30 minutes. Remove from the fire. Crush the berries with a wooden spoon and drain through a strainer. Measure the juice and add an equal amount of sugar. Boil gently until it becomes frothy. Skim and pour into hot clean glasses and let it stand 2 days before covering with paraffin. Store in a cool, dry place.

620. Cherry Jam   *Confitures de cerises*

1 quart currants   sugar
2 quarts cherries

Extract the juice from the currants (614). Remove the stems and stones from the cherries. Measure the juice and cherries together. For every cup of combined juice and cherries add ¾ cup sugar. Boil the sugar and fruit 30 minutes. Skim and pour into clean, hot jars or glasses. Let it stand 2 days before covering with paraffin. Store in cool, dry place.

621. Four-Fruit Jelly   *Gelée de quatre-fruits*

2 cups raspberries   2 cups strawberries
2 cups cherries   sugar
2 cups currants

Wash the fruit. Remove the stones from the cherries. Pick over the currants and raspberries and hull the strawberries. Crush the fruit in the bottom of a heavy saucepan. Heat over a low flame until the juice is extracted. Be careful not to let the fruit stick to the pan. Place the fruit in a jelly bag or in a double thickness of cheesecloth and allow the juice to drip into an earthenware bowl. For every cup of juice measure ¾ cup of sugar. Boil sugar and juice 30 minutes. Pour into clean, hot glasses and let it stand 2 days before covering with paraffin.

622. Strawberry Jam   *Confitures de fraises*

strawberries   water
sugar

Wash and hull the strawberries. Weigh the berries. Weigh an equal amount of sugar. For every pound of sugar allow 1 cup of water. Bring water and sugar to a full boil. Add the strawberries and boil 2 minutes. Remove the strawberries with a skimmer and place in clean, hot jars. Each jar should be half filled. Boil down the syrup until quite thick and pour over the fruit, filling the jar almost to the top. Let it stand 2 days before covering with paraffin.

623. Grape Jam   *Confitures de raisins*

grapes   water
sugar

Remove the stems and seeds from very ripe grapes. Tante Marie suggests a goose feather to remove the seeds; a toothpick will do. Weigh the grapes. Measure half the weight in sugar. Add ½ cup water for every cup of sugar. Boil the sugar and water. Add the grapes and boil 2 minutes. Remove the grapes with a skimmer and place in hot, clean jars, filling them half full. Boil down the syrup until thick and pour over the fruit. Fill the jars almost to the top. Let the jars stand uncovered for 2 days before covering them with paraffin.

624. Apricot Jam   *Confitures d'abricots*

apricots   water
sugar

Wash the apricots and cut in two. Remove the stones but do not throw them away. Weigh the apricots and weigh an equal amount of sugar. Add ½ cup of water to every cup of sugar. Bring the sugar and water to a boil and add apricots. Boil 30 minutes. Remove the apricots with a skimmer and place in clean, hot jars. Boil down the syrup until thick and pour over the fruit. Break the shells of the stones and extract the nuts. Soak them in hot water to remove the skins. Divide each nut in half and place 4 or 5 halves in each jar. Let it stand uncovered for 2 days before covering with paraffin.

625. Peach Jam   *Confitures de pêches*

peaches   water
sugar

Place the peaches in boiling water for 30 seconds and then in cold water. This will make it easy to remove the skin. Halve and stone the peaches. Proceed as in recipe 624.

626. Apple Marmalade   *Marmelade de pommes*

Follow directions for French Applesauce (503). Pour the hot sauce into clean, hot jars and cool before covering with paraffin.

627. Apricot Marmalade   *Marmelade d'abricots*

apricots   sugar

Peel and stone the apricots. Measure the fruit. For every cup of fruit use ¾ cup of sugar. Let the apricots and sugar stand in an earthenware bowl for 24 hours. Cook gently until the fruit becomes brilliant. Test by placing a little on a cold plate. If it jells in a moment or two, it is ready. Stir often to prevent burning. The marmalade should be cooked in 30 or 40 minutes. Pour into hot, clean jars. Use the stones as in Apricot Jam (624). Let it stand until cooled. Cover with paraffin.

628. Greengage Marmalade
Marmelade de prunes de reine-Claude

greengage plums   water
sugar

This marmalade is made like Apricot Marmalade (627). Do not peel the plums and do not use the stones.

629. Plum Marmalade *Marmelade de prunes*

plums   sugar

This marmalade is made like Apricot Marmalade (627). Do not peel the plums and do not use the stones.

630. Bar-le-Duc *Confitures de groseilles de Bar*

Wash the currants. Remove the seeds carefully with a toothpick or goose feather. Do not break the skin of the berry. Weigh the fruit. For every pound of fruit measure 1½ pounds of sugar. For every pound of sugar allow 1 cup of water. Boil the sugar and water until it registers 250°F. or until it reaches the *hard-ball stage* (see recipe 635). Skim the syrup and add the currants. Boil 2 minutes and pour into clean, hot, porcelain jars. Keep forcing the berries down into the syrup until they no longer float on top. Do not try to make too much of this at one time. It takes care to make it, but the result is delicious.

631. Melon Rind Jam   *Confitures d'écorce de melon*

Peel thick slices of melon rind and cut into 1-inch pieces.
Weigh equal amounts of sugar and melon rind. Add enough
water to keep the sugar from scorching and heat in a heavy
saucepan. Stir until the sugar is dissolved. Add 1 teaspoon of
lemon rind for every cup of sugar. Cook 2 hours over low
flame. Place in clean, hot jars and let it stand 2 days before
covering with paraffin.

632. Burgundy Jam   *Raisiné de Bourgogne*

dark blue or black grapes   pears

Wash and stem the grapes. Heat the grapes over a low flame
to extract the juice. Just before it reaches the boiling point,
remove from the fire and strain the juice through a strainer or
cheesecloth. Boil the juice down to half its original quantity.
Stir often. Peel, quarter, and core the pears. Simmer in the
grape juice until tender. Take care not to let the jam burn.
Pour into clean hot jars and let it stand 2 days before covering with paraffin.

633. Candied Quince Paste   *Pâte de coings*

Peel, quarter, and core ripe quinces. As the quinces are prepared, place in cold water so that they will not darken. Cover
with cold water and boil until they are soft. Put in a strainer
placed over a bowl. Use the juice to make Quince Jelly (616).
Weigh the drained quince and weigh an equal amount of
powdered sugar. Pound the sugar and fruit together with a
pestle or potato masher. Line the bottom of pie plates with
this mixture ⅛ inch thick. Let it stand 4 or 5 days before

cutting into narrow strips. The strips may be stored in a covered jar and used as a candy or garnish. It will remain good for a year.

634. Candied Apricot Paste *Pâte d'abricots*

Follow the directions in the preceding recipe substituting apricots for the quinces. Spread the paste ¼ inch thick. When it is dry cut into narrow strips. Each layer should be separated by a piece of wax paper and it should be stored in a dry place.

635. Sugar Testing

A thermometer is very useful in candy making. However, sugar can be tested by putting a little of the hot sugar syrup into cold water and testing the sugar between the thumb and finger. Candy and syrup recipes call for different stages of consistency. The following table is helpful in determining these stages.

238°F.	thread stage	*le filet*
240°F.	soft ball	*petit boulet*
244°F.-250°F.	medium ball	*boulet*
270°F.-290°F.	hard ball	*grand boulet*
290°F.-310°F.	brittle	*grand cassé*

636. Fondant

3 cups sugar   1 cup water

Boil the sugar and water to the soft-ball stage or approximately 240°F. Wash down the sides of the pan with a wet pastry brush to prevent the sugar from sticking. When the sugar has reached the proper stage, pour onto a well-oiled enamel table top or marble slab. Let the syrup cool. Work the syrup with a broad spatula, turning in the edges toward the center. The syrup will become creamy and white. The fondant may be flavored with almond or peppermint oil. It may be used as a coating for strawberries or cherries or may be colored and shaped into little candies. It may also be placed in a covered jar and stored until needed.

637. Pralines

3 cups sugar	1 pound almonds, hazel nuts, or
½ cup water	pistachio nuts

Blanch the nuts in boiling water for 2 minutes. Place in cool water and peel. Boil sugar and water until it registers between 244°F. and 250°F.—the medium-ball stage. Add nuts and cook 3 minutes. Pour on well-oiled marble slab or enamel top table. Cool before breaking into pieces.

638. Caramels   *Bonbons au caramel*

1¼ cup sugar	1 cup heavy cream
½ cup light corn syrup	

Boil the ingredients in a heavy pan. Stir often and wash down the sides of the pan with a wet pastry brush to prevent crystallizing. Boil to the medium-ball stage (244°-50°F.) Pour into a well-oiled, square cake tin and cool. Cut into small squares with a sharp knife.

639. Chocolate Caramels   *Caramels mous au chocolat*

1¼ cups sugar	1 cup cream
½ cup light corn syrup	⅓ cup cocoa

Combine ingredients and follow instructions in preceding recipe.

640. Nougat   *Nougat*

½ pound almonds   1 cup sugar

Blanch almonds by dropping them into boiling water and then removing the skins. Melt sugar in a heavy frying pan. Add the almonds, which have been coarsely chopped. Stir for a moment and pour on a well-oiled marble slab or enamel-top table. Cool before breaking into pieces.

641. Chocolate Truffles   *Truffes au chocolat*

6 ounces chocolate   1 teaspoon vanilla
½ cup butter   cocoa
1 cup powdered confectioner's
    sugar

Melt the chocolate and butter in the top of a double boiler. Add sugar and stir until the sugar is well blended. Add vanilla and if the mixture is too dry add a little cream. It should be firm and moist enough to form into small balls. Roll the little balls in cocoa and place in individual candy papers.

642. Tea *Thé*

The secret of making good tea lies not only in the choice of tea but in the brewing of it. Allow 1 teaspoon of choice tea leaves for 3 teacups of water. Fill the teapot with hot water before making the tea. Pour out the water and put in the tea leaves. Pour fresh boiling water over the leaves. Serve with milk or light cream, lemon, or rum.

643. Coffee *Café*

Allow 1 generous tablespoon of freshly ground coffee for every coffee cup of water. Tante Marie recommends the 'drip method.' Pour 1½ cups boiling water through the coffee and when it has filtered through, add the rest of the water. Coffee should be made just before serving.

644. Café au lait *Café au lait*

Café au lait is made with coffee extract. It is not, as is generally supposed, ordinary coffee mixed with milk. To make the extract allow 2 tablespoons powdered coffee and 1 teaspoon chicory to 1 cup of water. Filter it as in making 'drip' coffee. The extract may be made in quantity and kept in a covered jar or bottle. Use 1 to 2 tablespoons of the hot extract with 1 cup of hot milk.

645. Hot Chocolate   *Chocolat*

3 1-oz. squares of cooking chocolate	6 cups milk, scalded
	6 to 8 tablespoons sugar

Melt the sugar and chocolate in the top of a double boiler. Add 2 cups of the milk and stir until the mixture is smooth. Add the rest of the milk and beat with a rotary beater until frothy. Serve very hot. Serve a bowl of Sweet Whipped Cream (523) with the chocolate.

646. Hot Rum Punch   *Punch pour soirée*

3 teaspoons tea leaves	1 lemon sliced, peeled, and seeded
boiling water	1 pound of sugar
grated rind of 1 lemon	1 quart of rum

Place the tea leaves in a mixing bowl. Add lemon rind, the slices of lemon, and sugar. Pour 4 cups of boiling water over the tea leaves. Cover and let it stand 30 minutes. Strain and add the rum. Reheat but do not let it boil. Serve in large, stemmed wine glasses.

Qui a bu n'a point de secrets.

647. Hot Wine *Vin chaud*

1 quart red wine (Bordeaux type)
1¼ cups sugar

1 small piece of cinnamon stick
lemon slices

Heat the wine, sugar, and cinnamon stick to the boiling point. Just before the wine reaches the boiling point remove the cinnamon stick and pour into stemmed wine glasses. Place a slice of lemon in each glass.

648. Lemonade and Orangeade *Limonade et Orangeade*

lemons or oranges
sugar

cold water

Allow ½ lemon or 1 orange (or both) and ¼ cup sugar to each glass of water. Slice the lemon or orange quite thin and remove the seeds. Place in a large bowl and add sugar and water. Let this stand 2 hours before serving. Serve with cracked ice.

649. Cold Grog *Grog froid*

1 lemon
¼ cup sugar

2 teaspoons brandy
1 glass ice water

Press the juice from the lemon and mix with sugar and brandy. Add to ice water. This makes a good summer drink.

650. Hot Grog *Grog chaud*

Place a slice of lemon in an 'old-fashioned' glass. Add 1 teaspoon sugar. Fill ¾ full with boiling water. Add 1 jigger of brandy or rum. Serve very hot.

651. Russian Punch   *Punch à la russe*

2 bottles of champagne	1 pound sugar
1 large fresh pineapple, peeled and cut in pieces	1 cup kirsch, rum, or cognac

Combine the ingredients in a large silver punch bowl. Touch with a lighted match. Let it burn until the punch is hot—a matter of a few moments—and pour into punch glasses. There should be a piece of pineapple in each glass.

652. American Punch   *Punch à l'américaine*

Combine the ingredients of the preceding recipe. Stir until the sugar has dissolved and add a large quantity of cracked ice. Serve very cold.

There is a real economy in making liqueurs at home. They will not be as good as commercial liqueurs but they will be very good and will serve the same purpose as those bought from the wine dealer.

Liqueurs should be brilliantly clear. This is achieved by very careful filtering. It is best to use filter paper instead of cheesecloth since the liqueur is apt to take on a taste of cloth.

TANTE MARIE

653. Black Currant Liqueur   *Cassis*

1 pound black currants   ⅔ cup sugar
2 quarts of pure alcohol

Wash and stem the currants. Crush them a little and place in a heavy crock. Add the alcohol and cover tightly. If half the recipe is made, a 2-quart preserving jar may be used. Cover and let stand in a cool dark place for 2 months. Filter the juice and add the sugar. Put back into clean crock and let it stand 3 days before bottling.

654. Curaçao   *Curaçao*

6 tangerines
1 quart domestic brandy
2 cups sugar

½ cup water
4 teaspoons sugar

Peel the tangerines and let the skin dry until almost brittle. Place the skins in a wide-mouthed jar and cover with brandy. Cover the jar. Let it stand 2 or 3 months. When it is time, filter the liqueur. Combine water and sugar and boil for 2 minutes. Skim and cool. Caramelize 4 teaspoons sugar by heating it in a heavy frying pan until dark brown. Add both sugars to the filtered liqueur. Mix well and bottle.

655. Gin   *Genièvre*

⅛ pound juniper berries
2 quarts pure alcohol

1 pound sugar
½ cup water

Pour alcohol over very ripe juniper berries. Let it stand in a covered crock for 6 weeks. Filter the liqueur. Heat sugar and water until the sugar is completely dissolved. Skim the syrup and add to the liqueur. Mix well and cool thoroughly before bottling.

656. Orange Blossom Liqueur   *Liqueur de fleurs d'oranger*

¼ pound orange blossom petals
2 quarts of pure alcohol

8 cups sugar
1 cup water

Cover the orange blossom petals with alcohol and let the mixture stand in a covered crock for 6 weeks. Filter the liqueur. Combine sugar and water and bring to a full rolling boil. Skim the syrup and add to the liqueur. Cool thoroughly before bottling.

657. Apricot Brandy   *Noyau*

apricot stones	1¼ cups sugar
1 quart pure alcohol	¼ cup water

Fill a jar half full of cracked apricot stones. Fill the jar with alcohol and cover. Let it stand 6 weeks. Shake the jar once a week. Boil the sugar and water 2 minutes. Skim and mix with the liqueur after it has been filtered. Cool thoroughly before bottling.

658. Brandied Fruits   *Fruits à l'eau-de-vie*

4 quarts raspberries	sugar
2 quarts strawberries	domestic brandy
2 quarts cherries	

Wash and pick over the fruit. The cherry stems should be clipped if they are very long and the strawberries should be hulled. Weigh the fruit and weigh an equal amount of sugar. Place a layer of cherries in the bottom of a wide-mouthed jar or crock. Cover with sugar and place a layer of strawberries on the sugar. Cover this with sugar and place a layer of raspberries on the sugar. Continue this process until the crock is ¾ full. Cover the fruit with brandy and seal tightly. Let this stand for 1 month. This makes an excellent dessert in itself or may be used as a sauce for ice cream.

659. Brandied Candied Fruits   *Fruits confits à l'eau-de-vie*

2 pounds candied fruits (plums, apricots, peaches, or pears)	domestic brandy

Place the fruit in a crock or jar. Cover with brandy. Seal and keep in a cool dry place for at least 2 weeks before using.

660. Brandied Cherries   *Cerises à l'eau de vie*

cherries   domestic brandy
sugar

Choose perfect cherries that are not too ripe. Clip the stems of the cherries if they are very long. Place the cherries in a jar or crock. Cover with brandy and seal the jar or crock tightly. Let this stand 3 weeks before adding sugar. Allow 1 pound of sugar for every quart of brandy. Mix well and cover again. It is important that the jar be hermetically sealed. Let the cherries stand 2 months before using.

TANTE MARIE offers no rules or suggestions about the choice and use of wines. In most French homes dinner is accompanied by a wine, or wines, of the family's choice. Usually it will be *vin ordinaire* and for special occasions there will be wines of rarer vintage.

In America wine-drinking is not such an accepted part of the daily diet; therefore, a word of guidance about wines seems appropriate.

Americans are becoming increasingly aware of the delights and satisfaction that a bottle of good wine may add to a good meal. Worries about the 'appropriate' wines and the decorum with which they are to be served are fast giving way to the realization that the only important thing is to enjoy wine-drinking. Gourmets as well as wine dealers rejoice in this fact.

The United States is capable of producing fine wines. Prohibition and the two World Wars did much to retard the wine industry here, but rapid progress is now being made and many growers may be proud of their efforts. It will be a long time—if ever—before the really great French wines can be equalled here. Nevertheless, some excellent wines are being produced in the United States, although still in comparatively small quantity.

For a long time producers of wine have considered it necessary to give the wines the names of their French, Spanish, or Italian prototypes in order to sell them. This practice is discouraged by the government and by wine lovers, and fortunately is diminishing.

Choice wine is the product of expensive and patient viticulture. Potable and commercially successful wines of inferior quality are produced on a large scale with comparative ease; and as long as the consumer continues to buy this grade of wine in large quantities the finer wines will unfortunately be scarce.

Wine experts know that certain climatic and soil conditions, combined with good grapes and careful production methods, will assure fine wines; and usually it is best to rely on these experts for guidance. Reliable wine dealers almost always print the names of the grapes used and the area in which the grapes are grown on the labels of the bottles.

The region around San Francisco is the largest area in this country well adapted to wine making, but even there varying geographical conditions plus diverse commercial aims create a wide range in the quality and quantity of wines. Certain counties produce better wines than others. If the label bears the name of one of the following areas and any of the grapes listed in the following table, the chances of a good bottle of wine are excellent.

AREAS

Napa Valley (especially red wine)

Sonoma County (many excellent varieties, including Champagne)

Santa Cruz

Santa Clara

Alameda (particularly Livermore Valley)

GRAPES

For Red Wine:
  Cabernet
  Pinot Noir
  Gamay
  Duriff
  Zinfandel (varies greatly)
  Refosco
  Grignolino

For White Wine:
  Pinot Chardonay
  Reisling
  Pinot Blanc
  Sylvaner
  Sauvignon Blanc
  Folle Blanche
  Sémiilon
  Pineau de la Loire
  Grey Reisling
  Ugni Blanc

The Finger Lakes district of New York State is the second region best adapted to the production of good wine. Two areas within this region are notable. The Lake Keuka area produces an American champagne made from Delaware, Catawba, Iona, Elvira, and Isabella grapes. The wine from these grapes is combined with some California white wine to make a very acceptable champagne. The red wines are generally sold as 'Burgundy,' 'Bordeaux,' or 'Claret,' which is regrettable since they are apt to be discredited for not resembling their European original instead of being credited for their own good qualities. The white wines, sold as 'Sauterne,' 'Chablis,' and

'Rhine Wine,' are made from the same grapes that the Champagne is made from and are superior to the red wines.

The Lake Canandaigua or Neopolitan area boasts many fine vineyards that produce a wide variety of wines. The dry white wines are particularly good. A few wines, such as Champagne, Sparkling Burgundy, Sherry, Rhine, Sauterne, Chablis, and Burgundy cling to the European name, but one of the best producers lists a large number of 'Varietal Wines.' Thus Diana, Delaware, Elvira, Vergennes, Catawba, Isabella, Moore's Diamond, Dutchess, and Reisling are sold under their grape names and are of the same high grade.

The Lake Erie Islands known as North Bass, Middle Bass, Put-In-Bay, and Kelly, and the near-by Ohio mainland have large and flourishing vineyards. Some wine—particularly white wine—is produced in its natural form and is very fine. Unfortunately, too many of the wines of this area are fortified or blended with other wines. This practice tends to destroy their flavor and distinction.

Other regions in Southern California, Virginia, and North Carolina produce wines, but so far these products cannot be placed in the same category as the finest wines produced in the regions that have been described.

Fortified wines such as Sherry and Port are produced in large quantities in many vineyards. The bulk of this production is very ordinary, not only because it is difficult to grow the proper grapes but also because the method of making first-class Sherry and Port is costly and takes a long time. Some good Muscatel is produced—but again a far cry from its European prototype.

There are a few fundamental rules in the use of wine that are dictated by taste rather than by tradition or arbitrary fashion. Fortified wines such as Sherry or Sweet Vermouth may be served in place of cocktails. Too many glasses of either tend to cloud the sense of taste, and moderation is urged before a good TANTE MARIE meal. A slightly chilled, dry white wine goes best with sea foods, with white meats (chicken, turkey, etc.) and with some entrées (mushrooms, sweetbreads, etc.). Red-meated roasts are enhanced by good red wine, served at room temperature. The richer varieties of red wines go well with game. A sweet wine such as Tokay, American Muscatel, or Sweet Catawba may be served with dessert.

Cooking wines deserve more respect than they usually receive. Cooking with poor wine is a culinary crime, since it can spoil the most carefully prepared dish. Many recipes in this book call for wine. The drier varieties are best unless otherwise specified.

English Index

(*For* French index, *see page* 309.)

291

TABLE des MATIERES